Lecture Notes in Artificial Intelligence 12832

Subseries of Lecture Notes in Computer Science

More information about this subseries at http://www.springer.com/series/1244

Phatthanaphong Chomphuwiset ·
Junmo Kim · Pornntiwa Pawara (Eds.)

Multi-disciplinary Trends in Artificial Intelligence

14th International Conference, MIWAI 2021
Virtual Event, July 2–3, 2021
Proceedings

Editors
Phatthanaphong Chomphuwiset (iD)
Mahasarakham University
Maha Sarakham, Thailand

Pornntiwa Pawara (iD)
Mahasarakham University
Maha Sarakham, Thailand

Junmo Kim
Korea Advanced Institute of Science
and Technology
Daejeon, Korea (Republic of)

ISSN 0302-9743   ISSN 1611-3349 (electronic)
Lecture Notes in Artificial Intelligence
ISBN 978-3-030-80252-3   ISBN 978-3-030-80253-0 (eBook)
https://doi.org/10.1007/978-3-030-80253-0

LNCS Sublibrary: SL7 – Artificial Intelligence

This Springer imprint is published by the registered company Springer Nature Switzerland AG
The registered company address is: Gewerbestrasse 11, 6330 Cham, Switzerland

Preface

The Multi-disciplinary International Conference on Artificial Intelligence (MIWAI), formerly called the Multi-disciplinary International Workshop on Artificial Intelligence, is a well-established scientific venue in the field of Artificial Intelligence (AI). The MIWAI series started in 2007 in Thailand as the Mahasarakham International Workshop on Artificial Intelligence and has been held every year since then. It has emerged as an international workshop with participants from around the world. In 2011, MIWAI 2011 was held outside of Thailand for the first time, in Hyderabad, India, so that it became the "Multi-disciplinary International Workshop on Artificial Intelligence". Then the event took place in various Asian countries: Ho Chi Minh City; Vietnam (2012); Krabi, Thailand (2013); Bangalore, India (2014); Fuzhou, China (2015); Chiang Mai, Thailand (2016); Brunei Darussalam (2017); Hanoi, Vietnam (2018); and Malaysia (2019). In 2018, MIWAI was renamed to the "Multi-disciplinary International Conference on Artificial Intelligence."

The MIWAI series of conferences serves as a forum for AI researchers and practitioners to discuss and deliberate cutting-edge AI research. It also aims to elevate the standards of AI research by providing researchers and students with feedback from an internationally renowned Program Committee.

AI is a broad research area. Theory, methods, and tools in AI sub-areas encompass cognitive science, computational philosophy, computational intelligence, game theory, multi-agent systems, machine learning, multi-agent systems, natural language, representation and reasoning, data mining, speech, computer vision, and the Web. The above methods have broad applications in big data, bioinformatics, biometrics, decision support systems, knowledge management, privacy, recommender systems, security, software engineering, spam filtering, surveillance, telecommunications, Web services, and IoT. Submissions received by MIWAI 2021 were wide ranging and covered both theory and applications.

This year, amid the COVID-19 pandemic, the 14th edition of MIWAI was organized as a virtual conference during July 2–3, 2021. This volume contains papers selected for presentation at MIWAI 2021. MIWAI 2021 received 33 full papers from authors in 10 countries including Bangladesh, Brunei Darussalam, China, France, Germany, India, Malaysia, South Korea, and Thailand. Following the success of previous MIWAI conferences, MIWAI 2021 continued the tradition of a rigorous review process.

In the end, a total of 16 papers were accepted (an acceptance rate of 48.48%), of which 7 papers received positive reviews and were accepted as regular papers, and the rest were deemed suitable for publication as short papers. Each submission was carefully reviewed by at least two members from a Program Committee consisting of 82 AI experts from 23 countries, and some papers received up to four reviews when necessary. The reviewing process was double-blind. Many of the papers that were excluded from the proceedings showed promise but the quality of the proceedings had to be maintained. We would like to thank all authors for their submissions. Without their contribution, this conference would not have been possible.

In addition to the papers published in the proceedings, the technical program included a keynote talk and we thank the keynote speaker for accepting our invitation. We are also thankful to the Korea Advanced Institute of Science and Technology (KAIST), Korea, for co-organizing this virtual conference.

We acknowledge the use of the EasyChair Conference System for the paper submission, review, and compilation process. Last but not least, our sincere thanks go to Ronan Nugent, Anna Kramer, and the excellent LNCS team at Springer for their support and cooperation in publishing the proceedings as a volume of Lecture Notes in Computer Science.

May 2021   Phatthanaphong Chomphuwiset
                                                                              Junmo Kim
                                                                       Pornntiwa Pawara

Organization

Steering Committee

Arun Agarwal	University of Hyderabad, India
Rajkumar Buyya	University of Melbourne, Australia
Patrick Doherty	University of Linköping, Sweden
Rina Dechter	University of California, Irvine, USA
Leon Van Der Torre	University of Luxembourg, Luxembourg
Peter Haddawy	Mahidol University, Thailand
Jérôme Lang	Université Paris-Dauphine, France
James F. Peters	University of Manitoba, Canada
Somnuk Phon-Amnuaisuk	UTB, Brunei
Srinivasan Ramani	IIIT Bangalore, India
C. Raghavendra Rao	University of Hyderabad, India

Honorary Advisors

Sasitorn Kaewman	Mahasarakham University, Thailand

Conveners

Richard Booth	Cardiff University, UK
Chattrakul Sombattheera	Mahasarakham University, Thailand

General Chairs

Dong Eui Chang	Korea Advanced Institute of Science and Technology, South Korea
Junmo Kim	Korea Advanced Institute of Science and Technology, South Korea

Program Chairs

Phatthanaphong Chomphuwiset	Mahasarakham University, Thailand
Heechul Jung	Kyungpook National University, South Korea
Pornntiwa Pawara	Mahasarakham University, Thailand

Program Committee

Arun Agarwal	University of Hyderabad, India
Grigoris Antoniou	University of Huddersfield, UK

Adham Atyabi	University of Colorado, Colorado Springs and Seattle Children's Research Institute, USA
Thien Wan Au	Universiti Teknologi Brunei, Brunei
Costin Badica	University of Craiova, Romania
Raj Bhatnagar	University of Cincinnati, USA
Richard Booth	Cardiff University, UK
Zied Bouraoui	CNRS and Artois University, France
Gauvain Bourgne	CNRS and Sorbonne Université, France
Maria do Carmo Nicoletti	UNIFACCAMP, Brazil
Rapeeporn Chamchong	Mahasarakham University, Thailand
Zhicong Chen	Fuzhou University, China
Suwannit-Chareen Chit	Universiti Utara, Malaysia
Phatthanaphong Chomphuwiset	Mahasarakham University, Thailand
Sook Ling Chua	Multimedia University, Malaysia
Todsanai Chumwatana	Rangsit University, Thailand
Abdollah Dehzangi	Morgan State University, USA
Juergen Dix	Clausthal University of Technology, Germany
Nhat-Quang Doan	University of Science and Technology of Hanoi, Vietnam
Abdelrahman Elfaki	University of Tabuk, Saudi Arabia
Lk Foo	Multimedia University, Malaysia
Hui-Ngo Goh	Multimedia University, Malaysia
Sheng He	Harvard Medical School, USA
Chatklaw Jareanpon	Mahasarakham University, Thailand
Himabindu K	Vishnu Institute of Technology, India
Manasawee Kaenampornpan	Mahasarakham University, Thailand
Ng Keng Hoong	Multimedia University, Malaysia
Kok Chin Khor	Universiti Tunku Abdul Rahman, Malaysia
Suchart Khummanee	Mahasarakham Univesity, Thailand
Ven Jyn Kok	National University of Malaysia, Malaysia
Satish Kolhe	North Maharashtra University, India
Raja Kumar	Taylor's University, Malaysia
Chee Kau Lim	University of Malaya, Malaysia
Chidchanok Lursinsap	Chulalongkorn University, Thailand
Sebastian Moreno	Universidad Adolfo Ibañez, Chile
Sven Naumann	University of Trier, Germany
Atul Negi	University of Hyderabad, India
Thi Phuong Nghiem	University of Science and Technology of Hanoi, Vietnam
Dung D. Nguyen	Vietnam Academy of Science and Technology, Vietnam
Thi-Oanh Nguyen	VNU University of Science, Vietnam
Pornntiwa pawara	Mahasarakham University, Thailand
Jantima Polpinij	Mahasarakham University, Thailand

Tho Quan	Ho Chi Minh City University of Technology, Vietnam
Srinivasan Ramani	IIIT Bangalore, India
Alexis Robbes	University of Tours, France
Annupan Rodtook	Ramkhamhaeng University, Thailand
Harvey Rosas	University of Valparaiso, Chile
Junmo Kim	Korea Advanced Institute of Science and Technology, South Korea
Adrien Rougny	National Institute of Advanced Industrial Science and Technology, Japan
Jose H. Saito	Universidade Federal de São Carlos, Brazil
Nicolas Schwind	National Institute of Advanced Industrial Science and Technology, Japan
Peter Scully	Mahasarakham University, Thailand
Myint Myint Sein	University of Computer Studies, Yangon, Myanmar
Jun Shen	University of Wollongong, Australia
Guillermo R. Simari	Universidad del Sur, Argentina
Alok Singh	University of Hyderabad, India
Dominik Slezak	University of Warsaw, Poland
Chattrakul Sombattheera	Mahasarakham University, Thailand
Heechul Jung	Kyungpook National University, South Korea
Panida Songrum	Mahasarakham University, Thailand
Frieder Stolzenburg	Harz University of Applied Sciences, Germany
Olarik Surinta	Mahasarakham University, Thailand
Ilias Tachmazidis	University of Huddersfield, UK
Thanh-Hai Tran	MICA, Vietnam
Suguru Ueda	Saga University, Japan
Chau Vo	Ho Chi Minh City University of Technology, Vietnam
Chalee Vorakulpipat	NECTEC, Thailand
Kewen Wang	Griffith University, Australia
Kevin Wong	Murdoch University, Australia

Publicity Chairs

Khanabhorn Kawattikul	Rajamangala University of Technology Tawan-ok, Thailand
Potchara Pruksasri	Mahasarakham University, Thailand
Oralik Surinta	Mahasarakham University, Thailand

Financial Chair

Rapeeporn Chamchong	Mahasarakham University, Thailand

Web Master

Panich Sudkhot	Mahasarakham University, Thailand

Bias, Trust, and Doing Good: The Impacts of Digital Technology on Human Ethics, and Vice Versa (Abstract of Keynote Speaker)

Joanna Bryson

The Hertie School, Germany

Abstract. Is artificial intelligence compromising or complementing human ethics? In this talk I focus on a third option: that as we introduce digital technologies into our lives, we are changing our society in ways that exposes the nature and origins of our own social behavior. This gives us an opportunity to know our selves better, and to behave well if we choose. I begin the talk by introducing the concept of public goods, then show how these relate to sustainability, trust, bias, and political polarization. I conclude speaking about remedies including how we as individual nations and collections of nations might regulate these technologies to improve our future lives.

Biography: Joanna Bryson is Professor of Ethics and Technology at the Hertie School. Her research focuses on the impact of technology on human cooperation, and AI/ICT governance. From 2002-19 she was on the Computer Science faculty at the University of Bath. She has also been affiliated with the Department of Psychology at Harvard University, the Department of Anthropology at the University of Oxford, the School of Social Sciences at the University of Mannheim, and the Princeton Center for Information Technology Policy. During her PhD she observed the confusion generated by anthropomorphised AI, leading to her first AI ethics publication "Just Another Artifact" in 1998. In 2010, she co-authored the first national-level AI ethics policy, the UK's Principles of Robotics. She holds degrees in psychology and artificial intelligence from the University of Chicago (BA), the University of Edinburgh (MSc and MPhil), and Massachusetts Institute of Technology (PhD). Since July 2020, Prof. Bryson has been one of nine experts nominated by Germany to the Global Partnership for Artificial Intelligence.

Bias, Trust, and Doing Good: The Impacts of Digital Technology on Human Ethics, and Vice Versa (Abstract of Keynote Speaker)

Joanna Bryson

Hertie School, Berlin, Germany

Abstract.

Contents

3D Point Cloud Upsampling and Colorization Using GAN

Beomyoung Kim[✉], Sangeun Han, Eojindl Yi, and Junmo Kim

Korea Advanced Institute of Science and Technology (KAIST), Daejeon, South Korea
{qjadud1994,bichoomi,djwld93,junmo.kim}@kaist.ac.kr

Abstract. Progress in LiDAR sensors have opened up the potential for novel applications using point clouds. However, LiDAR sensors are inherently sensitive, and also lack the ability to colorize point clouds, thus impeding further development of the applications mentioned above. Our paper presents a new end-to-end network that upsamples and colorizes a given input point cloud. Thus the network is able to manage the sparseness and noisiness resulting from the sensitivity of the sensor, and also enrich point cloud data by giving them the original color in the real world. To the best of our knowledge, this is the first work that uses a voxelized generative model to colorize point clouds, and also the first to perform both upsampling and colorization tasks in a single network. Experimental results show that our model is able to correctly colorize and upsample a given input point cloud. From this, we conclude that our model understands the shape and color of various objects.

Keywords: GAN · Point cloud · Colorization · Upsampling

1 Introduction

Recent developments in deep learning have shown great success in many 2D domain computer vision tasks such as classification, object detection and segmentation. This success can be attributed to deep convolutional neural networks (CNNs) [10] - an architecture that is able to capture local interaction and induce translation invariance - and a large dataset [3] that has become public for academic use. The field is now making progress towards generative tasks as well. Generative adversarial nets (GANs) [4] have succeeded in creating real-like fake images by letting a generator and a discriminator enter a minimax game. With GAN as its cornerstone, models like pix2pix [7] have emerged to solve the image-to-image translation task, whose objective is to translate images between different domains.

The paradigm that the proliferation of available data leads to advances in technology can be found in other domains as well. Due to the advancement in LiDAR sensor technology, 3D point cloud data have become more available, and therefore large progress is being made in 3D domain computer vision tasks. Typical 3D domain computer vision tasks include discriminative tasks such as object classification and part segmentation, and generative tasks such as colorization

ⓒ Springer Nature Switzerland AG 2021
P. Chomphuwiset et al. (Eds.): MIWAI 2021, LNAI 12832, pp. 1–13, 2021.
https://doi.org/10.1007/978-3-030-80253-0_1

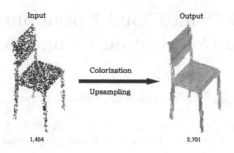

Fig. 1. Overview of our works. Our method colorizes and upsamples colorless point clouds in a single model.

and upsampling. Object classification is a task to predict the object category of a given input point cloud and part segmentation is a task to predict each prescribed part of an object for each point.

Point cloud colorization is a task that aims to colorize a given input point cloud with its original color in the real world. This task is important because applications in robotics, medical image, virtual/augmented reality can benefit from colorized point clouds. Since it is a generative task that requires the generation of colors, GANs which have shown great success in 2D domain tasks, are generally selected as baselines. Existing work in this domain [2] heavily relies on the PointNet [12] architecture which, although has received tremendous attention in recent years, may not be well suited for this task. Because the colorization task inherently requires a hierarchical understanding of point clouds, we need a model that is able to take both global overview and local structure into account. Although PointNet has solved many issues that point cloud data are facing, its design makes it impossible to recognize how each of the points is locally interacting with its neighboring points. This necessitates other design choices to solve the colorization task. Therefore, we choose to preprocess the point clouds to a voxelized grid structure, and use 3D convolutional neural networks instead. As it has been less preferred due to excessive computation and memory consumption issues, we properly preprocess the data and adjust the model capacity to circumvent these issues. Based on the aforementioned base architecture, we build a Unet-like network [13] that generates the color for a voxelized point cloud, and another discriminator network which is introduced to confirm the validity of the generated color values.

In addition to point cloud colorization, our paper aims to perform the point cloud upsampling task. As the LiDAR sensors that generate point clouds are essentially very sensitive to noise and perturbation, the generated point clouds are sparse and noisy. We solve this problem by training the model to naturally upsample an input point cloud by matching it with its ground truth point cloud that contains more points than the input. The model succeeds in generating a denser output point cloud that is both visually and semantically appealing. As a result, as described in Fig. 1, our method not only colorizes the colorless point clouds but also makes them denser in a single model.

To the best of our knowledge, the contributions of our paper is as follows:

- We propose the first generative model that colorizes point clouds using 3D convolution.
- Our model is the first to perform both colorization and upsampling in a single network.
- Compared to existing models for the same task, our model is better in that it can be trained using a single network and extracts features that better reflect local information.

2   Related Work

Image-to-Image Translation. Pix2pix [7] is a conditional GAN that translates an image in one domain to an image in another domain. It takes an input image, generates an output image in the target domain, and trains a discriminator to classify between the fake generated images and the ground truth images in the target domain. U-Net [13] is used as a generator architecture, which uses an encoder-decoder architecture with skip connections. Our task can be thought as translating an image from colorless domain to colored domain. Thus, we use pix2pix [7] as our base architecture. The architecture is modified to be compatible with 3D input data, and the size of the network is increased such that it can have enough capacity to learn various color information just by looking at the point cloud of an object.

Point Cloud Colorization. [2] is the only existing work that aims to solve the 3D point cloud colorization task. The network structure is also based on Pix2pix [7] and uses PointNet [12] as a feature extractor. PointNet [12] is a model that is able to induce permutation invariance and transformation invariance on the point cloud features. However, this design choice only enables each of the points to recognize the global features only, and is not sufficient to capture how the points interact locally. Furthermore, [2] overly simplifies the task by training each category of objects in separate networks. To address these two issues, our model converts the input point cloud to voxelized grid representations and performs 3D convolution on them, and trains all of the objects on a single network.

Point Cloud Reconstruction and Upsampling. [1] jointly trains an autoencoder with a generative model to reconstruct point clouds. [6] trains a generative network that ensures that point clouds with missing parts and even with corrupted latent representation can be reconstructed. [14] uses multilevel features to reconstruct an upsampled point cloud that has points with better uniformity and better represents the underlying surface. Compared to the above methods, our approach uses a much simpler method by making the number of points in the output to be larger than that of the input point cloud.

3   Method

In this section, we introduce more details about our framework, including how we convert a 3D point cloud into a 3D voxelized grid representation and how we perform 3D point cloud upsampling and colorization.

3.1   Data Pre-processing

The first step of our proposed framework is data pre-processing. Whereas point clouds are generally in $(n * 3)$ form, where n is the number of points and 3 indicates the XYZ coordinates, we find this representation inappropriate for our task, due to their lack of ability to capture spatial information in a structured way. In contrast, as mentioned in Sect. 1, a voxelized representation enables us to use a 3D convolutional network, where a model can better exploit the local geometry of 3D data. For this reason, we modify raw point clouds into voxelized representations before feeding them to the network. The whole process is illustrated in Fig. 2.

Point Cloud Voxelization. Our goal is to convert an XYZ point cloud of size $(n * 3)$ into a 3D volume of size $(N * N * N)$. First, we normalize the XYZ coordinate values of the point cloud to $[0, N]^3$, where N is the desired volume size. Then we round down each of them to its nearest integer. Although some fine-grained details are lost in this step, we set N such that it best balances the trade-off between information loss and computational efficiency. Finally, we construct two volumes; one is a binary volume of shape $(N * N * N)$, where each voxel indicates the presence of the point in that location, and the other is an RGB volume of shape $(N * N * N * 3)$, where each voxel contains the RGB values of the corresponding point. The binary volume is used as the input to the network, and the RGB volume is used as the ground truth.

Cutting Out Redundancy. One problem caused by voxelization is that most of the voxels are redundant. The region of our interest is located around the center of the volume, and its size is even smaller than $(N/2 * N/2 * N/2)$ out of $(N * N * N)$. In other words, it has a large outer shell that contains no useful information. Therefore for computational efficiency and training stability, we cut

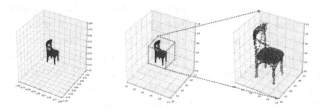

Fig. 2. The whole process of data pre-processing. (Left) A raw point cloud is in the form of $(n * 3)$. (Middle) We perform voxelization by mapping each point to a voxel in an $(N * N * N)$ 3D volume. (Right) Finally we cut out the outer shell, leaving the meaningful part only.

out the outer part of the volume in every direction by R, producing the final input of size $(N - 2R) * (N - 2R) * (N - 2R)$. In our experiments, we choose $N = 128$ and $R = 38$.

3.2 Network Architecture

Inspired by pix2pix [7], we design an adversarial network for 3D point cloud upsampling and colorization task, as illustrated in Fig. 3. The network consists of two sub-networks, a generator and a discriminator. The generator G performs 3D convolutions in a U-Net [13]-based structure, which is advantageous in capturing both local features and global context. It takes a 3D binary volume as input and outputs a 3D colorized volume with denser representation. G is trained to produce a dense, colored object, given an input point cloud that is sparse and binary. The discriminator D is trained to distinguish between the fake data generated by G and the ground truth. Joint training of these networks results in a global optimum in which G succeeds in deceiving D, which means that G has fully learned to colorize and densify point clouds.

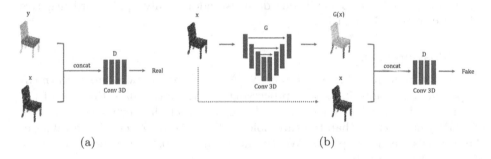

Fig. 3. The architecture of our proposed network. The input x is a 3D binary volume data and y is the ground truth volume with RGB color information. (a) The discriminator D is trained to recognize real data as real. (b) The generator G that has a U-Net [13]-like structure with 3D convolutions is trained to produce dense, colored samples that look realistic. The discriminator D is trained to recognize them as fake.

3.3 Objective

The goal of the generator is to reconstruct and colorize data with realistic color, intending to make it hard for the discriminator to distinguish from real colored data. On the other hand, the goal of the discriminator is to enhance the ability of differentiating the generated data from the real, colored ones. To achieve these goals, we adopt the MSE loss from [11] and the L1 loss from [7], which are defined as follows:

$$L_{MSE}(D) = \frac{1}{2}\mathbb{E}_{x \sim p_{data}(x)}[(D(x, y) - 1)^2]$$
$$+ \frac{1}{2}\mathbb{E}_{z \sim p_z(z)}[(D(x, G(x, z)))^2] \tag{1}$$

$$L_{MSE}(G) = \frac{1}{2}\mathbb{E}_{z \sim p_z(z)}[(D(x, G(x, z)) - 1)^2] \qquad (2)$$

$$L_{L_1}(G) = \mathbb{E}_{x,y,z}[\|y - G(x, z)\|_1], \qquad (3)$$

where x is the input volume without RGB values, y is the ground truth with RGB values, and z is a random noise vector which ensures the variation of the output. For the MSE loss, 0 and 1 are the labels for fake data and real data, respectively.

The MSE loss helps the generator to create realistic samples with reasonable colors and density. At the same time, it learns to generate samples that are similar to the ground truth, using the L1 loss. The benefit of using the MSE loss lies in its stability and fast convergence.

Our final objective function for the generator is as follows:

$$G^* = \arg\min_G L_{MSE}(G) + \lambda L_{L_1}(G), \qquad (4)$$

where λ is a hyperparameter that controls the balance between the two losses.

Although we cut out redundancy at data pre-processing step, foreground points still occupy only a small part of the entire volume. To balance between foreground and background in our data, we additionally apply hard negative mining of ratio 1:3 on L1 loss.

3.4   Post-processing

To convert from the volume with $(N*N*N*3)$ shape to raw points with $(n*3)$ shape, we apply additional post-processing. First, we calculate the sum of the normalized RGB values for each voxel. Next, we get the voxels with the sum of RGB value greater than the threshold τ. Then the XYZ coordinate values of these voxels mean raw points. We set the τ value to 0.1 when the initial value of the background is 0.

4   Experiments

In this section, we first introduce details of the dataset and implementation. Next, we explain experimental settings and investigate the impact of each component. Our experimental results show that our method achieves competitive performance on colorization as well as upsampling.

4.1   Dataset

We use DensePoint [2] dataset that contains over 7,000 single objects across 16 categories. Among them, we only use three categories (chair, airplane, table) for our training set, which together take up almost 70% of the entire dataset. Each point cloud is in form of $(n*7)$, where n is the number of points and 7 channels consist of 3 channels for coordinate values, 3 channels for RGB and 1 channel for part annotation. There are two types of the dataset; one is n_{2048} with $n = 2,048$ and the other is n_{4096} with $n = 4,096$. Since we do not need part annotation in our work, we use $(n*3)$ data with XYZ channels for input and $(n*6)$ data with XYZ-RGB channels for ground truth.

Upsampling + Colorization

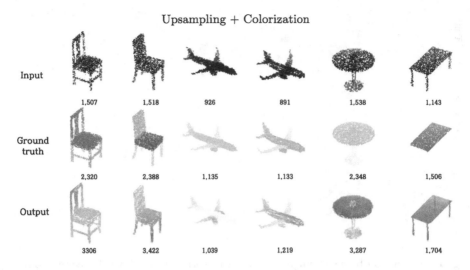

Fig. 4. The results of our model for both upsampling and colorization. The number below each figure represents the number of points. The results show that our model can generate denser points and colorize them reasonably. (Best viewed in color.) (Color figure online)

4.2 Implementation Details

We train for three categories in a single network. For data augmentation, we apply rotation to the points with randomly selected axis and angle. The generator and discriminator were trained using Adam [9] optimizer with a learning rate of 0.0001 and 0.00001 respectively and momentum parameters $\beta_1 = 0.5$, $\beta_2 = 0.999$. To settle down the early vanishing gradient of the generator, we do warm-up training the generator with only L1 loss during 2k iterations, then training both generator and discriminator with the whole losses defined in Sect. 3.3. The batch size is 32 and we set λ for L1 loss with hard negative mining to 20 and train the network for 200 epochs. We implement the model using Pytorch on GeForce TITAN X GPUs.

4.3 Upsampling and Colorization Results

We train the network for both upsampling and colorization. For training both tasks, x is a binary volume that is voxelized from ($n_{2048} * 3$) raw points and y is an RGB volume that is voxelized from ($n_{4096} * 6$) raw points. In Fig. 4, each resulting color and the number of points of our model show that our model can generate denser points and colorize them reasonably. Also, our model seems to have the ability to distinguish parts and color new points. However, because of the over-upsampling, our model generates some noisy color points. We will describe this issue in Sect. 4.5.

Fig. 5. Comparison between our results and the work of Cao [2] which was reproduced using their official TensorFlow code. Our work produces colors that are more uniform within each part of an object, and are also more distinct between different parts of an object.

4.4 Only Colorization Results

In this experiment, we trained only for the colorization without upsampling. For this, x is a binary volume that is voxelized from $(n_{4096} * 3)$ raw points and y is an RGB volume that is voxelized from $(n_{4096} * 6)$ raw points. In Fig. 5, the result points for the only colorization shows that our model paints in reasonable colors. Compared to the upsampling and colorization results, it seems to have fewer noisy color points and learns quickly and stably. Given that the number of input and output points is almost the same, it appears to learn that the position of the output points should be the same as the input, so it can focus more on colors and parts.

4.5 Ablation Study

Hard Negative Mining on L1 Loss. In Fig. 6, we conduct experiments on the effect of hard negative mining on L1 loss. The model without hard negative mining paints in almost the same colors with many noisy color points. It does not seem to focus on the foreground points and colors because the background voxels are dominant. On the other hand, the model with hard negative mining paints in reasonable colors and generate points denser than the model without hard negative mining, and this seems that hard negative mining helps the model more focus on the foreground points and colors.

Value of λ on L1 Loss. In this experiment, we analyze the effect of the value of λ on L1 loss. When λ is small, about 1, it takes a very long time for a model to converge and paints in a disorderly variety of colors. But when λ is large,

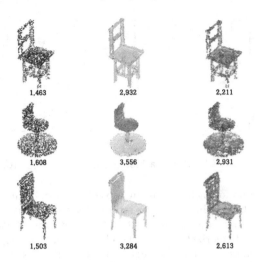

Fig. 6. (Left to Right) Input points, output points with hard negative mining, output points without hard negative mining. The model with hard negative mining paints in reasonable colors but the model without hard negative mining paints in almost the same colors with many noisy color points and it does not generate points as denser as the model with hard negative mining. Based on those results, hard negative mining seems to help the model focus more on points and colors. (Color figure online)

about 100, it converges very fast, and it is very difficult to balance generator and discriminator. We found that the value of λ between 10 and 20 results in the most desirable outputs, and that learning is stable.

5 Evaluation

We evaluate our results using three different metrics: color distribution and part color variance ratio for the colorization task, and point density for the upsampling task.

5.1 Evaluation Metrics

Color Distribution. To investigate how well our model performs colorization, we analyze the distribution of colors. According to [7], the similarity between the output and the ground truth color distributions is a measure of the colorfulness of the results. Adopting the idea, we convert the color space from RGB to Lab and plot the histogram for each channel. Having distributions close to the ground truth distributions means that the model produces natural and reasonable colors. For a more quantitative evaluation, we get the histogram intersection score against the ground truth. This score indicates how similar the distribution is to ground truth, and a high score means that the model colorizes with natural and reasonable colors.

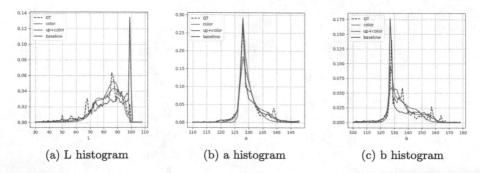

(a) L histogram   (b) a histogram   (c) b histogram

Fig. 7. Color distribution for each channel in Lab color space. We used the black dotted line for the ground truth distributions, the red line for the output distributions of our model for only colorization, the green line for the output distributions of our model for both upsampling and colorization, and the blue line for the output distributions of Cao [2]. The histogram intersection score calculated from this distribution is in Table 1. Both of our two models show similar color distributions with those of the ground truth. This demonstrates that our models colorize point clouds more naturally and reasonably compared to the baseline model. (Color figure online)

Part Color Variance Ratio. A successful model should generate a uniform color within each object part. However, intra-part color uniformity is not sufficient to evaluate the model's performance, because it does not penalize for painting in a single color over the entire object, which is undesirable. If a model has learned to recognize the object shape and distinguish different parts, it should be able to paint in different colors across parts. Therefore, we want our model to generate colors that are uniform within a part (*i.e.* low intra-part variance), and at the same time, different from those in the other parts (*i.e.* high inter-part variance). Based on this idea, we adopt Part Color Variance Ratio(PCVR) as the second evaluation metric for colorization, which is defined as follows:

$$PCVR = \frac{inter\ part\ color\ variance}{intra\ part\ color\ variance}. \tag{5}$$

Since a high PCVR score is assigned to a model with large inter-part variance and small intra-part variance, we can compare colorizing performances of different models using this metric.

Point Density. In the upsampling task, we train our model to produce compact samples. By defining the point density as the average number of points per unit volume, we quantitatively evaluate how dense the upsampled outputs are compared to their original inputs. For $(52 * 52 * 52)$ data, we use the unit volume of size $(5 * 5 * 5)$.

5.2 Evaluation Results

We report the color distributions in Fig. 7 and Table 1, the PCVR per class in Table 2, and the point density per class in Table 3. For all metrics, a higher score means better performance. Note that the color evaluation is the comparison between Cao [2] and our model, whereas the point density scores are compared between the original data and the upsampled outputs generated by our model.

The color distribution results in Fig. 7 shows that our two models, one for the only colorization and the other for both upsampling and colorization, have more similar color distributions with the ground truth. Together with the histogram plots, high scores in Table 1 and Table 2 ensure that our approach encourages realistic colors that resemble the ground truth distribution. It is noteworthy in Table 2 that our single model trained on all three classes outperforms the baseline in every class, although Cao [2] trained one model for each class.

Our model achieves the desired performance for the upsampling task as well, as shown in Table 3. The point density increases in the upsampled data by 96.16% on average, indicating that our model successfully generates dense outputs.

Table 1. Histogram intersection against ground truth

Method	L	a	b
Cao [2]	0.745	**0.893**	0.719
Only colorization	**0.833**	0.836	**0.804**
Upsampling and colorization	0.810	0.821	0.775

Table 2. Part color variance ratio result

Method	Chair	Airplane	Table
Cao [2]	0.177	0.062	0.254
Ours	**1.307**	**2.322**	**1.225**

Table 3. Point density result

	Chair	Airplane	Table
Original input	0.916	0.566	0.895
Ours	**1.307**	**2.322**	**1.225**
Upsampled output	**2.057**	0.744	**2.080**

6   Conclusion and Discussion

In this paper, we propose a model that is able to colorize and upsample a given input point cloud. To achieve both upsampling and colorization simply, we have chosen to discard conventional architectures for processing point clouds, e.g. PointNet [12]. Instead, we have opted for voxelized representations to take advantage of 3D convolution. The quantitative, qualitative results demonstrate that our choice is justified.

Although the release of DensePoint [2] dataset was one of the cornerstones on which we have built our work, it was also one of the main obstacles throughout our research. The dataset itself has some inherent problems that impede the progress of training. There were many noisy labeled instances, such as objects that were colored in primary colors or peculiar colors that do not have any semantic connections with the class it belongs to, or there were also objects with extraordinary shape. Class imbalance is also a great issue because three out of sixteen object classes take up 70% of the total number of instances. Because of this, the model severely suffered from low performance when it was asked to colorize classes with the small number of training instances. We conjecture that class imbalance is the main reason why Cao [2] has failed to build a unified network that is able to colorize all of the object classes.

In future works, we plan to propose a model that does not require a fully colorized point cloud dataset to learn the colorization task. One possible way is to develop a model that is able to colorize a given point cloud by taking an additional 2D image as input. We have two suggestions on what this 2D image could be. First, it could be an image of texture or material such as wood or marble, so that the network learns to colorize appropriate parts of the point cloud with the given texture. Second, it could be a 2D image of the object that is given as the input point cloud to the model. In this case, we plan to use attention [5] mechanisms or spatial transformer networks [8] to ensure that the model can ignore background clutter and only concentrate on the color of the object, and use that color to colorize point clouds.

References

1. Achlioptas, P., Diamanti, O., Mitliagkas, I., Guibas, L.J.: Representation learning and adversarial generation of 3D pointclouds. CoRR, abs/1707.02392 (2017)
2. Cao, X., Nagao, K.: Point cloud colorization based on densely annotated 3D shape dataset. In: Kompatsiaris, I., Huet, B., Mezaris, V., Gurrin, C., Cheng, W.-H., Vrochidis, S. (eds.) MMM 2019. LNCS, vol. 11295, pp. 436–446. Springer, Cham (2019). https://doi.org/10.1007/978-3-030-05710-7_36
3. Deng, J., Dong, W., Socher, R., Li, L.-J., Li, K., Fei-Fei, L.: ImageNet: a large-scale hierarchical image database. In: 2009IEEE Conference on Computer Vision and Pattern Recognition, pp. 248–255. IEEE (2009)
4. Goodfellow, I.: Generativeadversarial nets. In: Advances in Neural Information Processing Systems, pp. 2672–2680 (2014)
5. Graves, A., Wayne, G., Danihelka, I.: Neural turing machines. CoRR, abs/1410.5401 (2014)
6. Gurumurthy, S., Agrawal, S.: High fidelity semantic shape completion for point clouds using latent optimization. CoRR, abs/1807.03407 (2018)
7. Isola, P., Zhu, J.-Y., Zhou, T., Efros, A.A.: Image-to-image translation with conditional adversarial networks. In: Proceedings of the IEEE Conference on Computer Vision and Pattern Recognition, pp. 1125–1134 (2017)
8. Jaderberg, M., Simonyan, K., Zisserman, A., et al.: Spatial transformer networks. In: Advances in Neural Information Processing Systems, pp. 2017–2025 (2015)
9. Kingma, D.P., Ba, J.: Adam: a method for stochastic optimization. CoRR, abs/1412.6980 (2015)

10. Krizhevsky, A., Sutskever, I., Hinton, G.E.: ImageNet classification with deep convolutional neural networks. In: Advances in Neural Information Processing Systems, pp. 1097–1105 (2012)
11. Mao, X., Li, Q., Xie, H., Lau, R.Y.K., Wang, Z., Smolley, S.P.: Least squares generative adversarial networks. In: 2017IEEE International Conference on Computer Vision (ICCV), pp. 2813–2821 (2017)
12. Qi, C.R., Su, H., Mo, K., Guibas, L.J.: PointNet: deep learning on point sets for 3D classification and segmentation. In: Proceedings of the IEEE Conference on Computer Vision and Pattern Recognition, pp. 652–660 (2017)
13. Ronneberger, O., Fischer, P., Brox, T.: U-net: convolutional networks for biomedical image segmentation. CoRR, abs/1505.04597 (2015)
14. Yu, L., Li, X., Fu, C.-W., Cohen-Or, D., Heng, P.-A.: PU-Net: point cloud upsampling network. In: Proceedings of the IEEE Conference on Computer Vision and Pattern Recognition, pp. 2790–2799 (2018)

Learning Behavioral Rules from Multi-Agent Simulations for Optimizing Hospital Processes

Daan Apeldoorn[1,2(✉)], Lars Hadidi[1], and Torsten Panholzer[1]

[1] IMBEI Medical Informatics, University Medical Center of the Johannes Gutenberg University Mainz, Mainz, Germany
daan.apeldoorn@uni-mainz.de
[2] Z Quadrat GmbH Mainz, Mainz, Germany

Abstract. Hospital processes are getting more and more complex, starting from the creation of therapy plans over intra-hospital transportation up to the coordination of patients and staff members. In this paper, multi-agent simulations will be used to optimize the coordination of different kinds of individuals (like patients and doctors) in a hospital process. But instead of providing results in form of optimized schedules, here, behavioral rules for the different individuals will be learned from the simulations, that can be exploited by the individuals to optimize the overall process. As a proof-of-concept, the approach will be demonstrated in different variants of a hospital optimization scenario, also showing its robustness to several changes in the scenario.

Keywords: Multi-agent simulation · Hospital process optimization · Knowledge base learning

1 Introduction

1.1 Motivation

The hospital daily life is getting more and more complex: Besides larger amounts of patients being emerged from growing cities, also the complexity of hospital processes can quickly increase due to more diverse therapies or growing organizational structures. This leads to the idea of using simulation and other optimization software. However, software solutions for optimizing different kinds of hospital processes still seem to be underrepresented in the hospital domain. This might be the case, since—even if the software is able to provide adequate results—it can be hard to implement these results in the hospital daily life due to the diversity and the interdisciplinarity of the hospital working environment: Solutions require to be easy to communicate and to implement for every individual participating in a hospital process (e. g., doctors, patients, etc.).

In this paper, an approach will be presented that has the potential to deal with the aforementioned challenges: Hospital processes are proposed to be modeled and simulated as multi-agent systems to improve their schedules. However,

P. Chomphuwiset et al. (Eds.): MIWAI 2021, LNAI 12832, pp. 14–26, 2021.
https://doi.org/10.1007/978-3-030-80253-0_2

instead of communicating these resulting schedules directly to the different participants of the hospital process, rule-based knowledge will be extracted for every group of participants. This knowledge can then be communicated in a simplified form to all individuals that are relevant for the process to be optimized.

More concretely, the main contributions of this paper are:

- An approach for optimizing hospital processes by learning rule-based knowledge from multi-agent simulations that can be easily simplified and communicated to all participatory individuals.
- A *knowledge base extraction algorithm* that is able to extract such rule-based knowledge from a larger data set in a human-readable way.

As a *proof-of-concept*, the approach will be demonstrated, by equipping the agents from the original multi-agent setting with a simplified version of the rule-based knowledge that was learned by means of the knowledge base extraction algorithm. It will be shown that (1) the agents are able to improve the (simulated) hospital process by exploiting the learned rules in comparison to a random baseline and (2) that the rules are robust against changes of the environment.

1.2   Related Work

An established approach that allows for gaining insights into the inherent structure of data is that of learning a decision tree (see, e. g., [4], pp. 105–120). In [7], decision trees are extracted from learning agents, which can help the agent developer to analyze and create adequate agent behavior. Similar to a decision tree, the approach used here also represents knowledge from general to more specific. However, unlike decision trees, where often entropy-based measures are used to build the tree, the concept presented here only needs conditional probabilities, which makes it much more intuitive.

In contrast to other knowledge representation approaches, the approach used here is only loosely coupled to logic and is therefore also readable and comprehensible for people that do not have a strong background in logic. The comprehensibility of the approach in comparison to ASP [6] has been studied in [8].

In [3], two approaches are proposed that are able to extract knowledge bases with knowledge represented on several levels of abstraction from learning agents. These knowledge bases are also used here to extract and simplify the rules learned by agents in a hospital process. However, the algorithms proposed in [3] to create such knowledge bases from data lack transparency, since it is not easy to comprehend whether the resulting knowledge is complete regarding the original data.

Also in [9], the same kind of knowledge representation approach from [2] and [3] is used to represent human intuitions for optimizing job-shop problems. This work is already closely related to optimization, however it does not focus on the extraction of the knowledge rather than exploiting it for optimization.

2   Mutli-agent Simulation Setting

2.1   Scenario Description

In the hospital process used here, patients, doctors and nurses have to be coordinated to achieve a smooth workflow: Patients have to visit a doctor and additionally need an X-ray and/or a blood draw appointment. Doctors have to be available in a treatment room at the respective time and nurses have to perform X-raying and blood drawing or have to be on standby to be able to support a doctor, if necessary. The different locations have different distances between them, such that, e. g., patients need a certain time to get from X-ray to a doctor's treatment room.

2.2   Modeling of the Scenario

The described scenario will be modeled using the ABSTRACTSWARM system [1], where agent types are represented as *circles* and station types are represented as *squares*. The scenario is divided into three so-called *perspectives* (see Fig. 1).

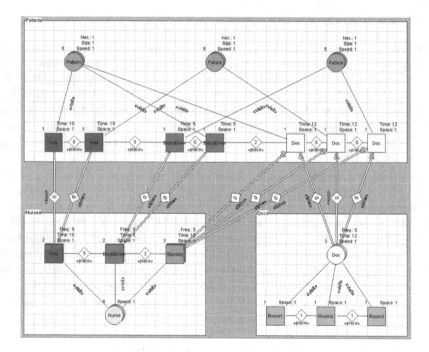

Fig. 1. Hospital process modeled as multi-perspective scenario using the modeling and simulation system ABSTRACTSWARM [1].

In the *Patients* perspective (upper part of Fig. 1), there are three different types of patient agents that have to visit a doctor, an X-ray and/or a blood draw station, which is indicated by the «visit»-labeled edges. In the *Doctors* perspective (lower right part of Fig. 1), doctor agents are assigned to rooms and in the *Nurses* perspective (lower left part of Fig. 1), nurse agents are assigned to X-ray, blood draw and a Standby station. Distances between the different locations are modeled by the «place»-labeled edges, whose weights indicate the distance (in *units of time*, where one unit can be considered to be approximately one minute in this scenario). The «time»-labeled double edges that are spanned across the perspectives are used to synchronize the visits of the different agents: Every time a patient agent is visiting an X-ray or a blood drawing station, a nurse agent must be present there. In case of a patient agent is visiting a doctor, both a nurse agent must be on standby and a doctor must be present in a treatment room (indicated by the &-symbols in Fig. 1). The annotated attributes determine how long a station has to be visited (*Time*), how often such visit events have to occur at an agent or station/at each connected agent or station (*Freq./Nec.*), or how many agents are able visit a station simultaneously (*Space*).[1] These parameters will not be considered explicitly later, but the agents will learn a rule-based behavior that can deal with the scenario.

Details about the agents' sensory input will be explained later in Sect. 3.3.

2.3 Simulation Results as Gantt Charts

The simulation's results are usually presented in form of Gantt charts [10], a type of bar chart which lays out tasks on the vertical axis and their temporal position on the horizontal axis. This chart shows the schedule of tasks in a compact visual way, but needs to be refreshed each time some parameter changes. It can quickly grow incomprehensible with an increasing number of tasks to be scheduled. Therefore simple rules, formulated as conditional statements, are more accessible to each individual within the diverse field of daily clinical practice. Such rules will be generated by an algorithm presented in following Sect. 3.

3 Alternative Solution: Learning Behavioral Rules

Instead of learning a static schedule in form of a Gantt chart (as described in Sect. 2.3), in this section, it is proposed to learn behavioral rules for every group of participating agents that can be easily simplified and communicated. Theses rules should be able to reproduce similar optimization results when being implemented by every participatory agent.

As knowledge representation paradigm to represent the behavioral rules, hierarchical knowledge bases (HKBs) [3] will be used.[2] A novel algorithm will be introduced here, that is able to learn HKBs from data collected by the agents during a simulations. Unlike other algorithms for learning HKBs presented in [2,3], the algorithm introduced here is able to handle higher-dimensional data as well as being more transparent than the algorithms used in the past.

---

[1] Detailed explanations of the attributes, can be found in [1].

[2] Not to be confused with the hierarchical knowledge base approach in [5].

3.1   Preliminaries

This section provides the preliminaries needed for introducing the knowledge extraction algorithm. The presentation closely follows [2,3], where alternative and less transparent algorithms for learning HKBs were provided.

Basic Agent Model. To be able to learn a knowledge base that comprises behavioral rules of an agent, a basic agent model will be assumed, where an agent is equipped with n sensors. Each of the agent's sensors can provide sensor values that are represented by a sensor value set. Thus, the agent's state space is defined as $\mathbb{S} := \mathbb{S}_1 \times ... \times \mathbb{S}_n$, where every $\mathbb{S}_i$ is the sensor value set of the agent's i-th sensor. Furthermore, the agent can perform actions that are represented by an action set $\mathbb{A}$.

The trace of such an agent's run in its environment can be represented as a sequence of state-action pairs, in form of an (ordered) set $\mathcal{SA}$. Every pair $\mathbf{p} \in \mathcal{SA}$ consists of a state $s_{\mathbf{p}} = s_1 \wedge ... \wedge s_n$ and an action $a_{\mathbf{p}} \in \mathbb{A}$ that was performed by the agent in state s. The notion $s_1 \wedge ... \wedge s_n$ is used to indicate that the state $s_{\mathbf{p}}$ is composed of the sensor values $s_1, ..., s_n$ where every $s_i \in \mathbb{S}_i$ represents the perceived sensor value of one of the agent's sensors.

Based on the agent model described here, an HKB can now be defined.

Hierarchical Knowledge Bases. An HKB [2], [3] is a knowledge base containing rule-based knowledge that is organized on several levels of abstraction: The topmost level contains the most general rules and the bottommost level contains the most specific rules. Rules on a level j represent exceptions of rules of the next higher abstraction level $j - 1$. As one is usually interested in a compact representation, HKBs with fewer rules on the lower levels are preferable.

States and rules in the context of HKBs can be distinguished according to the following definitions from [3]:

Definition 1 *(Complete States, Partial States). A complete state is a conjunction* $s := s_1 \wedge ... \wedge s_n$ *of all sensor values* s_i *that are currently perceived by an agent, where* n *is the number of sensors. A partial state is a conjunction* $s := \bigwedge_{s' \in S} s'$ *of a subset* $S \subset \{s_1, ..., s_n\}$ *of the sensor values of a complete state.*

Definition 2 *(Complete Rules, Generalizing Rules). Complete rules and generalized rules are of the form* $p \to a\ [w]$, *where* p *is either a complete state (in case of a complete rule) or a partial state (in case of a generalized rule), the conclusion* $a \in \mathbb{A}$ *is one of the agent's actions and* $w \in \mathbb{R}$ *is the rule's weight (determining the "strength" of the rule).*[3]

According to Definition 1 and Definition 2, complete rules can conclude an action from a given complete state and generalized rules can conclude an action from a partial state. Based on that (still following [3]), an HKB can be defined:

---

[3] When learning such rules from data, as will be done here, the weight will represent the conditional probability $P(a|p)$.

Definition 3 (Hierarchical Knowledge Base/HKB). *An HKB is an ordered set* $\mathcal{KB} := \{R_1, ..., R_{n+1}\}$ *of* $n+1$ *rule sets, where* n *is the number of sensors (i. e., the number of state space dimensions). Every set* $R_{j<n+1}$ *(short hand for "R_j with $j < n+1$") contains generalized rules and the set* R_{n+1} *contains complete rules, such that every premise* $p_\rho = \bigwedge_{s \in S_\rho} s$ *of a rule* $\rho \in R_j$ *is of length* $|S_\rho| = j - 1$.

Reasoning Algorithm. $\mathfrak{R}$ for HKBs. To infer an action $a \in \mathbb{A}$ from a given state $s = s_1 \wedge ... \wedge s_n$ by using the knowledge contained in an HKB $\mathcal{KB}$, the reasoning algorithm searches the HKB from bottom to top (starting on the bottommost level R_{n+1}) for the first rule, whose premise is satisfied by the state s and a set containing the found rule's conclusion will be returned. In case the premises of multiple rules with different conclusions are satisfied by s and all of these rules are having the same maximum weight, the returned set will contain the conclusions of all of these rules. (One of these "equally good" conclusions can be selected randomly later). The described reasoning algorithm ensures that the inference is always based on the most specific rule that fits to the given state s. A formalization of the algorithm can be found in [2].

In the following, the reasoning algorithm for HKBs will also be denoted as $\mathfrak{R}(\mathcal{KB}, s)$. As an *abbreviated form*, $\mathfrak{R}(\mathcal{KB}, s) = a$ will be used to state, that a is the only action that is inferred for state s and $\mathfrak{R}(\mathcal{KB}, s) \neq a$ will be used to state that a cannot be inferred as the only action for state s.

3.2 An Advanced Algorithm for Learning HKBs from Data

Learning Algorithm. The approach presented here to learn an HKB from data is that of representing a state-action sequence in a compact way (i. e., with few rules having few exceptions).

Unlike the algorithms introduced in [2,3], the algorithm introduced here can deal better with higher dimensional inputs and is much more transparent.[4]

The algorithm expects a *deterministic* state-action sequence $\mathcal{SA}$ as input (i. e., there are no two pairs $\mathbf{p_1}, \mathbf{p_2} \in \mathcal{SA}$ with $s_{\mathbf{p_1}} = s_{\mathbf{p_2}}$ and $a_{\mathbf{p_1}} \neq a_{\mathbf{p_2}}$). In case of $\mathcal{SA}$ being non-deterministic, the sequence must first be converted to a deterministic one by counting relative frequencies: This is done by keeping only those pairs $\mathbf{p} \in \mathcal{SA}$ with the most frequent action $a^{\max}$ for a given state s, i. e., those $\mathbf{p} \in \mathcal{SA}$ with $a_{\mathbf{p}} = a^{\max} = \arg\max_{a \in \mathbb{A}} P(a|s)$.[5]

The general idea of the algorithm is, to add on each level of an initially empty HKB those rules that cover as many state-action pairs of $\mathcal{SA}$ as possible, starting with the topmost level R_1. On each of the more specific levels, further rules are then successively added as exceptions to the rules of the previous level(s), until

---

[4] The proposed algorithm is implemented in the open-source toolbox INTEKRATOR, which allows for integrating machine learning, reasoning and revision: https://gitlab.com/dapel1/intekrator_toolbox.

[5] If $\arg\max_{a \in \mathbb{A}}$ is not unique, i. e., every $a \in A \subseteq \mathbb{A}$ is leading to the same maximum $P(a|s)$, one $a \in A$ is chosen randomly.

the HKB covers all state-action pairs of $\mathcal{SA}$—i. e., until the reasoning algorithm $\mathfrak{R}$ infers for every state-action pair $\mathbf{p} \in \mathcal{SA}$ the corresponding action $a_{\mathbf{p}}$ from the state $s_{\mathbf{p}}$. Algorithm 1 shows a formalization of the algorithm.

Note that in lines 17–29 of Algorithm 1, the number of iterations grows in principle exponentially with the number of sensors. However, if the algorithm is applied to data that is well-explainable in the form of rules with exceptions, usually only a small number of levels R_j will be needed here until the algorithm terminates. Also note that performing lines 44–49 at the end of each iteration allows that $\mathcal{KB}$ can be provided in its final form after each iteration (and the algorithm can, e. g, be stopped interactively if no more exceptions are needed).

Completeness of the Learning Algorithm. An important question is now, whether Algorithm 1 provides for an arbitrary deterministic state-action sequence $\mathcal{SA}$ an adequate HKB $\mathcal{KB}$, such that the reasoning algorithm $\mathfrak{R}$ infers for each state $s_{\mathbf{p}}$ of a state-action pair $\mathbf{p} \in \mathcal{SA}$ the correct corresponding action $a_{\mathbf{p}}$.

Algorithm 1 only terminates if there are no more state-action pairs remaining in $\mathcal{SA}^-$ (see line 11 of Algorithm 1 and line 42, where $\mathcal{SA}^-$ is updated once per iteration with all state-action pairs for which an incorrect inference is provided by $\mathfrak{R}$ being applied to each state-action pair of the *original* input state-action sequence $\mathcal{SA}$). This is the case for the following reasons:

(1) After the first step (lines 13–30) of the j-th iteration, it is ensured that correct conclusions can be provided by $\mathfrak{R}$ for all $\mathbf{p} \in \mathcal{SA}^-$, since corresponding rules are added for each subset of length j of each remaining state-action pair's state.

(2) In the second step (lines 32–34), rules are removed that are unused according to the *original* input state-action sequence $\mathcal{SA}$. Thus, after this step, at least one additional rule will remain here (otherwise the algorithm would have stopped in the previous iteration already).

(3) After adapting the new rules' weights to conditional relative frequencies in lines 36–39 (which does neither manipulate $\mathcal{SA}^-$ nor $\mathcal{KB}$), the set of remaining state-action pairs $\mathcal{SA}$ is updated by checking against the original input set $\mathcal{SA}$, for which of the state-action pairs the reasoning algorithm does not provide correct conclusion (lines 41–42): This only concerns those state-action pairs for which $\mathfrak{R}$ provided correct inferences in the previous $(j-1)$-th iteration and which are overridden now by the new rules added in the current j-th iteration.

If the algorithm is in the n-th iteration (where n is the number of sensors, i. e., the number of elements of a state-action pair's state), then by (1) a complete rule will be added for each state of all state-action pairs in $\mathcal{SA}^-$ on level R_{n+1} and thus by (2) no rules will be removed. Since only complete rules were added by (1), these rules cannot provide any inference except for the complete states in their premises. Thus, no inferences can be overridden by the newly added rules and after (3) $\mathcal{SA}^-$ will be empty.

Input:	Deterministic state-action sequence $\mathcal{SA}$
Output:	HKB $\mathcal{KB}$

```
01  % Create and add the most general rule
02  a_ρ := arg max_{a∈A} P(a)
03  w_ρ := P(a_ρ)
04  R_1 := {⊤ → a_ρ [w_ρ]}
05  KB := {R_1}
06
07  % Get remaining state-action pairs not covered by the current KB
08  SA⁻ := {p ∈ SA | a_p ≠ ℜ(KB, ⋀_{s∈S_p} s)}
09
10  j := 1
11  while SA⁻ ≠ ∅ do
12
13      % Create rules of the HKB's next level to cover as much
14      % state-action pairs as possible
15      R_{j+1} := ∅
16      for each p ∈ SA⁻ do
17          for each S_p^j ⊂ S_p do   % S_p^j is a subset of S_p of length j
18
19              % Create new rule
20              s_ρ := ⋀_{s∈S_p^j} s
21              a_ρ := a_p
22              w_ρ := P(⋀_{s∈S_p^j} s∧a_ρ)   % will be adapted to P(a_ρ | ⋀_{s∈S_p^j} s) in lines 36-39
23              ρ := s_ρ → a_ρ [w_ρ]
24
25              % Add rule if it does not exist yet
26              if ρ ∉ R_{j+1} then
27                  R_{j+1} := R_{j+1} ∪ {ρ}
28              end if
29          end for
30      end for
31
32      % Remove unused rules on the bottom most level of the HKB
33      % (delete all worse (i.e., less frequent) rules)
34      R_{j+1} := R_{j+1} \ {ρ ∈ R_{j+1} | ∄p ∈ SA: ρ fires to infer a_p = ℜ(KB ∪ {R_{j+1}}, ⋀_{s∈S_p} s)}
35
36      % Adapt rule weights
37      for each ρ ∈ R_{j+1} do
38          w_ρ := P(a_ρ | ⋀_{s∈S_p^j} s)
39      end for
40
41      % Get remaining state-action pairs not covered by the current KB
42      SA⁻ := {p ∈ SA | a_p ≠ ℜ(KB ∪ {R_{j+1}}, ⋀_{s∈S_p} s)}
43
44      % Remove unused rules on all levels of the HKB
45      % (delete rules that became superfluous either due to the new rules on
46      % level R_{j+1} or due to the adaption of the weights)
47      for each R ∈ KB do
48          R := R \ {ρ ∈ R | ∄p ∈ SA: ρ fires to infer a_p = ℜ(KB ∪ {R_{j+1}}, ⋀_{s∈S_p} s)}
49      end for
50
51      KB := KB ∪ {R_{j+1}}
52      j := j + 1
53  end while
```

Algorithm 1. Advanced Extraction Algorithm for HKBs

Since lines 44–49 are only removing rules that are unused according to the *original* input state-action sequence $\mathcal{SA}$, the completeness of the resulting HKB is not affected and the algorithm will terminate due to $\mathcal{SA}^-$ being empty.[6]

3.3   Application in the Hospital Process Multi-agent Simulation Setting

The algorithm introduced in Sect. 3.2 will now be applied to the hospital process modeled by the multi-agent simulation setting that was described in Sect. 2. At first, the state-action spaces of the different kinds of agents are considered. After that, it will be described how the behavioral rules are learned individually for each kind of agent and how the rules are simplified and adapted to better fit the needs of the hospital application domain.

State-Action Space of Agents. In the described multi-agent simulation setting, three kinds of agents exist: *Patients*, *Docs* and *Nurses* (see Fig. 1). The state-action spaces of these kinds of agents are modeled as follows, according to their respective visiting relations (indicated by the «visit»-labeled edges in Fig. 1):

– For *Patient*:
  $\mathbb{S}^{\text{Pat}} \times \mathbb{A}^{\text{Pat}}$ with $\mathbb{S}^{\text{Pat}} := \mathbb{S}^{\text{Pat}}_{\text{at}} \times \mathbb{S}^{\text{Pat}}_{\text{tasks}}$ and, depending on the kind of patients (cf. Fig. 1), either
  - $\mathbb{S}^{\text{Pat}}_{\text{at}} = \{\text{at\_Xray}, \text{at\_BloodDraw}, \text{at\_Doc}\}$ and $\mathbb{S}^{\text{Pat}}_{\text{tasks}} = \mathcal{P}(\{X, B, D\})$ and $\mathbb{A}^{\text{Pat}} = \{\text{to\_Xray}, \text{to\_BloodDraw}, \text{to\_Doc}\}$ or
  - $\mathbb{S}^{\text{Pat}}_{\text{at}} = \{\text{at\_Xray}, \text{at\_Doc}\}$ and $\mathbb{S}^{\text{Pat}}_{\text{tasks}} = \mathcal{P}(\{X, D\})$ and $\mathbb{A}^{\text{Pat}} = \{\text{to\_Xray}, \text{to\_Doc}\}$ or
  - $\mathbb{S}^{\text{Pat}}_{\text{at}} = \{\text{at\_BloodDraw}, \text{at\_Doc}\}$ and $\mathbb{S}^{\text{Pat}}_{\text{tasks}} = \mathcal{P}(\{B, D\})$ and $\mathbb{A}^{\text{Pat}} = \{\text{to\_BloodDraw}, \text{to\_Doc}\}$
  with $\mathcal{P}$ providing the power set and $X \in \{\text{Xray\_full}, \text{Xray\_free}\}$, $B \in \{\text{BloodDraw\_full}, \text{BloodDraw\_free}\}$, $D \in \{\text{Doc\_full}, \text{Doc\_free}\}$. $\mathbb{S}^{\text{Pat}}_{\text{at}}$ contains the stations where the patient agent can be located, $\mathbb{S}^{\text{Pat}}_{\text{tasks}}$ is a set containing the stations that still have to be visited and their current states and $\mathbb{A}^{\text{Pat}}$ contains the agent's possible target stations.
– For *Doc*:
  $\mathbb{S}^{\text{Doc}} \times \mathbb{A}^{\text{Doc}}$ with $\mathbb{S}^{\text{Doc}} := \mathbb{S}^{\text{Doc}}_{\text{at}} \times \mathbb{S}^{\text{Doc}}_{\text{tasks}}$, where
  $\mathbb{S}^{\text{Doc}}_{\text{at}} = \{\text{at\_Room}_1, \text{at\_Room}_2, \text{at\_Room}_3\}$, $\mathbb{S}^{\text{Doc}}_{\text{tasks}} = \mathcal{P}(\{R_1, R_2, R_3\})$ and $\mathbb{A}^{\text{Doc}} = \{\text{to\_Room}_1, \text{to\_Room}_2, \text{to\_Room}_3\}$. As for patients, $\mathbb{S}^{\text{Doc}}_{\text{at}}$ contains the stations where the doctor can be located, $\mathcal{P}$ provides the power set and $R_i \in \{\text{Room}_i\_\text{full}, \text{Room}_i\_\text{free}\}$ is indicating the current state of the respective room.

---

[6] The INTEKRATOR toolbox, which implements the algorithm, can also automatically determine the number of covered state-action pairs for non-deterministic state-action sequences.

- For *Nurse*:
  $\mathbb{S}^{\mathrm{Nur}} \times A^{\mathrm{Nur}}$ with $\mathbb{S}^{\mathrm{Nur}} := \mathbb{S}^{\mathrm{Nur}}_{\mathrm{at}} \times \mathbb{S}^{\mathrm{Nur}}_{\mathrm{tasks}}$, where
  $\mathbb{S}^{\mathrm{Nur}}_{\mathrm{at}} = \{\mathrm{at\_Xray}, \mathrm{at\_BloodDraw}, \mathrm{at\_Standby}\}$, $\mathbb{S}^{\mathrm{Nur}}_{\mathrm{tasks}} = \mathcal{P}(\{X, B, S\})$ and
  $A^{\mathrm{Nur}} = \{\mathrm{to\_Xray}, \mathrm{to\_BloodDraw}, \mathrm{to\_Standby}\}$. Again, $\mathbb{S}^{\mathrm{Nur}}_{\mathrm{at}}$ contains the stations where the nurse agent can be located, $\mathcal{P}$ provides the power set and $S \in \{\mathrm{Standby\_full}, \mathrm{Standby\_free}\}$ is indicating the state of the Standby station (X, B are the same as for patients).

Learning and Adaption of Behavioral Rules as Guidelines. To learn simple yet adequate behavioral rules as guidelines for each kind of participant in the scenario to be optimized, agents with random behavior are used at first to explore the state-action space. After a simulation run, in case the agents could find a solution, the state-action sequence of each agent is stored, according to the agent's respective state-action space. The stored data is weighted with the square of the global reward of all agents after a simulation run that is calculated from the total unused time of every single agent in the scenario: The lower the sum of the total weighting time of every single agent, the higher the global reward at the end of a simulation run.

After 300 runs, Algorithm 1 is applied on the state-action-sequences for every kind of agent (i. e., separately for patient, doctor and nurse agents). As an example, for patients, this results in the following HKB:

```
to_Doc [0.375]

at_Xray → to_BloodDraw [0.45]
at_BloodDraw → to_Xray [0.4]
at_Doc → to_BloodDraw [0.375]

at_Xray ∧ |Doc_full|Xray_full| → to_Doc [1.0]
at_Xray ∧ |BloodDraw_full|Doc_full|Xray_full| → to_Doc [1.0]
...                                                           (54 more)
```

The large number of exceptions on the bottommost level of the HKB are still quite unhandy. Thus, the bottommost level will be replaced by a set of rules that let the agents avoid occupied places.[7] The final rules for patients that will be reflected by the HKB and that will be used for evaluation is as follows:

"Usually go to the doctor first. Except if at X ray or at a doctor, then go to blood draw next; or if at blood draw, go to X-ray next. Except place is full, go to a free place."

This step is similarly done for the HKBs of doctor and nurse agents as well.

4   Demonstration and Basic Evaluation

To demonstrate the described approach and as a basic evaluation, the scenario from Fig. 1, which was used to learn the behavioral rules, will serve as a test scenario. Additionally, to show that the learned rules also work under changed

---

[7] Besides being intuitive, such rules turned out to be efficient in earlier experiments.

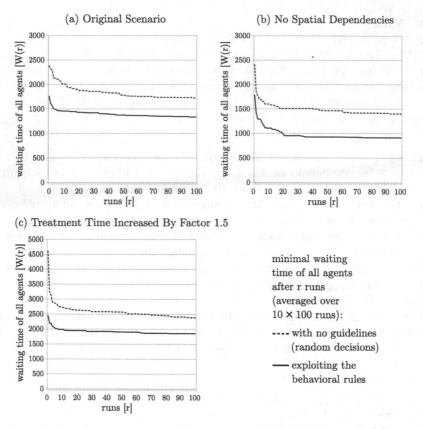

Fig. 2. Comparison of the minimal total waiting time for all agents found after r runs.

circumstances, they will also be evaluated in two variants of the original scenario: without considering spatial dependencies (i. e., all stations can be reached in zero time) and with all treatment times being increased by factor 1.5. Agents choosing their stations randomly[8] will be compared with agents that select their stations according to the simplified adapted rules from Sect. 3.3. Both kinds of agents were performed for 100 runs and the minimal total waiting time of all agents that emerged after the r-th run was measured. The results were averaged over 10 repetitions (see Fig. 2): It can be seen that agents exploiting the behavioral rules lead to overall *much less waiting times* ($\approx 300\text{--}500$ time units). Even if state-of-the-art optimization algorithms could possibly outperform the presented approach, the idea here is to be able to provide rules as guideline to every single

---

[8] When not being provided with rules/guidelines, at least a part of the participants in the process might not select the tasks in a specific order. Note that this is a *basic* evaluation only, as a proof-of-concept that the presented approach in principle works; also other rules/guidelines (e.g., "shortest distance") appear to be promising here.

individual of the scenario. Note that the algorithm presented in Sect. 3.2 can in principle also be applied in more complex environments—both the performance and the benefit depend on whether the environment follows certain rules (which can usually be assumed in many man-made environments).

5   Conclusion and Future Work

In this paper, it was proposed to optimize hospital processes by learning behavioral rules from multi-agent simulations. Unlike the obvious approach of simply providing optimized static Gantt charts as results, it was proposed here to provide the learned behavioral rules to all individuals involved in a process. In real life, this would require the learned rules to be *easily comprehensible*.

Using the proposed *knowledge base extraction algorithm*, such rules have been learned here from multi-agent simulations and the rules were simplified and complemented to fit the needs. Intuitions on the completeness of the extraction algorithm have been outlined. Compared to random agent behavior, exploiting the learned rules improved the simulated hospital process, resulting in reduced waiting times. The benefit of the rules was robust to several changes in the scenario.

However, further experiments need to be done, since other strategies (like "shortest distance") seem to be promising here as well (which would require different sensory inputs for learning). The implementation and evaluation of such optimizations in real world clinical settings could be possible future work.

References

1. Apeldoorn, D.: AbstractSwarm – a generic graphical modeling language for multi-agent systems. In: Klusch, M., Thimm, M., Paprzycki, M. (eds.) MATES 2013. LNCS (LNAI), vol. 8076, pp. 180–192. Springer, Heidelberg (2013). https://doi.org/10.1007/978-3-642-40776-5_17
2. Apeldoorn, D., Kern-Isberner, G.: When should learning agents switch to explicit knowledge? In: 2nd Global Conference on Artificial Intelligence. EPiC Series in Computing, GCAI 2016, vol. 41, pp. 174–186. EasyChair Publications (2016)
3. Apeldoorn, D., Kern-Isberner, G.: Towards an understanding of what is learned: extracting multi-abstraction-level knowledge from learning agents. In: Rus, V., Markov, Z. (eds.) Proceedings of the Thirtieth International Florida Artificial Intelligence Research Society Conference, pp. 764–767. AAAI Press, Palo Alto (2017)
4. Beierle, C., Kern-Isberner, G.: Methoden wissensbasierter Systeme - Grundlagen, Algorithmen, Anwendungen (4. Auflage). Vieweg+Teubner (2008)
5. Borgida, A., Etherington, D.W.: Hierarchical knowledge bases and efficient disjunctive reasoning. In: Brachman, R.J., Levesque, H.J., Reiter, R. (eds.) Proceedings of the First International Conference on Principles of Knowledge Representation and Reasoning, pp. 33–43. Morgan Kaufmann Publishers Inc., San Francisco (1989)
6. Brewka, G., Eiter, T.: Truszczyński: answer set programming at a glance. Commun. ACM **54**(12), 92–103 (2011)
7. Junges, R., Klügl, F.: Learning tools for agent-based modeling and simulation. KI - Künstliche Intelligenz **27**(3), 273–280 (2013)

8. Krüger, C., Apeldoorn, D., Kern-Isberner, G.: Comparing answer set programming and hierarchical knowledge bases regarding comprehensibility and reasoning efficiency in the context of agents. In: Proceedings of the 30th International Workshop on Qualitative Reasoning (QR 2017) at International Joint Conference on Artificial Intelligence (IJCAI 2017) in Melbourne, Australia. Northwestern University, Evanston (2017)
9. Kuhn, I.: Heuristische optimierung durch menschliche intuition - das beste aus zwei welten. In: Becker, M. (ed.) SKILL 2019 - Studierendenkonferenz Informatik, pp. 97–108. Gesellschaft für Informatik e. V. (2019)
10. Pinedo, M.: Scheduling: Theory, Algorithms, and Systems. Springer, New York (2012). https://doi.org/10.1007/978-1-4614-2361-4

An Open-World Novelty Generator for Authoring Reinforcement Learning Environment of Standardized Toolkits

Sangho Lee[1,2], Junbeom Park[2], Ho Suk[1], Taewoo Kim[1], Pamul Yadav[2], and Shiho Kim[1(✉)]

[1] School of Integrated Technology, Yonsei University, Incheon 21983, South Korea
`shiho@yonsei.ac.kr`
[2] Department of Research, GREW Creative Lab. Inc., Incheon 21983, South Korea
`gamecrew@gamecrewlab.com`

Abstract. Current research in Reinforcement Learning (RL) is based on closed-world learning environment where the environment remains fixed and unchanged throughout the agent's training and application session. The fixed environment may be prone to failure when the agents incorporate under novel unseen situations. To overcome the drawback of the existing closed-world model, an Open-world learning model is required which can classify the novelty occurring in an environment in a hierarchical manner. The proposed control suite with open world novelty generator is an attempt to augment the machine learning environment for authoring the novelty in actors, interactions, and environment of standardized Reinforcement learning toolkits such as UnityML, OpenAI Gym, and DeepMind Control Suite in real-time. Such a tool will provide an opportunity to the RL researchers to simulate the Open-world learning model and test their algorithms within the standardized closed-world learning environments of the standardized RL toolkits.

Keywords: Reinforcement learning · Open-world learning · Control suite · Novelty-generator · RL toolkits

1 Introduction

In recent years, the Reinforcement Learning (RL) research domain has witnessed a soaring interest ever since Google Deepmind developed and played its AlphaGo [1] program and won against the world's best Go players [2]. Most of the current research in RL heavily focuses on the AI systems which solve the challenges where the rules of the environment are known beforehand and usually remain unchanged during the course of action. In the situations where the novelty is expected to be encountered into the environment (often termed as closed-world learning environment), RL researchers or practitioners have to rely on crafting the system to be suitable for handling such novel situations and thus fail to generalize in solving the problems in other domains [3].

© Springer Nature Switzerland AG 2021
P. Chomphuwiset et al. (Eds.): MIWAI 2021, LNAI 12832, pp. 27–33, 2021.
https://doi.org/10.1007/978-3-030-80253-0_3

To tackle the challenges encountered in the existing model of closed-world learning environment, a new paradigm has been proposed to develop AI systems based on the Open-World learning model [4]. The goal of the Open-World learning model [5] is to allow a system to learn novel situations occurring in the real-world like environment and update its knowledge on-the-go by eliminating the need for training from scratch. Open-world learning requires the characterization of the types of novelty that can occur in an environment. Such a classification can be done in a hierarchical manner starting from the most specific to the most abstract way possible. Novelty Hierarchy of an environment can be roughly categorized as: Entities and attributes, Interactive configurations, and External configurations. It is to be noted that research progress in the field of RL is primarily dependent on strong mathematical theory and state-of-the-art experimental results. RL being a relatively old discipline in the field of Machine Learning is already well-equipped with sufficient mathematical theory. On the other hand, in the past few years, various RL training toolkits, such as OpenAI Gym [6], Unity ML [7], Google DeepMind Control Suite [8], GazeboSim [9], and WeBots [10] , have been introduced in the market to accelerate the research in the RL and Robotics domain. Despite their popularity among the RL researchers, such toolkits are only able to provide a closed-world learning environment where the state space and reward functions are defined at the beginning of the training session and cannot be modified easily and require scripting in real-time during the process of the training session if and when a novel situation occurs. There have been attempts to formulate Open-world learning by designing and testing the multi-robot systems in an open environment [11]. Task and Motion Planning of a robot in a simulated physical environment has also been an interesting approach towards Open-world learning [12] but it lacks real-time changes in the environment. Therefore, the proposed Control Suite can simplify the training process, be more accessible and with wider possibilities to encourage more and better general intelligence learning for agents.

In this paper, we propose CSONG, a control suite with an ability to simulate an open-world learning environment. It can generate unseen environments by allowing the user to change the suitable values of actions, interactions, and environment for the training agents in real-time during the on-going training episode. It aims at allowing the practitioners to create and test intelligent agents which can work appropriately in real-world domain under novel situations that violate experienced environmental condition during training stages. It has been demonstrated that Agricultural Robotics requires simulation to identify the variations in the agricultural fields before employing the robot on the ground [13]. Thus it can contribute to the development of simulated agent learning and ease the real-world training of robots for a wide variety of applications. The goal of CSONG (Fig. 1) is to augment the existing closed-world learning environment simulator such as Unity ML to provide the RL researchers an opportunity to train and test their algorithms in a real-world like environment and possibly serve as a benchmark in extending the Open-world learning based RL research.

The paper is organized as follows. Section 2 discusses the architectural design and functionality of CSONG. Section 3 describes the implementation progress of CSONG in its preliminary developmental stage. Section 4 discusses the findings of CSONG implementation on UnityML and highlights the future works.

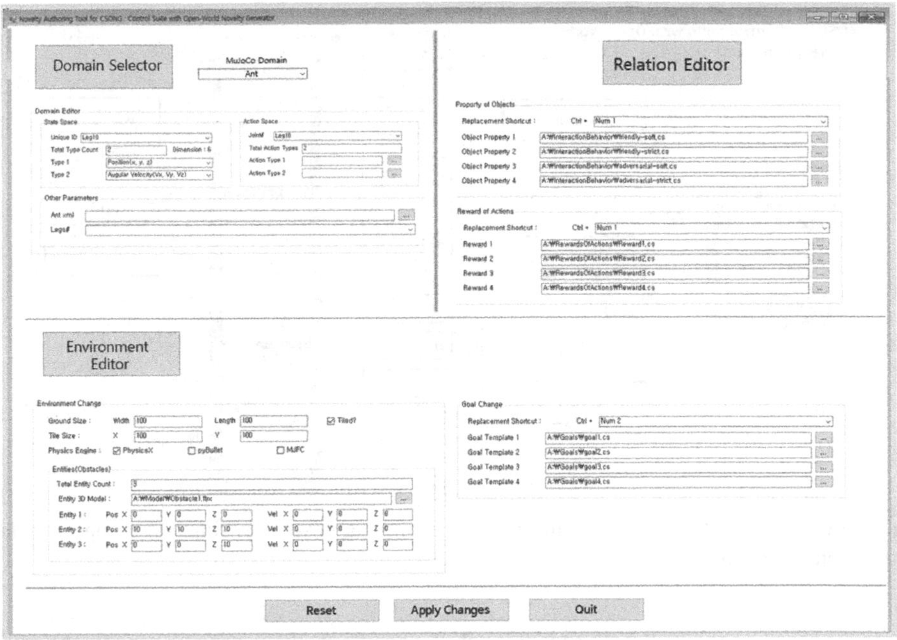

Fig. 1. Proposed Control Suite User Interface for changing the parameters of Actor, Environment and Interaction.

2   System Architecture

Open-world learning model requires a system to be able to categorize and classify various kinds of configurations responsible for bringing changes in the environment and thus termed as novelty generators. One possible way of classifying the possible configurations is into a hierarchical novelty level ranging from the most abstract configurations to the most domain-specific configurations. The proposed system is a Novelty-Generator Suite in the Open-World domains (Fig. 2), which aims at changing the configurations at various levels in the learning environment on the go without the need of stopping a training session. Doing so allows the learning agent to treat the typical closed-world environment as an Open-world learning environment It is divided into three independent changers namely, Actor Changer (or Domain Editor), Interaction Changer (or Relation Editor) and Environment Changer (or Environment Editor). Different Changers affect different configurations such as agent's characteristics, interaction configurations, environment and entity configurations. These configurations can be directly used to bring changes in several standardized RL agent toolkits such as UnityML, OpenAI Gym, and DeepMind Control Suite while learning agent's training and inference.

Actor Changer allows the user to change the State Space, Action Space, and model-specific parameters. State Space allows the user to designate the type of value that can be extracted through Observation. Action Space specifies what type of output can be defined for a given action. Actor Changer makes it possible to set the categories of

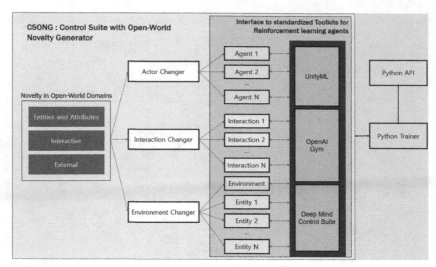

Fig. 2. Proposed Control Suite Architecture for generating novelty to simulate an open-world learning environment.

actions that can be taken at each object level. It also allows the user to change the overall model or parts of the model.

Interaction Changer allows the user to change the relationship between objects and rewards for the predefined actions. The property of an object defines its relationship with the first-class actor when there are two or more dynamic objects present in the environment. It is hypothesized that the relationship cannot be formalized because it can vary depending on the characteristics of the object. Therefore, the object property for relationship setting is written as a script file that can be added or removed to the Actor object in the form of a simulator-specific component. Interaction Changer is also responsible for changing the action rewards dynamically. It is typically a difficult job to develop a standard reward function for all the possible scenarios in the training environment, therefore depending on the given scenario, arguments and parameters are used to create a function suitable for each scenario and written directly into a script file and added to the Actor object in the simulator.

Environment Changer allows the user to change the environment and goal related properties. Entities (Obstacles) define the property values for static obstacles existing in the current environment. The current version of the Control Suite supports only one type of actor (3D object model) at a time, and multiple interactions (objects) with the relevant shapes can be placed in the environment.

3   Experimental Results

We applied the control suite over the UnityML toolkit that served as the closed-world training environment and used the MuJoCo [14] physics engine-based Marathon-envs environments for testing the pre-existing trained benchmarks of several actor(agent) models such as Ant and Hopper. MuJoCo XML model file in the MuJoCo environment contains the environment's configurations such ground size, tile size etc. and actor's attributes such as state space, action space etc. A Python API was used to communicate the changes in the MuJoCo XML model file via UnityML. The correctness of the implementation was tested by changing the parameters in the UI and observing the real-time changes in the MuJoCo based model's attributes and the environment configurations.

3.1 Domain Editor Results

Fig. 3. Experimental setup showing the real-time modification of MuJoCo-based Ant agent from having 6 legs (left) to 4 legs (right) during the on-going training session using the Domain Editor UI (center).

In Fig. 2 above, it can be seen that the actor's legs attributes were initialized with a value of 6, i.e. it had 6 legs at the beginning of the training session. The training session runs for some time and while it was on-going, the number of legs were modified using the control suite's domain editor to four and the Ant agent continued to walk with 4 legs in the environment without the need of restarting the session from the beginning (Fig. 3).

3.2 Environment Editor Results

Fig. 4. Experimental setup showing the environment map with initialized tile size values (left) and the real-time updated map with modified tile size values (right) using Environment Editor UI (center).

In Fig. 4 one of the possible utility of the control suite's environment editor is shown, where it was used to change the tile size of the hopper's learning environment. The tile size was initialized with the values for X and Y axes to be both 100 units. While the hopper was "hopping" in the environment, the tile size was changed to 10 and 20 units for X and Y-axes respectively during the on-going training session, while the hopper continued to hop in the environment space, using the Environment editor.

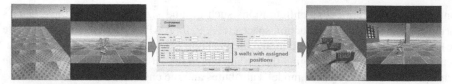

Fig. 5. Experimental setup showing the initialized environment map with no obstacles (left) and the modified environment map with 3 walls placed at designated positions during the on-going training session (right) using the Environment Editor UI (center).

Besides changing the tile size, one of the most impressive utility of the control suite's environment editor is that it can be also used to add obstacles in the environment in real-time. In Fig. 5, it is shown that the hopper environment was initialized with no obstacles, and after some time passed during the training session, three obstacles (walls) were placed at certain designated positions in the environment in real-time, while the hopper continued to hop in the environment. It was observed that the hopper continued to train with the presence of new obstacles added in the environment.

4   Discussion and Future Work

The proposed Control Suite aims at simplifying the training procedure of RL agents (or intelligent agents in real world) by helping automate the processes of changing the characteristics of the actors, environments, and the interactions through the User Interface. It is expected to perform quicker modifications and simulate the real-world like situations to help train the agent deal with the novel and irregular situations in the physical world. Control Suite demonstrate the changes in a simulated environment and were experimented with MuJoCo agents which were able to adjust with the modifications done on them and continued learning according to the novel situation. In the course of our experiment, we found that the agent's state space and environment space were modified in real-time and the corresponding changes in the Marathon-envs environment took place with insignificant amount of time lag. The current version of the CSONG uses PhysX physics engine with predefined mass values for the agents. In our future work, we aim to vary the mass values and other physical attributes of the agents to observe the possible effect of CSONG control suite on the agent's attributes and environment space in real-time. Further constraints required for changes made in Actors, Interactions, and Environments shall be explored in the future works too.

Acknowledgments. This work was support by the Ministry of Science and ICT (MSIT), Korea, by (No. 2020–0-00056, to create AI systems that act appropriately and effectively in novel situations that occur in open worlds) supervised by IITP.

References

1. Silver, D., Huang, A., Maddison, C., et al.: Mastering the game of Go with deep neural networks and tree search. Nature **529**, 484–489 (2016)

2. AlphaGo Homepage. https://deepmind.com/research/case-studies/alphago-the-story-so-far
3. Science of Artificial Intelligence and Learning for Open-world Novelty (SAIL-ON), HR001119S0038
4. Chen, Z., Liu, B.: Open-World Learning, 2nd edn. Morgan & Claypool Publishers. Lifelong Machine Learning (2018)
5. Fei, G., Wang, S., Liu, B.: Learning cumulatively to become more knowledgeable. In: KDD (2016)
6. Brockman, G., et al.: OpenAI Gym. arXiv preprint arXiv:1606.01540 (2016)
7. Juliani, A., et al.: Unity: a general platform for intelligent agents. arXiv preprint arXiv:1809.02627 (2018)
8. Tassa, Y., et al.: DeepMind Control Suite. ArXiv e-prints (2018)
9. Koenig, N., Howard, A.: Design and use paradigms for gazebo, an open-source multi-robot simulator. In: Intelligent Robots and Systems, (IROS 2004) (2004)
10. Webots. Mobile Robot Simulation Software. http://www.cyberbotics.com.Open-source
11. Alkilabi, M.H.M., Narayan, A., Tuci, E.: Cooperative object transport with a swarm of e-puck robots: robustness and scalability of evolved collective strategies. Swarm Intell. 11(3–4), 185–209 (2017). https://doi.org/10.1007/s11721-017-0135-8
12. Gan, C., et al.: The ThreeDWorld transport challenge: a visually guided task-and-motion planning benchmark for physically realistic embodied AI. arXiv preprint arXiv:2103.14025 (2021)
13. Rizzardo, C., Katyara, S., Fernandes, M., Chen, F.: The importance and the limitations of Sim2Real for robotic manipulation in precision agriculture. In: 2nd Workshop on Closing the Reality Gap in Sim2Real Transfer for Robotics, RSS (2020)
14. Todorov, E., Erez, T., Tassa, Y.: MuJoCo: a physics engine for model-based control. In: IEEE/RSJ International Conference on Intelligent Robots and Systems, Vilamoura 2012, pp. 5026–5033 (2012)

Book Cover and Content Similarity Retrieval Using Computer Vision and NLP Techniques

Chatklaw Jareanpon[1]([⊠]) and Khanabhorn Kawattikul[2]

[1] Polar Lab, Department of Computer Science, Faculty of Informatics,
Mahasarakham University, Kantharawichai, Thailand
`chatklaw.j@msu.ac.th`
[2] Department of Information Technology, Faculty of Social Technology,
Rajamangala University of Technology, Tawan-Ok, Thailand
`khanabhorn.ka@rmutto.ac.th`

Abstract. This paper proposes a computer vision and machine learning application for recognizing book covers and automatically retrieve similar book contents from the database. Recognizing the book covers relies on extracting the key points from the images of the book covers before they are used in a matching process. Moreover, the book description will automatically extract, retrieve, and generate a book representation using a Bag of Word (BOW) algorithm. The similarity function will use to measure the contents of the books. The experiments are conducted and evaluate the performance using the 30 real-image book covers. The output shows that the accuracy of book cover image recognition is 89.33% and from book description is 63.33%.

Keywords: Textural feature · Longest matching · Image recognition · SURF descriptor · Image matching · BOW

1 Introduction

Mostly, books in the shops are encased with plastic covers to prevent the damages from unexpected flipping. However, some people need to read the sample or other related contents of the books to decide for purchasing the books. One of the methods for people who buy the book is using online book catalogs to search book details using titles and some other associate information. It would be convenient, when uses are able to search the details of the books by the book cover (as images) using mobile devices, such as smart phones or tablets.

With advanced and modern computer vision and machine learning techniques, computer vision applications become essential and have been deliberately applied in many areas such as security, medicine, and biology. Image detection and recognition are among the common takes that are implemented to cope and solve various computer vision problems. In low-level perspective, discriminative descriptions are generally extracted from input images as to computationally represent the image for the recognition task [4]. These descriptors can be global/local presentation (decomposing as some key-points,

© Springer Nature Switzerland AG 2021
P. Chomphuwiset et al. (Eds.): MIWAI 2021, LNAI 12832, pp. 34–44, 2021.
https://doi.org/10.1007/978-3-030-80253-0_4

for example) depending on the applications and purposes. Examples of the descriptors include Harris descriptors, SURF (Speeded Up Robust Feature), SIFT (Scale-invariant Feature Transform), and MSER (Maximally Stable Extremal Regions [2–4]. For SURF, the advantage of SURF descriptor is computational and robust against different image size transformations, and various brightness that is proper for capturing images in uncontrolled environments such as from mobile devices in various location and time. Therefore, this paper presents an application of computer vision and machine learning to recognize book covers and retrieve the similar books based on their context. This work is divided into 2 folds, (i) the book-cover recognition is performed based around on SURF descriptor and a matching technique and (ii) related-book retrieval is carried out by a natural language processing technique that considers book's description as a context and results top k of similar books.

The rest of the paper is organized as follows: Sect. 2 overviews some related works before the proposed method for implementing the application is explained in Sect. 3. The experiments and results are highlighted in Sect. 4. This includes a discussion of the experimental results. Last, the conclusion and future work is given in Sect. 5.

2 Literature Review

Many researches interested to apply SURF algorithm in various areas. Jian et al. [1] proposed the comparative study between SIFT and SURF for face feature descriptors. These two descriptors are robust and invariant for scale change, blur, rotation, illumination change and transformation images. However, SURF algorithm is faster than SIFT with the same performance. Xingteng et al. [2] proposed the image matching method for improving SURF algorithm. This paper proposed to construct the k-d tree and BBF algorithm instead of the linear algorithm to increase the speed of matching. Hachemi et al. [3] proposed the evaluating image matching methods for book cover identification from SIFT, SURF, ORB (Oriented FAST and Rotated BRIEF), and AKAZE(Accelerated Kaze). The result showed that the SURF and AKAZE were the same accuracy and computational time consuming. Wei et al. [4] proposed the improvement of matching accuracy of SURF using Lowe optimization algorithm, (the descriptor dimension extension algorithm and the direct optimization method). Yoo et al. [5] proposed the invariant color information and global content to solve the problem of illumination variation and local pattern matching. The high recall rate came from the perfect matching between the corresponding points. Huijuan and Qiong [6] proposed the Fast-Hessin detector for SURF using the FAST (Features from Accelerated Segment Test) corner detector for increasing the speed in the real-time images.

From the previous research, the SURF is fast, tested in real time image, and tested in book cover images, that it is able to apply in book cover recognition from capturing mobile image.

3 Proposed Method

This paper proposes a technique to implement a computer vision application for recognizing book cover using SURF descriptor and the content-similarity retrieval using a

Bag of Word (BOW) and distant similar functions. The diagram of the proposed method is shown in Fig. 1. Our proposed method consists of the two parallel processes: (i) book cover recognition, extracting the key-points as the descriptors for the matching task to recognize books in a database (ii) extracting the representation of book description for the retrieval task.

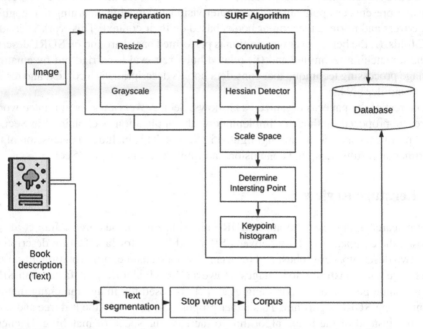

Fig. 1. Overall process of the proposed techniques to implement the application.

1. Book cover recognition consists of two sub processes, which image preprocessing and feature extracting using SURF, and matching process.
2. Book similarity retrieval consists of 4 processes i.e. (i) word segmentation using Longest-matching algorithms, (ii) stop word removal, (iii) feature generation, and (iv) matching process.

3.1 Image Preprocessing

This image pre-processing is aimed at preparing an input image (I) for the subsequence processes. The preparing is as follows:

- Image resizing: The input image is resized to 300 x 500 pixels.
- Grayscale conversion: The resized images are converted to Grayscale using Eq. 1 and shown in Fig. 1.

$$I_g = R(0.299) + G(0.587) + B(0.114) \tag{1}$$

where $I(R, G, B)$ is the color density of red, green and blue respectively, an example is depicted in Fig. 2.

Fig. 2. Grayscale conversion of the book cover

3.2 Feature Extraction Using Speed-Up Robust Features (SURF Descriptor)

This section explains the details of a technique used to extract a discriminative feature from the images of book covers. SURF descriptor is deployed in this stage. SURF is originally derived based on local geometric feature and SIFT [4]. The technique provides optimal computation, comparing to SIFT [1].

1. SIFT descriptors
   In general, SIFT extracts a local feature from images. It is able process a scale invariability, rotation, and affine invariance, and keep high matching rate by reducing noise, occlusion, and confusion. SIFT algorithm is decomposed by 5 steps:
   - Scale-space extreme detection – It detects some points on a book cover known as key-points. It is applied by the difference of the Gaussian function. The maxima or minima key points is calculated by the scale-space of an image that uses the convolution of the Gaussian $G(x, y, \sigma)$ with an input image $I_g(x, y)$, and the scale space of the image defined by (2)

$$L(x, y, \sigma) = G(x, y, \sigma) * I_g(x, y) \tag{2}$$

where the Gaussian convolution kernel $G(x, y, \sigma)$ of the second order derivative with the image shown as (3)

$$G(x, y, \sigma) = \frac{\left(\frac{1}{2\Pi\sigma^2}\right)e^{-(x^2+y^2)}}{2\sigma^2} \tag{3}$$

where (x, y) is the pixel coordinates of the input image,
σ is scale factor, and.
$L(x, y, \sigma)$ is the scale-space image.
Nearby scales are differentiated by multiplicative factor k to calculate local maximum or minimum of $D(x, y, \sigma)$ [7] as demonstrated in Eq. (4).

$$\begin{aligned} D(x, y, \sigma) &= (G(x, y, k, \sigma) - G(x, y, \sigma)) * I(x, y) \\ &= L(x, y, k, \sigma) - L(x, y, \sigma) \end{aligned} \tag{4}$$

The maxima or minima of $D(x, y, \sigma)$ is calculated by the comparison between sample point with respect to 8 neighbors at same scale and the neighboring pixels in each scale. The key-points, when it shows a local maxima or minima among all compared pixels, are considered as candidate sets.

- Key point localization – given a set of the candidate key-points, the found potential key-point locations must be delicate to keep more regular results. Taylor series expansion of scale space is used to obtain more regular location of extreme.
- Orientation assignment – image rotation achieves the invariance for each key-point. The key-point location is depended on the scale that considers the neighborhood coping with the gradient magnitude and the direction that it calculated in local regions. An orientation histogram with 360 degrees separated to 36 bins is created and weighted by the gradient magnitude and Gaussian-weight circular windows (setting σ equal to 1.5 times the scale of key point). The highest histogram peak is considered by the calculated orientation. It creates the stability matching key point, same location and scale, and different direction.
- Feature description of key point – a 16x16 key-point neighborhood is a created key -point descriptor around the key point. The 16 sub-blocks of 4x4 size are divided from a key point descriptor, that are 8 bin histograms. So, the total of each feature key point descriptor is 128 elements.
- Feature matching – The nearest neighbors identify the key point between the two matched images. The ratio of the first closest distance and the second closest distance is obtained. The false matching is rejected if the matched distance is greater than a predetermined threshold.
2. SURF descriptors

SURF has the major process to be like SIFT, but it reduces the time consuming, using extracting the feature.

- Feature extraction – SURF algorithm uses Hessian matrix, that determines the maxima value point. In Hessian matrix, scale σ to a point $X = (x, y)$ in image is shown as [8]

$$H(X, \sigma) = \begin{bmatrix} Lxx(x, \sigma) & Lxy(x, \sigma) \\ Lxy(x, \sigma) & Lyy(x, \sigma) \end{bmatrix} \tag{5}$$

- Orientation assignment – Using Haar wavelet determine the detected key point.
- SURF descriptor – SURF descriptor is able to calculate from the Haar wavelet and with the integral images. The square region is constructed from around the key points. This window region, spatial information, is splitting into small sub-region (4×4 square), that is described by the values of a wavelet response in the x and y directions. The robustness of deformations and translations are created from the Gaussian weight centered at the interest point of the interested area. 64D ($4 \times 4 \times 4 = 64$) is the descriptor vector of the SURF algorithm. SURF descriptor is lighting invariant because of Haar wavelet.
- Interested point matching - The key-point matching is performed using Euclidean distance between the feature vectors. It matches the key point of input and training image using the distance.

3.3 Word Segmentation

The word segmentation is the main function in Natural Language Processing (NLP). It can be used and applied in various domains. In English, the words can be separated by the separator such as spaces and "." (dot). However, Thai language is not appliable to separate using that separator such as a space. Therefore, several segmentation techniques have been invented. This work applies Longest-matching algorithm to segment the words in the book descriptions, shown in Fig. 3. [9]. The technique starts with the whole of the sentence search, If the whole of the sentence is found in the dictionary, return the sentence as a word. Else, the algorithm will cut the rightmost alphabet and search again in the dictionary, repeat step until found the word in the dictionary or empty sentence (in case of non-word in dictionary for example miss spelling). The algorithm demonstrated below. The book description and the sample output of the Longest-matching word segmentation are shown in Fig. 4.

The output of this process is the list of words. However, the words are consisted of some types of words that they are large frequency and unable to identify the characteristic.

3.4 Stop Word Removal

Stop word removal is implemented to eradicate the non-significant words such as conjunction, preposition, pronoun, adverb, and Interjection. These types of word are mostly found in the sentence. In addition, this removal can reduce the computational time and the storage space. Moreover, it can improve the proficiency in the retrieval task.

An example sentence is "ฉันนั่งรอพบเธอ", this sentence consisted of the lists of words "ฉัน|นั่ง|รอ|พบ|เธอ"
BEGIN
    Step 1 Compared the sentence with the dictionary.
    Step 2
        if the sentence is found in the dictionary, it is the word, return the output else cut the rightest alphabet of the sentence and search in the dictionary again.
    Step 3 Repeat Step 1 to 3 until the sentence is empty.
END

Fig. 3. An example of book descriptions.

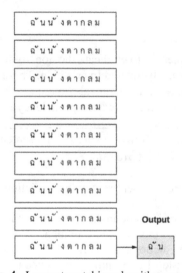

Fig. 4. Longest-matching algorithm sample.

3.5   Feature Generation

The descriptors of the book descriptions are generated using a BOW technique. A set distinct word is collected and stored in a database as a word corpus. For example.

Sentence 1: I / eat / rice.

Sentence 2: I / want / eat / rice.

Sentence 3: I / love / rice.

The corpus is [I, eat, rice, want, love] as shown in Fig. 5 and Fig. 6.

The word in the corpus is sorted by the number of appearances in the collected documents (book description). Top m of the most appearing in the collected documents is set as the codebook or template word (T). Given a book descriptor (D), the feature is

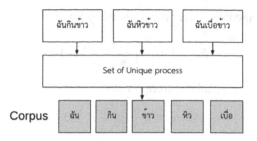

Fig. 5. The corpus construction

Fig. 6. The book description corpus construction sample

then generated by constructing a histogram of frequency of T on all words in D. Finally, min-max normalization is performed to result the final feature of the document.

3.6 Similarity Measurements

The distance function for image recognition is consisted of the 3 processes, i.e. (i) distance between point to point, (ii) percentage of the book cover and (iii) similarity score.

- The distance (D) between point to point is usually calculated from Euclidean Distance as shown in Eq. 6:

$$D = \sqrt{\sum\nolimits_{i=1}^{n} (p_i - q_i)^2} \tag{6}$$

where p is the feature of the database book, and.
q is the feature of the input book.

- The distance between the book cover is calculated by Eq. 7.

$$S_n = \sum\nolimits_{i=D}^{n} D_i \tag{7}$$

where S_n is the sum of the distance,
n is the number of key-points, and.
D is the distance between point to point.

- The percentage of the book cover is calculated by Eq. 8.

$$P_n = 100 - \left(\frac{S_n}{\max(s)}\right) \times 100 \tag{8}$$

- The similarity score is calculated from Eq. 9.

$$Score = n \times 0.9 + P \times 0.1 \tag{9}$$

where n is the number of paired points.

The distance measurement for content recognition (retrieving similar book contents) is performed by Eq. 6 using the generated histogram.

3.7 Performance Evaluation

The performance evaluation is carried out by determining the recall value of the recognition and retrieval of the books in the database. We consider top-k similarity for each query from the database. For any query, If the related items are in top-k, the result from the query is correct. The evaluation is divided into:

1. the image recognition evaluation is calculated by Eq. 10.

$$\frac{\sum a}{n} \times 100 \tag{10}$$

where a is the number of correct answers and n is the total of trials.
2. the content recognition evaluation is calculated by Eq. 11.

$$\frac{\sum p}{n} \times 100 \tag{11}$$

where p is the percentage of the book content.

4 Experiment and Result

This work collected 1,500 books (the covers and the descriptions) from the internet and manual collection as the dataset. 500 books were separated from the total dataset to generate the words corpus. A set of random books (30 books) was used in the experiment. The input book covers were captured from mobile devices taking on the actual book covers. Each of the book was experiment 10 trails to result a set of similar books in terms of the book covers and contents. The result is demonstrated in Table 1 and 2.

From Table 1, the accuracy of the book cover recognition is 89.33%. The incorrect answers are come from the same color, same picture of cover books such as from picture 1 and 2 in Table 2.

The accuracy of the content is 63.33%. The incorrect answers are from the same frequent words such as JAVA programming and C programming, the same content but it is different programming language.

Table 1. The experimental result.

Detail	Sum of correct or correct percentage	Sum of trails	Average
Accuracy of the book cover recognition	268	30	89.33% ± 5.34
Accuracy of the book cover content similarity	1600	30	63.33% ± 8.23

Table 2. Example of the experiment results

Image	Book Cover		Book Content	
	correct	Incorrect	correct	Incorrect
	9	1	5	0
	8	2	5	0
	10	0	2	3

5 Conclusion

This presents an application of computer vision and machine learning to recognize book covers and retrieve the similar books based on their context. This work is divided into 2 folds, (i) the book-cover recognition is performed based around on SURF descriptor and a matching technique and (ii) related-book retrieval is carried out by a natural language processing technique that considers book's description as a context and results top k of similar books. In the experiment, book data is collected from different source over the internet and manual collection. The experiments are conducted and evaluate the performance using the 30 real-image book covers. The output shows that the accuracy of book cover image recognition is 89.33% and from book description is 63.33%. The incorrect results are from the fact that there is variation of image color of the book cover and some same frequent words appear in a number of books that are not related.

The future work is aimed to improve the accuracy of the content using graph similarity or try the key word of the book. Moreover, some book sealed with the plastic makes the reflection and overshadowed.

References

1. Jain, S., Kumar, S., Shettigar, R.: Comparative study on SIFT and SURF face feature descriptors. In: 2017 International Conference on Inventive Communication and Computational Technologies, pp. 200–205 (2017)
2. Xingteng, J., Xuan, W., Zhe, D.: Image matching method based on improved SURF algorithm. In: 2015 IEEE International Conference on Computer and Communications (ICCC), Chengdu, pp. 142–145 (2015). https://doi.org/10.1109/CompComm.2015.7387556
3. Rabie, H., Ikram, A., Biasi, W., Mahfoud, S.A.M.: Evaluating image matching methods for book cover identification (2020)
4. Wei, Q., Qiao, L., Cheng, H., Yaohong, X., Hua, L.: Strategies of improving matching accuracy about SURF. In: 2017 First International Conference on Electronics Instrumentation & Information Systems (EIIS), Harbin, pp. 1–6 (2017). https://doi.org/10.1109/EIIS.2017.8298615
5. Hyunsup, Y., Hwan-Ik, C., Hernsoo, H.: SURF algorithm with color and global characteristics. In: ICCAS-SICE, Fukuoka, pp. 183–187 (2009)
6. Huijuan, Z., Qiong, H.: Fast image matching based-on improved SURF algorithm. In: 2011 International Conference on Electronics, Communications and Control (ICECC), Ningbo, pp. 1460–1463 (2011). https://doi.org/10.1109/ICECC.2011.6066546
7. Han, Y., Yin, J., Li, J.: Face recognition based on improved SURF. In: 2013 Third International Conference on Intelligent System Design and Engineering Applications (2013)
8. Sriram, E., Pinnamaneni, B.P.: Face recognition and person localization using SURF for automated attendance system. Int. J. Comput. Appl. (0975 – 8887) International Conference on Information and Communication Technologies (ICICT-2014) (2014)
9. Haruechaiyasak, C., Kongyoung, S., Dailey, M.: A comparative study on Thai word segmentation approaches. In: 2008 5th International Conference on Electrical Engineering/Electronics, Computer, Telecommunications and Information Technology, Krabi, pp. 125–128 (2008). https://doi.org/10.1109/ECTICON.2008.4600388

Fast Classification Learning with Neural Networks and Conceptors for Speech Recognition and Car Driving Maneuvers

Stefanie Krause[1,2] (iD), Oliver Otto[2] (iD), and Frieder Stolzenburg[2]([envelope]) (iD)

[1] Research Center Finance and Information Management, University of Bayreuth,
Bayreuth, Germany
stefanie.krause@fim-rc.de
https://www.fim-rc.de/en/
[2] Automation and Computer Sciences Department, Harz University of Applied
Sciences, Wernigerode, Germany
{ootto,fstolzenburg}@hs-harz.de
http://artint.hs-harz.de/

Abstract. Recurrent neural networks are a powerful means in diverse applications. We show that, together with so-called conceptors, they also allow fast learning, in contrast to other deep learning methods. In addition, a relatively small number of examples suffices to train neural networks with high accuracy. We demonstrate this with two applications, namely speech recognition and detecting car driving maneuvers. We improve the state of the art by application-specific preparation techniques: For speech recognition, we use mel frequency cepstral coefficients leading to a compact representation of the frequency spectra, and detecting car driving maneuvers can be done without the commonly used polynomial interpolation, as our evaluation suggests.

Keywords: Recurrent neural networks · Classification with conceptors · Fast learning · Speech recognition · Detecting car driving maneuvers

1 Introduction

The field of artificial intelligence nowadays is dominated by machine learning and big data analysis, in particular with deep neural networks. Deep learning in general means a class of machine learning algorithms that use a cascade of multiple layers of nonlinear processing units for feature extraction and transformation [2]. The tremendous success of deep learning in diverse fields of artificial intelligence such as computer vision and natural language processing seems to depend on a bunch of ingredients: deep networks with nonlinearly activated neurons, convolutional layers, and iterative training methods like backpropagation.

Since deep neural networks often consist of thousands of neurons, the corresponding learning procedures require a large number of training examples, usually several thousands per example class for classification tasks (cf., e.g., [17]).

© Springer Nature Switzerland AG 2021
P. Chomphuwiset et al. (Eds.): MIWAI 2021, LNAI 12832, pp. 45–57, 2021.
https://doi.org/10.1007/978-3-030-80253-0_5

Otherwise the networks do not generalize well, and overfitting is a problem. So it would be nice to work with smaller networks, which also reduces the time for training neural networks significantly. For this, we investigate small recurrent neural networks (RNNs) and their applicability to different tasks.

We demonstrate that a relatively small number of examples suffices to train neural networks with high accuracy by two applications, namely speech recognition and detecting car driving maneuvers. We employ RNNs, more precisely echo state networks (ESNs) with conceptors [8–10]. Training them is very fast, and they can effectively be learned by simply solving a linear equation system, backpropagation or similar methods are not needed. Moreover, we improve the state of the art by application-specific preparation techniques.

2 Background and Related Works

2.1 Recurrent Neural Networks

We now briefly introduce RNNs, following the lines of [9]. We use discrete-time RNNs where time is progressed in unit steps $n = 1, 2, \ldots$ and tanh (hyperbolic tangent) as activation function which squashes the neuronal activation values into a range between -1 and $+1$. For a network consisting of N neurons, the activations $x_1(n), \ldots, x_N(n)$ at time n are collected in an N-dimensional state vector $x(n)$. The random weights of the reservoir neurons are collected in a weight matrix W^{res} of size $N \times N$. $p(n)$ is the input signal fed to the network, where the input weights are collected in the weight matrix W^{in} of size $N \times d$ (for a d-dimensional input). b is a bias. The network update equation is:

$$x(n + 1) = \tanh\left(W^{\text{res}}x(n) + W^{\text{in}}p(n + 1) + b\right) \tag{1}$$

The network-internal neuron-to-neuron connections comprised in the matrix W^{res} are (and remain) random. This includes the existence of cyclic (recurrent) connections. The equation

$$y(n) = W^{\text{out}}x(n) \tag{2}$$

specifies that an output signal $y(n)$ can be read from the network activation state $x(n)$ via the output weights comprised in the matrix W^{out} of size $d \times N$. These weights W^{out} are computed by simply solving the linear equation system of Eq. 2 such that the output signal $y(n)$ is the prediction of the (next) input signal $p(n)$, i.e., $y(n) = p(n + 1)$.

2.2 Echo State Networks and Conceptors

ESNs provide a supervised learning principle for RNNs. They employ a randomly connected neural network with fixed random weights, called reservoir. Only the connections from the reservoir to the output readout neurons are modified in the training phase by learning [11]. The input signal of an ESN induces a non-linear response signal in each neuron within the reservoir network. A linear combination of these response signals is trained to obtain the desired output [9,11]. That is why training an ESN becomes a simple linear regression task [11] (cf. Sect. 2.1).

Conceptors, their basic mechanisms and characteristics and a mathematical definition are described in [9,10]. In [9, Sect. 3.13], the classification of Japanese vowels by means of conceptors is considered: Nine male native speakers pronouncing the Japanese di-vowel /ae/ should be recognized. The corresponding procedure employing conceptors has served as the basis for the tasks considered here: speech recognition and car driving maneuvers classification.

Let us now introduce conceptors in some more detail, following the lines of [9]: A conceptor matrix C for some vector-valued random variable $x \in \mathbb{R}^N$ is defined as a linear transformation that minimizes a loss function:

$$C(R, \alpha) = \mathrm{argmin}_C \, E\left[\|x - Cx\|^2\right] + \alpha^{-2} \|C\|_{\mathrm{fro}}^2 \qquad (3)$$

where α is a control parameter, called aperture, E stands for the expectation value (temporal average), and $\|\cdot\|_{\mathrm{fro}}$ is the Frobenius norm. The closed-form solution for this optimization problem is

$$C(R, \alpha) = R(R + \alpha^{-2}I)^{-1} = (R + \alpha^{-2}I^{-1})R \qquad (4)$$

where $R = E[xx']$ is the $N \times N$ correlation matrix of x, and I is the $N \times N$ identity matrix.

To understand Eq. 4, we have to look at the singular value decomposition (SVD) of C. If $R = U\Sigma V$ is the SVD of R (where Σ is a rectangular diagonal matrix with non-negative real numbers on the diagonal), then the SVD of $C(R, \alpha)$ can be written as USV where the singular values s_i of C (comprised in the diagonal matrix S) can be written in terms of the singular values σ_i of R: $s_i = \sigma_i/(\sigma_i + \alpha^{-2}) \in [0, 1)$, for $\alpha \in (0, \infty)$.

[9] finds that the non-linearity inherent in Eq. 3 makes the conceptor matrices come out almost as projector matrices because the singular values of C are mostly close to 1 or 0. In intuitive terms, C is a soft projection matrix on a linear subspace, where samples x are projected into this subspace. C almost acts like the identity: $Cx \approx x$.

Conceptor matrices are positive semi-definite matrices whose singular vectors are the axes of the conceptor ellipsoids. Their singular values in the unit interval $[0, 1]$ represent the lengths of the ellipsoid axes. In practice, the correlation matrix R is estimated from a finite sample $X = (x(1), \ldots, x(L))$ where the $x(n)$ are the reservoir states collected during a learning run. This leads to the approximation $R_{\mathrm{approx}} = XX^T/L$. An optimal aperture α, which can be interpreted as a scaling factor, can be found by a cross-validation search (cf. [4]). Using the correlation matrix R_j from a pattern p_j and α, one can compute the conceptor matrix $C^j = C(R_j, \alpha)$.

3 Classification with Conceptors

3.1 Conceptor Algebra

On matrix conceptors, operations that satisfy most laws of Boolean logic such as NOT ($\neg$), OR ($\vee$), and AND ($\wedge$) can be defined [4]. Although not all laws of Boolean algebra are satisfied, these operations bring a great advantage for conceptors, because if we get new patterns we need not train everything from the start, but use overlaps with other already saved patterns and just save the new components (which saves memory space) [9]. Furthermore, we can use Boolean operations to check how many patterns lie in one conceptor and not in any other and for similar considerations.

3.2 Classification

To use conceptors for a classification task, we first determine two conceptors, called positive and negative evidence, for each class, e.g., words, speakers, or car driving maneuvers, based on the training data. For instance, for the classification of nine speakers, we have twice as many conceptors. For every class, we compute (train) one conceptor C^j characteristic of class j and determine a second conceptor

$$N^j = \neg(C^1 \vee \cdots \vee C^{j-1} \vee C^{j+1} \vee \cdots \vee C^m) \tag{5}$$

where $\neg$ is the Boolean negation (NOT), $\vee$ is the Boolean operation disjunction (OR) and m is the number of different classes. This characterizes the condition that this class j is not any of the other classes $1, \ldots, j-1, j+1, \ldots, m$.

After the training phase, we can classify a sample by computing the evidence values for each conceptor as well as a combined evidence. The class corresponding to the conceptor with the highest evidence value is then assumed to be the correct classification. We get the positive evidence of a conceptor by computing $E^+(p,j) = z^T C^j z$ where z is the response signal of the network. This leads to a classification by deciding for $j = \text{argmax}_i \, z^T C_i^+ z$ to select class j. $E^+(p,j)$ is a non-negative number indicating how well the signal fits into the ellipsoid of C^j. The idea behind this is that, if the reservoir is driven by a class j, the resulting response signal z will be located in a linear subspace of the (transformed) reservoir state space whose overlap with the ellipsoids C_i ($i = 1, \ldots, m$) is maximal for $i = j$.

Similarly, the negative evidence $E^-(p,j) = x^T N^j x$ (which has a positive value despite its name) is computed. It describes that the sample p is of class j and not one of the other classes. Since $E^-(p,j) = x^T N^j x$ we can compute the negative evidence of a pattern using the Boolean operations NOT and OR (cf. Eq. 5). To obtain the combined evidence, we simply sum up the previous two values:

$$E(p,j) = E^+(p,i) + E^-(p,i) \tag{6}$$

Thus the combined evidence has a greater value if both the positive evidence $E^+(p,j)$ and the negative evidence $E^-(p,j)$ have high values. This is the case if the signal is inside the conceptor C^j and has low overlap with any other conceptor. For each utterance, we compute m combined evidences $E(p,1), \ldots, E(p,m)$. The pattern p can then be classified as class j by choosing the class index j whose combined evidence $E(p,j)$ was the greatest among the collected evidences.

4   Case Studies

4.1   Speech Recognition

In this case study, we consider two different tasks: A. recognition of isolated words and B. speaker recognition. We used speech samples of adults and children of age between 3 and 45 years, female and male. The datasets for both tasks overlap but are not identical.

Isolated Word Recognition: For the recognition of isolated words we have a total of 1320 samples, divided in a training set of 880 utterances (2/3 of all samples) and a test set of 440 utterances (1/3 of all samples). In this task we recognize the German isolated words "halt", "langsamer", "links", "rechts", "schneller", "stopp", "vor", and "zurück" pronounced by different speakers (adults and children, female and male). For each of our 8 different words we have 110 training and 55 test samples.

Speaker Recognition: For this task, nine persons spoke different distinct isolated German words (per speaker we used up to 26 different words). The number of speech samples differs per speaker. The training set of every speaker is the same with 65 samples. The amount of test samples varies per speaker. Overall we have 296 test samples. We choose samples of children and adults, female and male speakers to create a diverse dataset, with different speech rate and pronunciation.

The raw speech samples need to be preprocessed, before we can pass them to the neural network. Speech recognition performance and sensitivity depends heavily on preprocessing, because the amount of data supplied to the input of the neural network usually is reduced by this. Preprocessing differentiates the voiced or unvoiced signal and creates feature vectors [6]. We develop a speaker and isolated word recognition system based on the Japanese vowels classification system in [9] and employ the Matlab code from http://minds.jacobs-university. de/research/conceptorresearch/.

We apply application-specific preparation techniques and divide the signal into discrete sequences of feature vectors that only contain relevant information about the utterance. For this, we extract features by employing mel frequency cepstral coefficients (MFCCs) and obtain uncorrelated vectors by means of discrete cosine transforms (DCT). MFCCs are the most used spectral feature extraction method [3]. It is based on frequency analysis using the mel scale similar to the human ear scale. The coefficients are a representation of the real cepstral of a windowed short-time signal derived from the fast Fourier transform (FFT) of that signal, more precisely, the logarithm of the spectral amplitudes. In our experiments, we use 12 MFCCs and thus obtain 12-dimensional time series by means of a Python implementation using the `librosa` package for music and audio analysis (see https://librosa.org/). Each utterance is sampled with 512 data points. Since the length of the original audio files is between 0.6 and 2.0 s, the sampling rate is hence between 256.0 and 853.3 Hz.

4.2 Car Driving Maneuvers

In this case study, we investigate whether driving maneuvers can be classified by the use of conceptors. Driving behavior has already been analyzed in several papers, and possible applications have been presented [5,7,15,16]. We investigate here whether conceptors can also be used for car driving maneuver detection. Furthermore, we consider the influence of the number of reservoir neurons and whether very small training datasets are sufficient to train a conceptor.

The classification method we used for this task is based on the dynamic pattern recognition method in [9, p. 74]. In addition, we have investigated whether all components of the classification method in [9] are actually necessary for the car driving maneuver classification task (cf. Sect. 5.3). The data was recorded with a smartphone which was permanently installed in the car while driving. We took care of a fix position of the smartphone relative to the vehicle. An app (written by the second author, cf. [12]) continuously recorded the lateral, longitudinal, and gravitational acceleration acting on the vehicle as well as the GPS data. The speed was derived from the GPS data. The sampling rate was 10 Hz.

This test setup was used to collect the required data for seven different maneuvers. The types of car driving maneuvers and number of measurement series used for classification are shown in Table 1. For the classification task, only those sections of the measurement series were used whose features were typical for the car driving maneuver in question. This gives us the ground truth of the data. Typical measurement series are shown in Fig. 1. For the classification task, initially only the training data was classified. For each class j, the conceptors for the classification were calculated with 8 measurement series. The number of reservoir neurons N was varied between 2 and 60, and for $N = 10$ the number of training examples was varied.

Table 1. Overview of car driving maneuvers.

Class index j	Maneuvers	Number of samples
1	Stop	10
2	Straight ahead	9
3	Start up	11
4	Slow down	8
5	Full braking	8
6	Left turn	15
7	Right turn	17

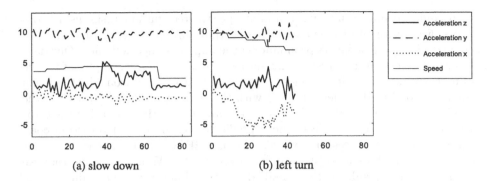

Fig. 1. Selection of examples of typical maneuver samples (acceleration in m/s^2 and velocity in m/s). Note that, following the lines of [9], we used only 4 states (called support points) for the conceptor calculation from all data series.

5 Evaluation

5.1 Speech Recognition

In both speech recognition tasks, we used 50 random ESNs to compare our results. Task A (word recognition) was to classify eight different German words. For each class of words, a positive and a negative conceptor is created (cf. Sect. 3.2). With them, we calculate the combined evidence (cf. Eq. 6) to classify test samples. We use the combined evidence classification, because its accuracy is higher in comparison to the positive or negative evidence classification alone. In Table 2, the error rates of Task A with and without conceptors as well as the error rate of a random guess are compared. With conceptors, our speech recognition system works nearly two times better than an ESN without conceptors. In addition, our method (with conceptors) is about 2.4 times better than a random guess, even if the samples of each class are not that similar.

The goal in Task B (speaker recognition) was to classify nine speakers. Without conceptors, we have a mean of 161 false classifications in 50 trials, which equals a mean error rate of 0.544. This misclassification rate is 3.5 times higher than the mean error rate of the same task with the use of conceptors. Our error rate of 0.155 with conceptors in Task B is much smaller than in Task A. The reason probably is that, in Task A, female and male speakers have different fundamental voice frequencies pronouncing the same isolated word. Therefore an analysis that is more invariant to voice frequencies would be desirable.

Table 2. Error rates of our two tasks: A. word recognition and B. speaker recognition.

Error rates	Task A	TaskB
With conceptors	0.366	0.155
Without conceptors	0.711	0.544
Random guess	0.875	0.889

Table 3. Program runtimes for Task A and Task B.

Runtime [s]	Task A	Task B
Training	0.1704	0.1396
Test	0.0057	0.0066

To compare our results with similar speaker recognition tasks using conceptors, we investigate the speaker classification task in [9] where it is tried to recognize nine male speakers pronouncing the Japanese di-vowel /ae/. Our data set is more diverse in contrast to this dataset, because we use samples of female and male speakers of different ages. We assume that is the reason why the mean error rate (combined evidence) 0.062 with the dataset of [9] is better than the rate of 0.155 for our dataset. We have to be careful directly comparing the error rates, however, because [9] uses linear predictive coding (LPC) cepstrum coefficients for data preprocessing, whereas we use MFCCs. Note that it is not our goal to improve the state-of-the-art word error rate. We aim to show that we already get good results with a small dataset within very short training time using ESNs and conceptors.

In Table 3, it is shown that the two experiments deliver fast in training and testing. Our Matlab implementation needs less than 1 s for the training from over 500 samples. This is due to the fact that we used ESNs where the majority of the weights in the network need not be trained. In comparison to other neural networks, like convolutional neural networks (CNNs) which need thousands of samples and a long training time to get good results, our study yields proper results already with limited training. Note that the reported accuracy of CNNs with error rates less than 1% eventually is higher. Since the error rate should be low in most speech recognition tasks, a direct comparison of the proportion of misclassifications with the results of the presented tasks would be necessary (with consideration of the dataset and used classification method). Nonetheless, we find using conceptors in both tasks reduces our error rate many times. This makes conceptors a very powerful means to improve speech recognition tasks, which should be tested and verified further, of course.

5.2   Car Driving Maneuvers

In this section, we describe our findings with which reservoir size and which amount of training data classification of car driving maneuvers is possible. Table 4 shows the results of classifications with different reservoir sizes. For each class of car driving maneuvers, h^+ and h^- are the positive and negative evidence vectors used for classification [9, p. 77] (cf. Sect. 3.2). One aim was to find out whether the reservoir size has a significant influence on the classification. The smallest reservoir we used had 2 neurons, the largest 60 neurons. For each reservoir size, 100 random reservoirs were generated. The conceptors of positive and negative evidence (cf. Sect. 3.2) were calculated for each driving maneuver and each reservoir. For each driving maneuver and reservoir, eight measurement series have been used to calculate the conceptors.

As it can be seen in Table 4, our experiments allow classification with very small reservoirs. In the first five classes, two neurons are sufficient for an almost 100% correct classification. Only for the driving maneuvers "straight ahead" and "full braking", the correctness is only 36% and 31% respectively. But the classification accuracy could be improved with larger reservoirs. With the exception of "full braking", every maneuver is classified correctly with at least 99%. In the case of emergency braking, we assume that significant features of the class are lost due to the previous data processing. Further investigations with alternative support points (cf. Figure 1) optimized for the class of emergency braking finally allow significantly better classifications.

Table 4. Classification of training data. The table shows the accuracy of the computed conceptors for positive and negative evidence in %.

Maneuver		Size of reservoir N								
		2	4	6	8	10	20	30	40	60
Start up	h^+	99.9	100	100	99.9	100	100	99.9	100	100
	h^-	2.9	11.1	38.4	50.1	51.0	60.1	69.5	79.6	82.0
Slow down	h^+	99.9	99.8	99.3	98.8	99.3	99.6	99.8	99.9	100
	h^-	1.0	10.8	38.6	39.6	41.3	39.1	41.5	44.1	49.4
Right turn	h^+	99.8	99.9	99.3	98.9	98.0	98.4	96.5	96.1	95.5
	h^-	78.4	92.6	97.9	98.0	96.4	100	100	100	100
Left turn	h^+	98.5	98.1	97.5	97.8	96.8	99.3	98.9	99.3	99.8
	h^-	36.1	36.9	79.4	92.6	93.9	98.0	100	100	100
Straight ahead	h^+	36.1	62.4	89.3	93.0	99.4	100	100	100	100
	h^-	0.0	0.0	0.0	0.0	0.0	0.0	0.0	0.0	0.0
Full braking	h^+	31.0	34.3	40.4	45.3	47.1	54.4	59.5	60.8	64.3
	h^-	0.0	0.0	0.0	0.0	0.0	0.0	0.0	0.0	0.0

Table 5 (left part) shows the results for classifications with different amounts of training data. For each driving maneuver, a minimum of two measurements series was used to calculate the conceptors. The number of measurement series for the training amount was then gradually increased to eight measurement series. 100 random reservoirs were generated and corresponding conceptors were calculated for each class. This time both the training data and the test data were classified. Since only a small number of measurement series was available, measurement series that were not used for training were automatically assigned to the test set.

Classifications with an accuracy of at least 70.7% and up to 100% could be achieved even with a very small amount of training, consisting of two measurement series. However, again the driving maneuvers "straight ahead" and "full braking" are an exception and are poorly classified. Nevertheless, Table 5 (left part) also shows that with increasing training size the accuracy of the classification improves significantly in many cases.

In summary, the accuracy of our car driving maneuver classification is rather good. Using random guessing as baseline, the accuracy of classifying seven different car driving maneuvers would reduce to $1/7 = 14.3\%$ which is far less than our values. Furthermore, in other experiments, often only the simpler task of binary classification is considered, e.g., only with respect to driver inattendance [7,15]. In our experiments, we also investigated open-set testing, i.e., considering also the case that the car driving behavior does not correspond to one of the given maneuvers. For this, the thresholds for the components of the evidence vectors have to be adjusted correctly (see also [12, Sect. 5.2]).

5.3   Identifying Essential Factors

Let us finally analyze essential factors of car driving maneuver detection, namely the influence of 1. using a linear activation function and 2. omitting polynomial interpolation, which are part of the method in [9], on the classification accuracy:

linear vs. nonlinear activation function: Motivated by linear neural networks [14] where all neurons are linearly activated, experiments with linear activation were carried out. Only the activation function of the existing classifier was changed for these analyses. Instead of tanh, a linear activation function is applied.

with vs. without polynomial interpolation: We have analyzed the influence of polynomial interpolation on the classifications of driving maneuvers. For this purpose, polynomial interpolation was not performed after data normalization. Here again tanh was used as the activation function in these analyses.

In total, 100 test runs (each with a randomly generated reservoir) with $n = 5$ and $n = 8$ training data sequences were performed. In Table 5 (right part), h^+ and h^- again are the positive and negative evidence vectors used for classification (cf. Sect. 5.2). We can see how much the classification with linear activation is better or worse than the classification with tanh as activation function. In the column "polynomial" it is shown how much the classification is better or worse if polynomial interpolation is not performed. The last column shows the results if both linear activation and no polynomial interpolation is performed. Results for the classification of training data and test data are presented separately for each car driving maneuver. The difference between the classification of the original implementation (with polynomial interpolation and the modified implementation) is given in percent. The calculation rule is: $\Delta_{quality} = quality_{original} - quality_{modification}$. If $\Delta_{quality}$ is negative, the classification of the original implementation is worse. These values are highlighted in Table 5 (right part).

Looking at the classification of the training measurement series, the classification with linear activation is 2.9% worse in the worst case ("straight ahead", h^+, $n = 8$). For emergency braking (h^+, $n = 5$) even better by 1.4%. For h^- there are also opposing values. For "start up", the linear activation achieves a better classification (4.0% or 6.8% better), whereas for "slow down" it achieves a significantly worse classification (23.2% or 29.0% worse). Finally, when classifying the training set with a linear activation for h^+ almost always the same quality is achieved as by the original implementation with tanh.

Table 5. Classification with a varying amount of training data (left part) and Comparison of the modifications (right part). Both with a constant reservoir size of $N = 10$ neurons. For each driving maneuver, the number of test series m of the test quantity is listed in the line "test". The number of training series n is listed at the top of the table.

			Classification							Modifications					
										linear		polynomial		linear and polynomial	
		n	2	3	4	5	6	7	8	5	8	5	8	5	8
start up	training	h^+	100	100	100	100	100	99.7	99.9	1.0	0.5	0	0	0.8	0.9
		h^-	93.0	74.0	63.5	47.6	48.5	53.4	52.1	−4.0	−6.8		−0.4	−4.6	−5.8
	test	m	9	8	7	6	5	4	3	6	3	6	3	6	3
		h^+	83.7	97.3	98.9	100	100	100	100	0	0	0	0	0	0
		h^-	37.7	54.6	50.6	49.3	69.8	72.5	88.0	−6.0	−1.3	−0.3	−1.0	−7.7	1.7
slow down	training	h^+	100	100	100	100	100	98.4	99.1	0	2.4	0	−0.6	0	1.5
		h^-	49.5	56.7	63.0	58.8	45.3	44.9	46.8	23.2	29.0	3.4	4.9	21.0	23.4
	test	m	6	5	4	3	2	1	0	3	0	3	0	3	0
		h^+	88.5	91.0	88.0	88.7	85.5	100	–	14.0	–	−1.7	–	5.7	–
		h^-	37.7	29.4	11.0	6.7	7.0	27.0	–	1.3	–	2.3	–	1.7	–
right turn	training	h^+	100	98.7	97.0	97.8	99.5	96.4	98.5	2.2	0.3	**-0.4**	**-0.5**	1.8	1.6
		h^-	98.0	99.0	96.0	100	99.3	98.0	96.8	1.2	**−1.5**	1.6	−0.6	3.0	0.1
	test	m	15	14	13	12	11	10	9	12	9	12	9	12	9
		h^+	98.5	97.4	95.6	97.7	99.1	97.5	99.2	1.8	**−0.3**	0	0.4	1.3	0.1
		h^-	94.1	96.6	95.2	97.5	97.1	97.0	96.0	1.5	**−3.0**	1.7	**−1.0**	1.4	−1.0
left turn	training	h^+	100	99.7	100	100	99.8	95.6	96.4	0	**−0.9**	0	−0.6	0	0.4
		h^-	94.0	95.7	95.0	96.0	95.0	93.0	93.9	2.8	**−0.6**	0.2	−0.6	3.0	−0.4
	test	m	13	12	11	10	9	8	7	10	7	10	7	10	7
		h^+	70.7	85.8	87.6	83.0	91.6	98.4	99.4	1.4	0	0	0	0.9	−0.1
		h^-	93.0	94.6	95.0	95.2	95.0	93.0	94.0	1.9	**−1.0**	1.1	**−1.0**	2.2	−1.0
straight ahead	training	h^+	93.5	95.7	99.5	95.0	97.7	96.6	95.6	0.6	2.9	**−2.6**	**−1.9**	**−2.0**	3.8
		h^-	0	0	0	0	0	0	0	0	0	0	0	0	0
	test	m	7	6	5	4	3	2	1	4	1	4	1	4	1
		h^+	45.4	74.3	89.6	82.3	80.0	74.5	48.0	2.0	7.0	**−4.3**	**−5.0**	**−2.3**	8.0
		h^-	0	0	0	0	0	0	0	0	0	0	0	0	0
full braking	training	h^+	87.0	63.0	30.8	34.2	32.8	40.0	46.3	−1.4	1.5	0.8	**−2.1**	**−1.6**	0.6˙
		h^-	22.0	2.3	0	0	0	0	0	−0.2	0	0	0	0	0
	test	m	6	5	4	3	2	1	0	3	0	3	0	3	0
		h^+	11.0	35.6	20.3	36.7	78.5	69.0	–	0.7	–	3.3	–	4.7	–
		h^-	0	0	0	0	0	0	–	0	–	0	–	0	–

Polynomial interpolation seems to have less impact on the classification. Although there are again classifications that achieve a worse quality without polynomial interpolation. Overall the quality of the modification is up to 5% better. The greatest (positive) deterioration compared to the original implementation is 4.9% for the "slow down" class (training measurement series, h^-, $n = 8$). Often even the same quality is achieved ($\Delta_{\text{quality}} = 0$). For further details the reader is referred to [12].

In conclusion, it should be noted that no uniform result could be achieved, thus a generally positive or negative effect can not be shown. The original and the modified implementations achieve similar quality. But from this we may conclude that the commonly used hyperbolic tangent function and polynomial interpolation is not really mandatory to solve classification tasks. Hence the procedure in [9] can be simplified significantly by using plain linear activation and omitting polynomial interpolation.

6 Conclusions

We have shown that fast learning with ESNs and conceptors is possible for diverse applications, in particular, speech recognition and detecting car driving maneuvers. With already hardly more than one hundred samples per class accurate classification is possible, in contrast to other neural networks like CNNs that require thousands of samples for each class. In addition, training conceptor networks for classification lasts only a few seconds. Nevertheless only with application-specific methods high accuracy is reachable, e.g., using MFCCs for speech recognition. Furthermore, existing procedures can be simplified, e.g., employing simple linear activation and omitting polynomial interpolation without loosing much accuracy, as done for car driving maneuver detection. Further work will consider even more applications and simplifications of RNNs (cf. [14]) and focus more on open-set testing, which seems to be important also for speech recognition [1]. While we use a common one-vs-all classification scheme with as many output units as there are classes in a dataset, a novel one-vs-one classification scheme that trains each output unit to distinguish between a specific pair of classes had recently been developed [13]. A comparison to our classification method could be of further interest.

References

1. Clopper, C.G., Pisoni, D.B., Tierney, A.T.: Effects of open-set and closed-set task demands on spoken word recognition. J. Am. Acad. Audiol. **17**(5), 331–349 (2006). http://www.ncbi.nlm.nih.gov/pmc/articles/PMC3324094/
2. Deng, L., Yu, D.: Deep learning: Methods and applications. Found. Trends Sign. Process. **7**(3–4), 198–387 (2014). http://research.microsoft.com/pubs/209355/DeepLearning-NowPublishing-Vol7-SIG-039.pdf
3. Dey, N.: Intelligent Speech Signal Processing. Academic Press, Cambridge (2019)
4. He, X., Jaeger, H.: Overcoming catastrophic interference using conceptor-aided backpropagation. In: ICLR 2018 – 6th International Conference on Learning Representations. Vancouver (2018). arXiv:1707.04853
5. Hong, J.H., Margines, B., Dey, A.K.: A smartphone-based sensing platform to model aggressive driving behaviors. In: Proceedings of the SIGCHI Conference on Human Factors in Computing Systems, pp. 4047–4056. CHI 2014, ACM, New York, NY, USA (2014). https://doi.org/10.1145/2556288.2557321
6. Ibrahim, Y.A., Odiketa, J.C., Ibiyemi, T.S.: Preprocessing technique in automatic speech recognition for human computer interaction: an overview. Ann. Comput. Sci. Ser. **15**(1), 186–191 (2017)

7. Islinger, T., Köhler, T., Ludwig, B.: Driver distraction analysis based on FFT of steering wheel angle. In: Adjunct Proceedings of the 3rd International Conference on Automotive User Interfaces and Interactive Vehicular Applications, pp. 21–22 (2011). http://www.auto-ui.org/11/docs/AUI2011_adjunctproceedings.pdf
8. Jaeger, H.: Echo state network. Scholarpedia **2**(9), 2330 (2007). https://doi.org/10.4249/scholarpedia.2330, revision #151757
9. Jaeger, H.: Controlling recurrent neural networks by conceptors. CoRR - computing research repository, Cornell University Library (2014). arXiv:1403.3369
10. Jaeger, H.: Using conceptors to manage neural long-term memories for temporal patterns. J. Mach. Learn. Res. **18**(1), 387–429 (2017). https://doi.org/10.5555/3122009.3122022
11. Jaeger, H., Haas, H.: Harnessing nonlinearity: predicting chaotic systems and saving energy in wireless communication. Science **304**(5667), 78–80 (2004)
12. Otto, O.: Analysis of smartphone sensor data with recurrent neural networks for classification of driving maneuvers. WAIT 03/2020, Automation and Computer Sciences Department, Harz University of Applied Sciences (2020). https://doi.org/10.25673/35931, in German
13. Pawara, P., Okafor, E., Groefsema, M., He, S., Schomaker, L.R., Wiering, M.A.: One-vs-one classification for deep neural networks. Pattern Recogn. **108**, 107528 (2020). https://doi.org/10.1016/j.patcog.2020.107528
14. Stolzenburg, F., Litz, S., Michael, O., Obst, O.: The power of linear recurrent neural networks. CoRR – computing research repository, Cornell University Library (2018). arXiv:1802.03308, latest revision 2021
15. Torkkola, K., Massey, N., Wood, C.: Driver inattention detection through intelligent analysis of readily available sensors. In: Proceedings of 7th International IEEE Conference on Intelligent Transportation Systems (IEEE Cat. No.04TH8749), pp. 326–331 (2004). https://doi.org/10.1109/ITSC.2004.1398919
16. Vaiana, R., Iuele, T., Astarita, V., Caruso, M.V., Tassitani, A., Zaffino, C., Giofré, V.: Driving behavior and traffic safety: an acceleration-based safety evaluation procedure for smartphones. Mod. Appl. Sci. **8**(1), 88–96 (2014). https://doi.org/10.5539/mas.v8n1p88
17. Warden, P.: Speech commands: A dataset for limited-vocabulary speech recognition. CoRR – computing research repository, Cornell University Library (2018). arXiv:1804.03209

Feature Group Importance
for Automated Essay Scoring

Jih Soong Tan[1]([envelope]) [iD] and Ian K. T. Tan[2] [iD]

[1] Priority Dynamics Sdn Bhd, E-05-01 & 02, Garden Shoppe, Jalan USJ 25/1C,
One City, 47650 Subang Jaya, Selangor, Malaysia
jsoong@prioritydynamics.com
[2] Monash University Malaysia, Bandar Sunway, 47500 Subang Jaya, Malaysia
ian.tan1@monash.edu

Abstract. One of the challenges in essay scoring is that it is highly
subjective to the human graders. There have been numerous research
projects conducted on improving computerised Automated Essay Scoring (AES). AES systems generally rely on hand-crafted linguistic features
to construct a classification model for essay scoring. The majority of the
AES systems' classification algorithm inputs are based on three main
feature groups; lexical, grammatical, and semantic feature groups. This
paper presents an empirical study to explore the influence of each feature group on the performance of AES classification models based on
a general approach of the AES system. The results uncovered that the
grammatical and semantic feature groups are lacking due to their poor
performance and typical over-fitting of the classification models when
using the features in the feature group.

Keywords: Auto essay scoring · Features · Importance · EASE ·
ASAP

1   Introduction

An essay is defined as a focused piece of writing in responding to a prompt.
Essay writing allows people to communicate thoughts that corresponds to a
prompt or topic question, and convince the reader that their stand is reasonable,
reliable, and conceivable. For academic purposes, assessors commonly use essays
to evaluate individual student's abilities, knowledge, and performance. However,
the human graders may be inconsistent and inaccurate due to high subjectivity
factors [25]. Thus, human essay grading requires a significant amount of time
and is labourious. Automated Essay Scoring (AES) systems were invented to
alleviate all these human graders' shortcomings. Automated Essay Scoring is an
implementation that makes computers to be the graders, where it allow them to
evaluate an essay written surrounding a prompt and provide a score to it.

The first work-related to Automated Essay Scoring is created in 1966 when
Page [21] shared the thoughts on the computer "grader" and invented a computing scoring software called Project Essay Grade (PEG). Over the succeeding

© Springer Nature Switzerland AG 2021
P. Chomphuwiset et al. (Eds.): MIWAI 2021, LNAI 12832, pp. 58–70, 2021.
https://doi.org/10.1007/978-3-030-80253-0_6

decades, there have been numerous new developments and creations in the AES field. Some of the noteworthy system are e-rater V2 [1], Schema Extract Analyse and Report (SEAR) [5], and Intelligent Essay Assessor (IEA) [9]. These systems are generally based on extracting three linguistic feature groups, which are lexical, grammatical, and semantic features.

In this study, we present an evaluation on a generic technique of feature engineering in AES. A well written essay required multiple key attributes including written surrounding the designated prompts, well organized structure, smooth flow, coherent, enough length, no spelling error and good punctuation usage [25]. Hence, we establish feature influence experiments to investigate the influence strengths and weakness of current feature engineering in AES using a generic feature engineering technique. The purpose of this research is to reveal the influence of various feature groups in AES that may further improve the performance of AES classification. Using known state-of-the-art learning algorithms for the classification models, the strengths and the weaknesses of the current feature engineering method are revealed.

2 Related Work

Feature engineering allows the system to improve its understanding of the data by leveling up the abstraction of data continuously. For feature engineering in AES, there has been several efforts done by the other researchers. Phandi et al. [22] have worked on AES by implementing the Enhanced AI Scoring Engine (EASE) engine to extract features and using the feature to train a Bayesian Linear Ridge Regression (BLRR) model which scored an average of 0.7045 Quadratic Weighted Kappa (QWK) score. The EASE engine mainly groups features into 4 main groups which are length, part-of-speech (PoS), bag of words (BoW), and prompt. It is often being used by others as the baseline feature engineering comparison to their own research projects [14,18,27] as it is invented by one of the top 3 winners of the Automated Student Assessment Prize (ASAP) competition. Hence the EASE engine is considered to be a robust and baseline engine for AES.

Yannakoudakis et al. [28] have implemented robust accurate statistical parsing (RASP) system [3] which is a similar feature extraction method to the EASE engine used by Phandi et al. [22]. Likewise, the RASP system can similarly group into 4 types of features which are lexical, PoS, syntactic, and others. However, the RASP system does not provide any prompt-specific features.

Coh-Metrix is a system proposed by Graesser et al. [10] where it is an integration of varying software modules that extract features based on language, discourse, cohesion, and world knowledge [15]. The Coh-Metrix allows the extraction of up to 106 features which can be grouped into 9 feature types; semantic, discourse, syntactic, text description, lexical diversity, text ease-ability, connectives, word information, and referential cohesion. Latifi and Gierl [12] have taken the ASAP dataset and built a random forest model based on Coh-Metrix features, which scored an average of 0.7 QWK score. The score reported is slightly lower compared to the model based on the EASE engine as reported by Phandi et al. [22]. Similarly, Chen and He [4] have defined 5 groups of features, which includes lexical, syntactical, grammatical, contextual, and prompt-specific features which are similar to the EASE engine. Eid and Wanas [8] have proposed to focus on lexical features for AES, where they gathered 22 lexical features from three other pieces of research on lexical features. They managed to improve the QWK score by 0.02 through the combination of lexical features.

Liu et al. [13] have proposed to use two types of feature groups; structure and textual. The structure feature group are consists of 24 features with a combination of grammatical and lexical features. The textual feature group is semantic features generated by an unsupervised learning algorithm based on word vector and subject vector. These were then used for an ensemble model of three learning algorithms (Extreme Gradient Boosting, Random Forest, and Gradient Boosting Decision Tree), which manage to outperform an open-source baseline model by 0.28 in terms of QWK score.

Cozma et al. [7] proposed a method to combine string kernel and word embeddings to extract features from essays, which were then feed into a regression and ranking model, as they hypothesized word embedding can help capture the features that the string kernel is lacking. String kernel's function helps to capture the similarity between strings in a specific theme [24]. Word embedding helps to extract significant alignment of word vectors that represent the context or meaning of the words [16].

Janda et al. [11] proposed 3 main groups of features; syntactic, semantic, and sentiment, that consists of 30 features and they worked on several feature selection methods to select the top features. These were then use for a classification model of a three-layer neural network that resulted in an average QWK score of 0.793, which shows near 0.1 improvements compared to BLRR as reported by Phandi et al. [22].

Yang et al. [27] proposed to use a finely-tuned pre-trained language model, the Bidirectional Encoder Representations from Transformers (BERT) model to extract deep semantics features out from the essays which result in a better result compare to the EASE engine. However, the BERT model requires significant effort to fine-tune the model to match each of the essay prompts, which is inefficient for the purpose of AES to lessen the effort to score essays. Ormerod et al. [20] have proposed to tackle the issue by ensembling multiple pre-trained natural language processing models and managed to get a QWK score of 0.782.

Overall, most AES systems feature engineering refers to mainly lexical, grammatical, and semantic feature groups. From our review of other related work, the results reported by Phandi et al. [22] using the EASE feature extractor is a good baseline for investigation as EASE uses all three main feature groups, namely lexical, grammatical and semantic refer to Table 1. We propose to base the evaluation on Phandi et al. to identify the influential feature groups.

3   Evaluation Methodology

Apart from evaluating the modeling part of AES, we target the investigation to focus on the generic approach of feature engineering for AES. The final goal of study is to discover the weak-point of the hand-crafted features and provide a direction for future improvement.

3.1 Data Preprocessing

Table 1. EASE feature groups and feature descriptions.

Feature group in EASE	Feature description	Main feature group
Length	Count of characters, words, commas, apostrophes, sentences, punctuation and average characters per words	Lexical
Part of speech (POS)	Count of bad POS n-grams, Count of bad POS n-grams divided by total words count	Grammatical
Prompt	Prompt words count, Synonym of prompt words count, Prompt words count divided by total words count, and Synonym of prompt words count divided by total words count	Semantic
Bag of words (BoW)	Count of unstemmed, and stemmed effective n-grams (unigrams and bigrams)	Lexical

We use the essay sets 1, 2, 7 and 8 from the dataset released for the ASAP competition. We have chosen these 4 essay sets so that we can focus on our investigation as these 4 have the same genres. The essay sets 1 and 2 are persuasive/narrative essays in the format of a letter to a newspaper. Similarly, the essay sets 7 and 8 are persuasive or narrative essays but in the format of story writing essays. The essay sets 1 and 2 have an average word length of 350. Also, essay set 7 has the least average word length at 250, whereas essay set 8 has the most average word length at 650. Despite that, essay set 8 has the smallest training set size of 918. Essay sets 1 and 2 have a similar training set size of around 1800, and essay set 7 has a training set size of 1569. Besides, essay sets 1, 2, 7, and 8 have different scores in range, where essay set 1 has 2 to 12, essay set 2 has 1 to 6, essay set 3 has 0 to 30, and essay set 8 has 0 to 60.

We extract the features from the dataset by using the functions in EASE. EASE has been used by multiple researchers over the years, and hence it is a suitable platform for generic feature engineering approach for AES [12,22,27]. EASE has 4 feature groups which are length, part of speech (PoS), bag of words (BoW), and prompt. Features generated by EASE are shown in Table 1.

We followed Phandi et al. [22] method of data preprocessing to get as close as the results they obtained with EASE. We scale the scores and later on will rescale the predicted score back and rounded to the nearest integer. For the features, we scale Length, PoS, and prompt features to range from 0 to 1, and for BoW features are recomputed to log(1+count). Splitting of train and test set required later on as the test data's scores of the competition were not released.

3.2   Learning Algorithms

Multinomial Naïve Bayes (NB) was added on top of the learning algorithms Support Vector Machine (SVM) and Bayesian Linear Ridge Regression (BLRR) that were applied in Phandi et al. [22]. Multinomial NB is included as it is known to be suitable for multinomial distributed data for short text classification. As reported by Phandi et al. [22], BLRR was chosen as it has been often proven to provide good results in natural language processing tasks, and SVM as the comparison against BLRR. The implementation of the learning algorithms is written in the Python (version 3.8) utilizing the Python scikit-learn library.

3.3   Evaluation Metric for Learning Algorithm

To evaluate the trained models, QWK was used to calculate the agreement between two raters, the human rater and the trained models. Cohen's kappa coefficient is a statistical method designed to measure the rate of agreement between two raters on a scale of 0 to 1, where 0 indicates agreement happening by chance and 1 indicates perfect agreement [6]. It is proven to be a robust measurement as it considers the possibility of the agreement happening by chance [26]. In addition, the QWK metric is the official evaluation metric being used for the ASAP competition. Also, the work by Phandi et al. [22], Yang et al. [27], Latifi & Gierl [12]; Janda et al. [11] use QWK for their evaluation.

3.4   Experimental Setup

For each essay set, the pre-processed data will be duplicated into 8 sets for the purpose of dividing them into 2 different types of dataset: "single feature group" and "exclude one feature group". "Single feature group" dataset will consist of 4 sets of data that only use one feature group, which are "Only Length", "Only PoS", "Only BoW", and "Only Prompt"; and the "exclude one feature group" dataset will consist another 4 sets of data that exclude one feature group which are "Exclude Length", "Exclude PoS", "Exclude BoW" and "Exclude Prompt". A set of pre-processed data will be kept for comparison. Hence, resulting in a total of 9 datasets for each essay set.

5-fold cross-validation used to generated the train and test set. The train set is a combination of 4-folds and the test set is 1-fold. The 9 train sets will then be the input to train the model of NB, SVM, and BLRR separately. Then, we use the trained model to predict the scores of each model of the test sets. The predicted scores will be taken into the QWK evaluation metric to compute the agreement between the human rater's scores and the AES predicted scores.

3.5   Feature Influence

The differences in QWK score between the processed dataset and the original dataset is compared to find the influence of the feature groups. For the dataset that uses only one feature group, the higher the differences of QWK score compared to the original dataset shows that is has a lower influence in the model.

The reason is the feature has no impact on the model and causes the model's QWK score to drop. Vice-versa, for the dataset excluding one feature group, the lower the differences of QWK score compared to the original dataset shows that the excluded feature has higher influence in the model.

3.6   Feature Selection

The three feature selection methods we applied to compare with previous results.

Chi-Squared. SelectKBest class from the scikit-learn library was applied and the score function of Chi-squared (CHI) was used. CHI compares two variables (feature and target variable) in a two-way contingency table, and find the relationship between the two variables. CHI is calculated as in Eq. 1

$$x^2(t,c) = \frac{N \times (AD - CB)^2}{(A+C) \times (B+D) \times (A+B) \times (C+D)} \tag{1}$$

Extra Tree Classifier. We use extra tree classifier (ET), a feature selection method from the scikit-learn library. The ET creates multiple trees and randomly split nodes using random features subsets, which is the strength of ET through the randomization attribute for numerical inputs [23]. This could be effective for the features in AES as the features generated are all numerical inputs.

Correlation. We compute the correlation to identify the relationship between features and the target variable and scores them. It is a classic feature selection method for machine learning methods, which helps improve the performance of the model by eliminating variables that are weakly related to target variable [2].

4   Results and Discussion

4.1   QWK Scores Result for Comparison

The QWK scores for "all features" dataset, the 4 "single feature group" datasets, and 4 "exclude one feature group" datasets were computed for the trained model

Table 2. Results using all EASE features

Essay set	Feature used	QWK score		
		NB	SVM	BLRR
1	All features	0.638	0.803	**0.824**
2	All features	0.517	0.601	**0.626**
7	All features	0.579	**0.760**	0.717
8	All features	0.430	0.636	**0.640**

of NB, SVM, and BLRR for each essay sets. The results for each essay set are shown in Table 2, where it shows the BLRR model outperforming the rest of the models, in agreement with Phandi et al. [22]. The best results are bold-faced.

Besides, the trained models' results of using "single feature group" are tabulated in Table 3. For each essay set, the most influential feature group is bold-faced and the least influential feature group is underlined. The length feature is the most influential feature group in essay set 1, 2 and 8, as it has the least differences in QWK scores compared to the "all features" trained model on average. On the contrary, the PoS feature is the least influential feature group.

Table 3. Results for single feature group

Essay set	Feature used	QWK score		
		NB	SVM	BLRR
1	Only Length	**0.619**	0.818	**0.795**
	Only PoS	<u>0.000</u>	<u>0.771</u>	<u>0.635</u>
	Only BoW	<u>0.000</u>	**0.822**	0.785
	Only Prompt	0.059	0.786	0.754
2	Only Length	**0.504**	0.580	**0.604**
	Only PoS	0.483	0.584	<u>0.536</u>
	Only BoW	<u>0.000</u>	**0.590**	0.574
	Only Prompt	0.246	<u>0.569</u>	0.543
7	Only Length	**0.533**	0.713	0.625
	Only PoS	<u>0.000</u>	<u>0.695</u>	<u>0.545</u>
	Only BoW	<u>0.000</u>	0.706	0.646
	Only Prompt	0.112	**0.729**	**0.665**
8	Only Length	**0.443**	**0.612**	**0.611**
	Only PoS	<u>0.000</u>	<u>0.431</u>	<u>0.343</u>
	Only BoW	<u>0.000</u>	0.468	0.470
	Only Prompt	0.098	0.558	0.500

The trained models' results of using "exclude one feature group" are summarized in Table 4. Likewise, the most influential feature group is bold-faced and the least influential feature group is underlined for each essay set. From Table 4, the length feature group is the most influential feature group among all essay sets. However, the PoS and prompt feature groups seems to be lacking. From the Table 4, the PoS feature group is slightly more influential comparing prompt feature group, as the prompt feature group has 5 out of 12 worst results among the four feature groups, and the PoS feature group only has 4. In essay sets 1 and 2, the QWK score of "exclude prompt" in SVM and BLRR compared to "all features" show it's overfitting the trained models. By overfitting, it means the prompt feature group has worsened the models.

Table 4. Results for except one feature group

Essay set	Feature used	QWK score		
		NB	SVM	BLRR
1	Excluding Length	**0.235**	0.802	**0.792**
	Excluding PoS	0.627	<u>0.814</u>	0.824
	Excluding BoW	<u>0.668</u>	**0.794**	0.799
	Excluding Prompt	0.576	0.804	<u>0.826</u>
2	Excluding Length	**0.444**	**0.565**	**0.601**
	Excluding PoS	0.511	0.583	0.617
	Excluding BoW	<u>0.546</u>	0.599	0.604
	Excluding Prompt	0.494	<u>0.636</u>	<u>0.657</u>
7	Excluding Length	**0.278**	**0.731**	**0.682**
	Excluding PoS	0.588	<u>0.752</u>	0.707
	Excluding BoW	<u>0.615</u>	0.749	0.685
	Excluding Prompt	0.556	0.749	<u>0.708</u>
8	Excluding Length	**−0.071**	**0.572**	**0.527**
	Excluding PoS	<u>0.424</u>	0.627	<u>0.640</u>
	Excluding BoW	0.412	0.615	0.591
	Excluding Prompt	0.402	<u>0.631</u>	0.637

From Tables 3 and 4, we believe the PoS and prompt feature groups have huge gaps of feature influence comparing to the other two feature groups as they often providing the worst result and overfitting the models. To determine the overfitting issue on the prompt feature, the EASE's prompt feature extraction function is evaluated. The prompt feature extraction function generates prompt features in an elementary method. The function uses the Python Natural Language ToolKit (NLTK) to tokenize the essay topic into prompt words. Subsequently, it finds the synonym of all the prompt words being used in the prompt through the WordNet corpus in NLTK. Then, the engine calculates the count of the synonym of prompt words and prompt words being used in each essay in the essay set. We postulate that the main reason for the prompt features to be the least influential and to overfit in the model is due to its weakness of extracting the semantic attributes from the essay and prompt. Semantic attributes are the attributes that correspond to the contextual meaning of words or a set of words [11]. It is crucial for essay evaluation that the essay is written around a prompt or essay topic semantically [19]. Hence, we believe that the EASE engine took into consideration of all types of parts of speech from essays and prompt, which caused the prompt feature to overfit the model. Like many types of parts of speech such as conjunctions and adpositions do not bring any contextual meaning, which could add noise to the dataset.

Also, it is noted that the method EASE to extract the semantic attributes from the essays and prompt is too brief and can be further improved in the future. It only takes into consideration the separate words instead of a pair of words or sentences, which makes it unable to capture context where a sentence or essay is starting to digress. The essays may have the prompt words or synonyms of the prompt words included, but the topic is not connected between a pair of words or sentences. As reported by Miltsakaki and Kukich [17], coherence between a pair of words or sentences is the key to make text semantically meaningful.

As the PoS feature group is almost equally poor to the prompt feature group, we evaluate the PoS feature extraction function to determine the issue. First, the function converts the words of the essay into n-grams of sizes 2 to 4. Subsequently, the function finds the PoS taggings of all the n-grams. Then, the function calculates the count of good PoS taggings n-grams by comparing it to a predefined good PoS n-gram set. We presume that the poor feature influence in the PoS feature group is due to the size limit of size in n-grams. Sentence structures are one of the crucial elements in essay evaluation [19]. However, the function only able to capture grammatical attributes within 2 to 4 n-grams.

4.2 Feature Selection Results

Chi-Squared (CHI). The results of the CHI feature selection technique for each essay set are tabulated in Table 5, where the best feature group is bold-faced, and the worst feature group is underlined (higher the feature importance score, closer the relationship to the target variable). As expected, the length feature group is the most important feature as it has the highest average feature importance scores among the four feature groups. Likewise, the BoW features outperform PoS and prompt features ranked second. Similar to previous experiment results, Both PoS and prompt feature groups are very poor in terms of feature importance scores comparing to Length and Bow feature groups.

Table 5. CHI-squared results.

Feature groups	Average feature importance scores			
	Set 1	Set 2	Set 7	Set 8
Length	**57442.281943**	**61908.621018**	**39413.094952**	**19729.548303**
BoW	53611.989232	48270.125619	36593.112551	11445.824239
Prompt	7200.552616	9321.183835	2906.868579	1971.995090
PoS	680.076900	576.846406	775.327027	229.616372

Extra Tree Classifier Feature Selection. The results from the ET feature selection are plotted as shown in Fig. 1. The feature groups are ranked in ascending order based on the feature importance score. Unlike previous results, the BoW feature group is the most important feature group in essay sets 1, 2, and 7 but the least important in essay set 8. We also see that the length feature group has the highest score in essay set 8 but lowest in essay set 7. The prompt feature group has a good score in essays set 7 and 8. However, the PoS feature group is the worst in all essay sets which corresponds with our previous results.

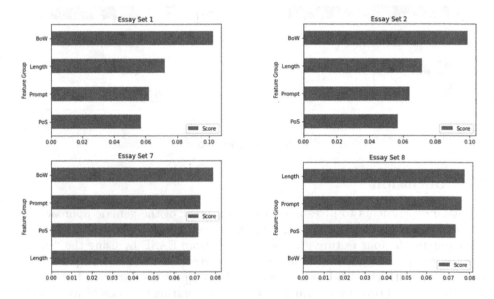

Fig. 1. Extra tree classifier feature selection results.

Correlation. The correlation of feature groups with the target variable (score) for each essay set is generated and visualized in a heat map as shown in Fig. 2, where the higher or greener the value is, the higher the correlation. Similar to the extra tree classifier, we see that the BoW feature group has the highest correlation with the target variable. Also, the length feature group is ranked second for all essay sets. Correspond to our feature influence and CHI-squared results, the prompt and PoS feature groups both were very poor in terms of correlation to the target variable. Given these points, the results from the correlation are inline with the results from the feature influence experiment.

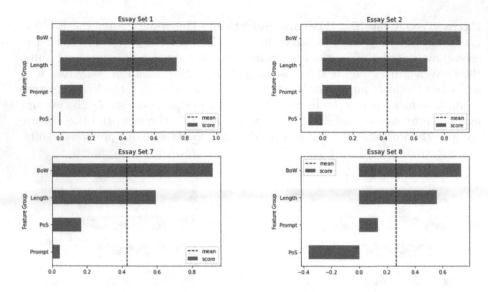

Fig. 2. Correlation score.

5   Conclusion

We have experiments to investigate the weak-point of the generic approach of feature engineering in AES through the EASE engine using the ASAP dataset. We compare the four feature groups extracted from EASE by using the "single feature group" sets and "exclude one feature group" sets, then compare their QWK score with the "all feature" set. As the comparison, our work has shown that the PoS and prompt feature groups are deteriorating the classification models. The "single feature group" set has represented that the PoS feature group is very poor in feature influence, and the "exclude one feature group" set has represented that the prompt features are better in performance in certain essay sets. Hence, we proved that the prompt feature is overfitting in the dataset. To ensure what we did to rank to feature influence is error-free, we have conducted multiple feature selection techniques to compare with the ranking we have done. Thus, it provides accurate information and sufficient details for us to work on the new PoS and prompt feature engineering in the future.

References

1. Attali, Y., Burstein, J.: Automated essay scoring with E-rater® v. 2. J. Technol. Learn. Assess. **4**(3) (2006)
2. Bisong, E.: Building Machine Learning and Deep Learning Models on Google Cloud Platform. Apress, Berkeley, CA (2019). https://doi.org/10.1007/978-1-4842-4470-8
3. Briscoe, T., Carroll, J.A., Watson, R.: The second release of the rasp system. In: Proceedings of the COLING/ACL 2006 Interactive Presentation Sessions, pp. 77–80 (2006)

4. Chen, H., He, B.: Automated essay scoring by maximizing human-machine agreement. In: Proceedings of the 2013 Conference on Empirical Methods in Natural Language Processing, pp. 1741–1752 (2013)
5. Christie, J.R.: Automated essay marking-for both style and content. In: Proceedings of the Third Annual Computer Assisted Assessment Conference, Loughborough University, Loughborough, UK. Citeseer (1999)
6. Cohen, J.: A coefficient of agreement for nominal scales. Educ. Psychol. Measur. **20**(1), 37–46 (1960)
7. Cozma, M., Butnaru, A.M., Ionescu, R.T.: Automated essay scoring with string kernels and word embeddings. arXiv preprint arXiv:1804.07954 (2018)
8. Eid, S.M., Wanas, N.M.: Automated essay scoring linguistic feature: comparative study. In: 2017 International Conference on Advanced Control Circuits Systems (ACCS) Systems & 2017 International Conference on New Paradigms in Electronics & Information Technology (PEIT), pp. 212–217. IEEE (2017)
9. Foltz, P.W., Laham, D., Landauer, T.K.: The intelligent essay assessor: applications to educational technology. Interact. Multimedia Electron. J. Comput. Enhanced Learn. **1**(2), 939–944 (1999)
10. Graesser, A.C., McNamara, D.S., Louwerse, M.M., Cai, Z.: Coh-Metrix: analysis of text on cohesion and language. Behav. Res. Methods Instrum. Comput. **36**(2), 193–202 (2004)
11. Janda, H.K., Pawar, A., Du, S., Mago, V.: Syntactic, semantic and sentiment analysis: the joint effect on automated essay evaluation. IEEE Access **7**, 108486–108503 (2019)
12. Latifi, S., Gierl, M.: Automated scoring of junior and senior high essays using cohmetrix features: implications for large-scale language testing. Lang. Test. (2020). https://doi.org/10.1177/0265532220929918
13. Liu, H., Ye, Y., Wu, M.: Ensemble learning on scoring student essay. In: 2018 International Conference on Management and Education, Humanities and Social Sciences (MEHSS 2018), pp. 250–255. Atlantis Press (2018)
14. Liu, J., Xu, Y., Zhu, Y.: Automated essay scoring based on two-stage learning. arXiv preprint arXiv:1901.07744 (2019)
15. McNamara, D.S., Louwerse, M.M., McCarthy, P.M., Graesser, A.C.: Coh-Metrix: capturing linguistic features of cohesion. Discourse Process. **47**(4), 292–330 (2010)
16. Mikolov, T., Sutskever, I., Chen, K., Corrado, G., Dean, J.: Distributed representations of words and phrases and their compositionality. arXiv preprint arXiv:1310.4546 (2013)
17. Miltsakaki, E., Kukich, K.: Automated evaluation of coherence in student essays. In: Proceedings of LREC, pp. 1–8 (2000)
18. Nguyen, H., Litman, D.: Argument mining for improving the automated scoring of persuasive essays. In: Proceedings of the AAAI Conference on Artificial Intelligence, vol. 32 (2018)
19. Norton, L.S.: Essay-writing: what really counts? High. Educ. **20**(4), 411–442 (1990)
20. Ormerod, C.M., Malhotra, A., Jafari, A.: Automated essay scoring using efficient transformer-based language models. arXiv preprint arXiv:2102.13136 (2021)
21. Page, E.B.: The imminence of... grading essays by computer. Phi Delta Kappan **47**(5), 238–243 (1966)
22. Phandi, P., Chai, K.M.A., Ng, H.T.: Flexible domain adaptation for automated essay scoring using correlated linear regression. In: Proceedings of the 2015 Conference on Empirical Methods in Natural Language Processing, pp. 431–439 (2015)

23. Sharaff, A., Gupta, H.: Extra-tree classifier with metaheuristics approach for email classification. In: Bhatia, S.K., Tiwari, S., Mishra, K.K., Trivedi, M.C. (eds.) Advances in Computer Communication and Computational Sciences. AISC, vol. 924, pp. 189–197. Springer, Singapore (2019). https://doi.org/10.1007/978-981-13-6861-5_17

24. Shawe-Taylor, J., Cristianini, N., et al.: Kernel Methods for Pattern Analysis. Cambridge University Press, Cambridge (2004)

25. Shermis, M.D., Burstein, J.C.: Automated Essay Scoring: A Cross-disciplinary Perspective. Routledge (2003)

26. Vanbelle, S., Albert, A.: A note on the linearly weighted kappa coefficient for ordinal scales. Stat. Methodol. **6**(2), 157–163 (2009)

27. Yang, R., Cao, J., Wen, Z., Wu, Y., He, X.: Enhancing automated essay scoring performance via cohesion measurement and combination of regression and ranking. In: Proceedings of the 2020 Conference on Empirical Methods in Natural Language Processing: Findings, pp. 1560–1569 (2020)

28. Yannakoudakis, H., Briscoe, T., Medlock, B.: A new dataset and method for automatically grading ESOL texts. In: Proceedings of the 49th Annual Meeting of the Association for Computational Linguistics: Human Language Technologies, pp. 180–189 (2011)

Feature Extraction Efficient for Face Verification Based on Residual Network Architecture

Thananchai Khamket[1] and Olarik Surinta[2(✉)] (iD)

[1] Applied Informatics Group, Department of Information Technology, Faculty of Informatics, Mahasarakham University, Mahasarakham, Thailand
thananchai.k@msu.ac.th
[2] Multi-Agent Intelligent Simulation Laboratory (MISL), Department of Information Technology, Faculty of Informatics, Mahasarakham University, Mahasarakham, Thailand
olarik.s@msu.ac.th

Abstract. Face verification systems have many challenges to address because human images are obtained in extensively variable conditions and in unconstrained environments. Problem occurs when capturing the human face in low light conditions, at low resolution, when occlusions are present, and even different orientations. This paper proposes a face verification system that combines the convolutional neural network and max-margin object detection called MMOD + CNN, for robust face detection and a residual network with 50 layers called ResNet-50 architecture to extract the deep feature from face images. First, we experimented with the face detection method on two face databases, LFW and BioID, to detect human faces from an unconstrained environment. We obtained face detection accuracy > 99.5% on the LFW and BioID databases. For deep feature extraction, we used the ResNet-50 architecture to extract 2,048 deep features from the human face. Second, we compared the query face image with the face images from the database using the cosine similarity function. Only similarity values higher than 0.85 were considered. Finally, the top-1 accuracy was used to evaluate the face verification. We achieved an accuracy of 100% and 99.46% on IMM frontal face and IMM face databases, respectively.

Keyword: Face verification · Face detection · Facial landmarks · Deep feature · Local descriptor

1 Introduction

Face verification is a sub-system of face recognition systems that can detect, extract features, and verify human identity from frontal faces [1]. Many algorithms and applications had been proposed to address face recognition systems. However, to achieve accurate face recognition many technical gaps need to be improved, such as insufficient training data, low quality of image source, and low light conditions.

Due to the computation time, various well-known computer vision techniques were proposed to challenge face recognition systems, such as scale-invariant feature transform (SIFT) [2] and histogram of oriented gradients (HOG) [3]. These techniques could

© Springer Nature Switzerland AG 2021
P. Chomphuwiset et al. (Eds.): MIWAI 2021, LNAI 12832, pp. 71–80, 2021.
https://doi.org/10.1007/978-3-030-80253-0_7

perform fast computation while training, and test without a graphics processing unit (GPU). Because of the high accuracy of measured face recognition, a deep learning technique [4] was proposed, called convolutional neural networks (CNNs). However, it requires a GPU while training.

A face verification system framework can be categorized into three sections; face detection or facial landmark localization, feature extraction or deep feature, and face verification [5–7].

In particular, a face verification system generally follows a common approach, and different solutions have been proposed for each step of it. These steps can be summarized as:

- **Face Detection.** In this step, face detection and facial landmark localization are applied to find human faces from the various devices, such as CCTV, web camera, video capture, and camera. Face detection mainly deals with finding the whole human face from the image and video. The facial landmark localization is defined as the localization of specific key points on the frontal face, such as eye contours, eyebrow contours, nose, mouth corners, lip, and chin [5, 7].
- **Feature Extraction Techniques.** The local descriptors, such as SIFT and HOG, are applied to extract the robust features (namely handcrafted features) from the face and key points detected as described in the first section. Instead of handcrafted features, CNN architectures have recently been applied to learn from the training images and then create the feature vector [8], called a deep feature. This method creates robust deep features from the whole face.
- **Similarity and Verification.** In this step, first, the similarity function is employed to find the similarity value between query faces and faces from the database. Second, a threshold value is used to verify if two faces are similar or not.

In this paper, we focus on enhancing the face verification system by proposing face detection and feature extraction methods based on convolutional neural networks (CNNs). As for face detection, the max-margin object detection (MMOD) method was designed to detect faces over the pyramid images. To define if that object is the face, we sent the object to the simple CNN model to extract the deep features and classify it as a face or not. The MMOD + CNN method discovered faces (even small faces) in unconstrained environment images. For face verification, we then proposed the ResNet-50 model to extract the deep feature from the specific face location that was extracted using the MMOD + CNN method. The face verification system can work in various face databases.

Paper Outline. The remainder of the paper is structured as follows: Sect. 2 explains and reviews related work in face verification. In Sect. 3, the proposed face verification system is described in detail. In Sect. 4, the experimental results, face databases, evaluation, and discussion are presented. In Sect. 5, the conclusion and suggestions for future work are given.

2 Related Work

Some approaches to face verification have focused on using computer vision techniques to generate the handcrafted feature. Recently, deep learning techniques have been used to train and create a deep feature. Furthermore, the facial landmarks localization technique is proposed to find the specific frontal face locations. To learn the achieving face verification systems, we briefly explain the research related to computer vision techniques, deep learning, and facial landmarks localization techniques.

Khunthi et al. [9] proposed a face verification system. Their system included two steps; face detection and face encoding. The face detection step found that the histogram of oriented gradients combined with the support vector machine (HOG + SVM) obtained an accuracy of 99.60% on the BioID dataset. In the face encoding step, the ResNet-50 architecture was used to extract the feature vector. The ResNet-50 architecture achieved 100% accuracy on the BioID and FERET datasets. It also provided a high accuracy of 99.60% on the ColorFERET dataset.

For the facial landmarks localization techniques, Kazemi and Sullivan [10] proposed a novel technique to estimate the location of facial landmarks using gradient boosting for learning an ensemble of regression trees. This technique could detect 194 facial landmarks in a millisecond. Khan [6] proposed a framework that detected only 49 facial landmarks from eyes (12 marks), eyebrows (10 marks), nose (9 marks), and lips (18 marks). Furthermore, Amato et al. [7] compared the effectiveness between facial landmarks features and deep feature or feature extraction for verifying faces. For facial landmarks features, it returned 68 key points located on the face. Then, the distance values between the 68 key points and the center key point were computed (68-point feature) and used as the feature vector. In addition, the 68 distance values were divided by the maximum distance value [8], called the pairs feature. The experimental results showed that the pairs feature provided better results than the 68-point feature. For deep feature, they used the VGGFace network to extract the deep feature. As a result, the deep feature outperformed the facial landmarks features.

For the deep feature, Taigman et al. [11] proposed a convolutional neural network to learn from a very large-scale labeled face dataset collected online. In their training CNN network, the 3D-aligned face with three channels, including red, green, and blue, were used as the input of the network. This network returned the deep feature of 4,096 dimensions. Subsequently, Srisuk and Ongkittikul [12] invented face recognition with weighted CNN architecture. In this method, the face components were extracted from the face image. The face components were then used as the input of the CNN network to extract the deep feature that represents the whole face. In addition, Parkhi et al. [13] introduced the VGGFace network based on the VGG network. The output of the first two fully connected (FC) layers was 4,096 dimensions. The last FC layer created 2,622 or 1,024 dimensions that depended on the loss functions.

Furthermore, Hof et al. [14] designed a device that included a mmWave radar sensor to capture human faces. Firstly, the mmWave radar sensor captured the energy reflected from the face at each distance from 8, 16, and 24 cm. Secondly, 6,000 real numbers were used as the input of the autoencoder network. Stochastic gradient descent (SGD) was used when training the network to reduce the reconstruction error. Finally, the mean square error (MSE) was proposed to find the reconstruction error between input and output faces reconstructed from the autoencoder network. The experimental results showed a correlation between different captures of the same face when tested on the 200 faces of different people.

As can be seen from the above, both well-known handcrafted and the deep feature have been accepted by researchers. We will present our proposed face verification system in the following section.

3 The Proposed Face Verification System

This paper presents a framework for accurate detection and verification of the human face. The proposed framework is shown in Fig. 1 and described in the following section.

3.1 Ace Detection Using MMOD + CNN

This section provides the concepts of max-margin objection detection (MMOD) combined with a convolutional neural network (CNN) that were applied to face detection.

King [15] proposed max-margin object detection to detect objects in images. In this method, to deal with small faces, small sliding windows with 50×50 pixels were slid through the image pyramid (see Fig. 2). This method skipped unnecessary sliding windows by considering only sliding windows that had a window scoring value larger than the max-margin value. Therefore, the sliding windows were sent to the simple CNN to extract the deep feature.

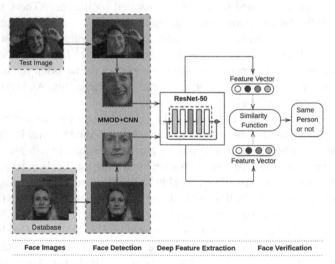

Fig. 1. Framework of the proposed face verification system.

To find more accurate faces, we can adjust more sub-image layers because the image pyramid is a sequence of an image defined as sub-image layers. The image sequence is obtained through the scale of the down-sampling. The bottom sub-image layer is the original image, and the size of the next layer is calculated according to the specific function.

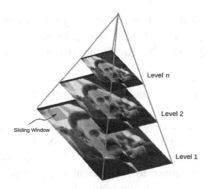

Fig. 2. Illustration of the image pyramid.

3.2 Deep Feature Extraction Using ResNet-50 Architecture

Deep feature extraction is the deep learning method proposed to extract the robust feature with the CNN architectures [16–18]. In this paper, the pre-trained ResNet-50 [19] model was applied to train a set of face images and then extracted the deep features from the layer before the fully connected layer. We then used the deep feature of the query face image to compare with other face images from the databases.

The purpose of the ResNet architecture was quite different from typical CNN architecture designed with a feedforward network without skipping any convolution layers. The ResNet architecture added the shortcut connections that allow skipping the next building block only when the number of feature maps was equal. Then, the output of the current building block was added to the outputs of the stacked layer.

4 Experiments

In this section, we report some experiments to evaluate the effectiveness of our approach on several face image databases; LFW, BioID, and IMM. We applied the face detection accuracy value for face detection to evaluate the face detection algorithms described in Eq. 1. For face verification, when verifying the person between the query face and faces in the database, we considered only the similarity value when the similarity value (see Eq. 2) was larger than 0.85. Furthermore, we used only Top-1 accuracy to verify if it was the same person.

4.1 Face Databases

Labeled Faces in the Wild (LFW). Huang et al. [20] provided the LFW face database to study face recognition in unconstrained environments. The LFW dataset consists of 13,233 images of 5,749 persons with the size of 250 × 250 pixels. We used this dataset only to evaluate the face detection algorithm. The LFW face database is shown in Fig. 3(a).

BioID Face Database. This dataset contains 1,521 grayscale images of 23 persons with a pixel resolution of 384 × 288 pixels [21]. We performed both face detection and face verification on the BioID dataset. The BioID face database is shown in Fig. 3(b).

IMM Face Database. In 2003, Stegmann et al. [22] proposed the IMM face database. This database is divided into two datasets; IMM face and IMM frontal face. First, the IMM face dataset contains 240 images of 40 different humans with a pixel resolution of 640 × 480 pixels and is stored in a color image. The humans were not allowed to wear glasses. This dataset aimed to define the shape model with the 58 facial landmarks. Second, the IMM frontal face dataset comprises 120 images of 12 persons. However, we applied the IMM face database to experiment with the proposed face verification system. The IMM face database is shown in Fig. 4.

(a)   (b)

Fig. 3. Sample images from (a) LFW and (b) BioID datasets.

(a)   (b)

Fig. 4. Example images from IMM face database. (a) IMM face and (b) IMM frontal face.

4.2 Evaluation Metrics

Face Detection Accuracy. The accuracy of face detection depends on two factors; detected and error faces [9]. The equation can be calculated as:

$$FDA = \frac{(p - n) * 100}{N} \tag{1}$$

where p is the number of positive faces detected after using the face detection method, n is the number of negative faces, and N is the number of face images.

Cosine Similarity for Face Verification. The cosine similarity measurement ($cos(\theta)$) [23, 24] between the feature vector of face a and face b can be defined as:

$$cos(\theta) = \frac{\sum_{i=1}^{n} a_i b_i}{\sqrt{\sum_{i=1}^{n} a_i^2} \sqrt{\sum_{i=1}^{n} b_i^2}} \tag{2}$$

where a_i and b_i are elements of vector a and b. The meaning of the similarity value of one is the same vector, while zero is the opposite.

Top-1 Accuracy. The result must be precisely the correct answer. In our study, the actual class matches with the highest similarity value calculated by the similarity function.

4.3 Evaluation

In order to evaluate the robustness of the face verification system, we divided the evaluation method into two steps; face detection and face verification.

For face detection, we made comparisons with three well-known face detection techniques; MMOD + CNN, Haar-Cascade, and HOG + SVM. The comparative results are shown in Table 1.

Table 1. Performance comparisons of face detection algorithms on LFW and BioID databases.

Face detection algorithms	Face detection accuracy (%) on face databases	
	LFW	BioID
Haar-Cascade	93.05	93.29
HOG + SVM	99.43	98.88
MMOD + CNN	**99.91**	**99.54**

From Table 1, the experimental results showed that the MMOD + CNN technique performed slightly better than the HOG + SVM method on both LFW and BioID face databases. A high accuracy above 99.5% was obtained from the MMOD + CNN method. Therefore, it can be seen that both the MMOD + CNN and HOG + SVM methods yielded an accuracy above 99% on the LFW face database, which was designed to detect faces in unconstrained environments.

To evaluate the face verification, we experimented with the effect of feature extraction techniques. Three feature extraction techniques; SIFT, HOG, and ResNet-50, were performed. Additionally, we extracted robust features, including SIFT and HOG features from 68-landmark localization (LL) and dense grid area (DG). The ResNet-50 extracted deep features from the face area. The experimental results are shown in Table 2.

We examined the face verification techniques on the IMM face databases. The IMM face databases were divided into training and test sets with a ratio of 60:40. Each of these face databases were split into two more face databases; IMM frontal face and IMM face. The IMM frontal face database contained only the frontal face images, while the IMM face database contained various face orientations and different light conditions.

Table 2 shows that ResNet-50 extracted robust 2,048 deep features and outperformed other local descriptor methods (SIFT and HOG). The ResNet-50 achieved 100% on the IMM frontal face database and 99.46% on the IMM face database. Consequently, the experimental result obtained an accuracy of 100% on the IMM frontal face database when extracting the local features from the 68-landmarks. Also, while extracting the local features with HOG and SIFT methods from the dense grid area obtained an accuracy of 100% and 96.2%, respectively. The high accuracy was achieved because the IMM frontal face contained only frontal faces. The results showed that extracting the local features with HOG and SIFT methods from the dense grid area performed better than extracting the local descriptors from the landmark localization on the IMM face database.

Table 2. Performance comparison of face verification with different feature extraction methods on IMM face database.

Feature extraction methods	Number of features	IMM frontal face	IMM face
LL + SIFT	8,704	100	90.81 ± 0.17
LL + HOG	544	100	94.35 ± 0.11
DG + SIFT	14,080	96.2 ± 0.23	95.79 ± 0.21
DG + HOG	880	100	98.82 ± 0.15
ResNet-50	2,048	100	99.46 ± 0.51

4.4 Discussion

In this section, we discuss the selection of the face verification system. Two main processes (face detection and face verification) are considered.

The MMOD + CNN face detection method can detect a small face because the small sliding windows with 50×50 pixels were sliding through the pyramid of images. Also, the max-margin value was used to consider the window scoring value from the overlap windows and rejected that window if it had a low score. Subsequently, we sent each window to a simple CNN architecture to create robust deep feature. It is quite fast because it created the deep feature from the window with high scoring.

A ResNet-50 architecture can be performed to extract the robust deep feature even when applied to extract from the unconstrained face, such as the face in different orientations, emotions, and light conditions (see Fig. 3(a)). It provided a high similarity value when comparing the query face and faces in the database were compared. By extracting robust deep feature with the ResNet-50 architecture, we can excluded face landmark localization and dense grid processes. We then selected the ResNet-50 architecture and set it into the face verification process.

5 Conclusion

In this research, we proposed a face verification system, including face detection and face verification. In face detection, we proposed to use the convolutional neural network and max-margin object detection, namely the MMOD + CNN method, to detect faces in unconstrained environments. It can detect a normal face, a small face, and even a part of a face. The results show that the MMOD + CNN method provided a high detection accuracy of more than 99.5% on the LFW and BioID databases. We then assigned the detected faces to the ResNet-50 model, the convolutional neural network (CNN) architecture, to extract the 2,048 deep features. We evaluated the ResNet-50 on the IMM face databases, including IMM frontal face and IMM face. The experimental results showed that the ResNet-50 model obtained 100% accuracy on the IMM frontal face database and 99.46% on the IMM face database. Additionally, the local descriptors (histogram of oriented gradients: HOG and scale-invariant feature transform: SIFT) that extracted the local features from the dense grid method outperformed the local descriptors that extracted the features from the face landmark localization method.

Acknowledgements. This work has been funded by the Faculty of Informatics, Mahasarakham University, Thailand [grant number it2-05/2560].

References

1. Bah, S.M., Ming, F.: An improved face recognition algorithm and its application in attendance management system. Array **5**, 100014 (2020). https://doi.org/10.1016/j.array.2019.100014
2. Lowe, D.G.: Distinctive image features from scale-invariant keypoints. Int. J. Comput. Vision **60**(2), 91–110 (2004). https://doi.org/10.1023/b:visi.0000029664.99615.94
3. Dalal, N., Triggs, B.: Histograms of oriented gradients for human detection. In: IEEE Computer Society Conference on Computer Vision and Pattern Recognition (CVPR), pp. 1–8 (2005). https://doi.org/10.1109/cvpr.2005.177
4. Prana, K.B., Manikandan, J.: Design and evaluation of a real-time face recognition system using convolutional neural networks. Procedia Comput. Sci. **171**, 1651–1659 (2020). https://doi.org/10.1016/j.procs.2020.04.177
5. Ouanan, H., Ouanan, M., Aksasse, B.: Facial landmark localization: past, present and future. In: 2016 4th IEEE International Colloquium on Information Science and Technology (CiSt), pp. 487–492 (2016). https://doi.org/10.1109/cist.2016.7805097
6. Khan, F.: Facial expression recognition using facial landmark detection and feature extraction via neural networks, pp. 1–7. arXiv https://arxiv.org/abs/1812.04510 (2018)
7. Amato, G., Falchi, F., Gennaro, C., Vairo, C.: A comparison of face verification with facial landmarks and deep features. In: 8th International Conference on Advances in Multimedia (MMEDIA), pp. 1–6 (2018)
8. Rassadin, A., Gruzdev, A., Savchenko, A.: Group-level emotion recognition using transfer learning from face identification. In: 19th ACM International Conference on Multimodal Interaction (ICMI), pp. 544–548 (2017). https://doi.org/10.1145/3136755.3143007
9. Khunthi, S., Saichua, P., Surinta, O.: Effective face verification systems based on the histogram of oriented gradients and deep learning techniques. In: 14th International Joint Symposium on Artificial Intelligence and Natural Language Processing (iSAI-NLP), pp. 215–219 (2019). https://doi.org/10.1109/isai-nlp48611.2019.9045237

10. Kazemi, V., Sullivan, J.: One millisecond face alignment with an ensemble of regression trees. In: IEEE Conference on Computer Vision and Pattern Recognition (CVPR), pp. 1867–1874 (2014). https://doi.org/10.1109/cvpr.2014.241

11. Taigman, Y., Yang, M., Ranzato, M., Wolf, L.: DeepFace: closing the gap to human-level performance in face verification. In: IEEE Conference on Computer Vision and Pattern Recognition (CVPR), pp. 1701–1708 (2014). https://doi.org/10.1109/cvpr.2014.220

12. Srisuk, S., Ongkittikul, S.: Robust face recognition based on weighted DeepFace. In: International Electrical Engineering Congress (iEECON), pp. 1–4 (2017). https://doi.org/10.1109/ieecon.2017.8075885

13. Parkhi, O.M., Vedaldi, A., Zisserman, A.: Deep face recognition. In: The British Machine Vision Conference, pp. 1–12 (2015). https://doi.org/10.5244/c.29.41

14. Hof, E., Sanderovich, A., Salama, M., Hemo, E.: Face verification using mmWave radar sensor. In: 2020 International Conference on Artificial Intelligence in Information and Communication (ICAIIC), pp. 320–324 (2020). https://doi.org/10.1109/icaiic48513.2020.9065010

15. King, D.E.: Max-margin object detection, pp. 1–8. arXiv https://arxiv.org/abs/1502.00046 (2015)

16. Chen, Y., Jiang, H., Li, C., Jia, X., Ghamisi, P.: Deep feature extraction and classification of hyperspectral images based on convolutional neural networks. IEEE Trans. Geosci. Remote Sens. **54**(10), 6232–6251 (2016). https://doi.org/10.1109/tgrs.2016.2584107

17. Mahmood, A., Bennamoun, M., An, S., Sohel, F.: Resfeats: residual network based features for image classification. In: IEEE International Conference on Image Processing (ICIP), pp. 1597–1601 (2017). https://doi.org/10.1109/icip.2017.8296551

18. Özyurt, F.: Efficient deep feature selection for remote sensing image recognition with fused deep learning architectures. J. Supercomput. **76**(11), 8413–8431 (2019). https://doi.org/10.1007/s11227-019-03106-y

19. He, K., Zhang, X., Ren, S., Sun, J.: Deep residual learning for image recognition. In: IEEE Conference on Computer Vision and Pattern Recognition (CVPR), pp. 770–778 (2016). https://doi.org/10.1109/cvpr.2016.90

20. Huang, G.B., Mattar, M., Berg, T., Learned-Miller, E.: Labeled faces in the wild: a database for studying face recognition in unconstrained environments. In: Workshop on Faces in 'Real-Life' Images: Detection, Alignment, and Recognition, pp. 1–14 (2008)

21. Jesorsky, O., Kirchberg, K.J., Frischholz, R.W.: Robust face detection using the Hausdorff distance. In: Audio- and Video-Based Biometric Person Authentication, pp. 90–95 (2001). https://doi.org/10.1007/3-540-45344-x_14

22. Stegmann, M.B., Ersbøll, B.K., Larsen, R.: FAME – a Flexible appearance modelling environment. IEEE Trans. on Med. Imaging **22**(10), 1319–1331 (2003). https://doi.org/10.1109/TMI.2003.817780

23. Nguyen, H.V., Bai, L.: Cosine similarity metric learning for face verification. In: Kimmel, R., Klette, R., Sugimoto, A. (eds.) ACCV 2010. LNCS, vol. 6493, pp. 709–720. Springer, Heidelberg (2011). https://doi.org/10.1007/978-3-642-19309-5_55

24. Zheng, L., Idrissi, K., Garcia, C., Duffner, S., Baskurt, A.: Triangular similarity metric learning for face verification. In: 11th IEEE International Conference and Workshops on Automatic Face and Gesture Recognition (FG), pp. 1–7 (2015). https://doi.org/10.1109/fg.2015.7163085

Acquiring Input Features from Stock Market Summaries: A NLG Perspective

Aristotle Tan[✉], Hui-Ngo Goh, and Lai-Kuan Wong

Multimedia University, 63100 Cyberjaya, Selangor, Malaysia
{hngoh,lkwong}@mmu.edu.my

Abstract. Generating text from structured data is challenging because it requires bridging the gap between the data and natural language. In the generation of financial data-to-text, stock market summaries written by experts require long-term analysis of market prices, thus it is often not suitable to formulate the problem as an end-to-end generation task. In this work, we focus on generating input features that can be aligned for stock market summaries. In particular, we introduce a new corpus for the task and define a rule-based approach to automatically identify salient market features from market prices. We obtained baseline results using state-of-the-art pre-trained models. Experimental results show that these models can produce fluent text and fairly accurate descriptions. We end with a discussion of the limitations and challenges of the proposed task.

Keywords: Data-to-text · Natural language generation

1 Introduction

The influence of neural data-to-text generation is a hot research topic in recent years. The goal of this task is to automatically generate natural language text, typically using non-lingustic representation of information as input [16], such as knowledge graphs [3,4], tables [14] and time-series data [1,11].

One challenging issue in building a dataset for data-to-text is to obtain the correct alignment between data and text. This is not a problem when there is a clear correspondence between data to text, such as when the annotator manually provide text for each input [12], or the annotator annotates the input features needed to generate the corresponding text description [14]. However, this is usually not a small problem, especially for summaries retrieved from human commentaries or news articles such as sportscasting [20] and stock market [11], where only loose alignment of data and text can be obtained.

In this paper, we investigate the task of generating stock market summaries from market prices data. An example is shown in Fig. 1. The market summary not only describes the price trend of the day, but also mentions the number of consecutive ups and downs, the record set and the best performance in a given period. However, the short-term weekly price chart shown in Fig. 1 can usually

© Springer Nature Switzerland AG 2021
P. Chomphuwiset et al. (Eds.): MIWAI 2021, LNAI 12832, pp. 81–93, 2021.
https://doi.org/10.1007/978-3-030-80253-0_8

be found in news articles, but it does not provide enough background information to support descriptions that require reference to long-term market data.

*The Dow Jones Industrial Average rose **for the sixth consecutive session and set a record**, boosted by signs that the domestic economy is revving up.*
*The blue-chip gauge added 293.05 points, or 0.9%, to 32778.64, **finishing its best week since November.** The S&P 500 edged lower for much of the session before turning higher and gaining 4 points, or 0.1%, to 3943.34, also **a fresh high.** The Nasdaq Composite lost 78.81 points, or 0.6%, to 13319.86. The Dow and S&P 500 gained 4.1% and 2.6%, respectively, this week. The Nasdaq added 3.1% for the week, **snapping a three-week streak of losses.** It is still **off 5.5% from Feb. 12's record.***

Fig. 1. An example of the Wall Street Journal's market summary on March 12, 2021. **Bold text**: Market summary that refers to long-term market data.

In this work, we present WSJ-Markets, a financial data-to-text generation dataset that summaries market movement of the day. This paper demonstrates a method of representing input features, and injects additional features retrieved or calculated from historical prices of stock market. It is used as a loose alignment method for data-to-text, by estimating common descriptions that are mentioned in market summaries without the need to manually annotate label data. We summarize our contributions as follows. (1) We propose the task of financial data-to-text by constructing a dataset that collects about 4,400 human-written stock market summaries (Sect. 3.1). (2) We introduce a dataset construction process that separate the stock market noise and the description summary (Sect. 3.2). (3) Based on the collected stock market summaries, we study the writing style and define a rule-based method to automatically identify salient market features from market prices data (Sect. 3.4). In this study, salient market features refer to the market price features often appearing or mentioned in the market summary. (4) We use state-of-the-art pretraining models to evaluate the proposed tasks (Sect. 4).

2   Related Work

Data-to-text generation aims to produce natural language output from structured input. Applications include generating weather forecasts [9], sports commentaries [20], knowledge-base description [3,4] and financial [1,5,11,19].

Traditional data-to-text models separates the generation process into different stages, such as content selection, document planning, microplanning and surface realization [16]. Recently, neural encoder-decoder models based on attention and copy mechanism has shown promising results [5,12,20]. More recently, recent advances in pre-trained language models (such as T5 [15] and BART[10]) have shown that by fine-tuning the model, very effective results can be obtained [6,14] for data-to-text task.

Financial Data-to-Text. Recent work in financial data-to-text systems has overwhelmingly focused on real-time generation of market data [1,5,11,19]. They employed customized architectures [1,11,19] to encode (numerical) time-series data as input to the learning model. However, the numerical encoding as the input of neural language model has some limitations: it requires additional pre-processing to replace all numerical values with the defined placeholder [19]. Therefore, we took a different approach by transforming numerical time-series inputs as seq2seq or "table-to-text" generation problem. In this study, we focuses on document-level generation task, while the existing financial NLG literature focuses on short market description from intraday data.

3   Dataset and Problem Formulation

3.1   Preliminary

The task can be formulated as $f(x) = y$, where x denotes the numerical market price features as inputs, y denotes the stock market summaries as target output, and f represents a learning model that learn the mapping from x to generate an equivalent market summary y.

We define a price feature $x_i = (x_{entity}^{(i)}, x_{attr-name}^{(i)}, x_{attr-val}^{(i)})$ a tuple of entity, attribute name and attribute value triples, and $x = \{x_i\}_{i=1}^{N}$ refers to a set of price features N.

Scope. Based on the dataset analysis in Sect. 4, we define the scope of study as generating stock market summaries that are only related to:

- Four Major U.S. stock market indices – Dow Jones Industrial Average, S&P 500, NASDAQ Composite, and Russell 2000 small-cap index
- Eleven sub-sectors of S&P 500 index – Consumer Discretionary, Consumer Staples, Health Care, Industrials, Information Technology, Materials, Real Estate, Communication Services, Utilities, Financials and Energy

Data Collection. For stock market summaries y, it is collected from the Wall Street Journal – *U.S. Markets*[1]. For numerical data x, we retrieved daily Open-High-Low-Close (OHLC) chart from TradingView.[2]

Align Numerical-Text Pair. Since stock market summaries y and market data x come from different sources, we use the publication date in the news article to align the numerical-text pair. Based on the publication date provided, we retrieve the closing price of the market index on that particular date and

---

[1] https://www.wsj.com/news/types/today-s-markets.
[2] https://www.tradingview.com/.

look for the number in the article that overlaps or refers to the closing price of the market index.

There are 13% of the stock market summaries that do not overlap the closing price of the index, mostly due to publication error. We manually correct the report date to ensure that all stock market summaries have at least one overlap with the market price, and those summaries that do not mention the closing price will be discarded.

Table 1. Examples of text preprocessing step. Deletion are indicated by red strikeouts, while grammar fixes are denoted in orange.

After Paragraph Extraction	After Phrase Deletion	After Grammar Correction
Stocks rose as minutes of the latest Federal Reserve meeting showed officials discussing another round of bond buying, helping push the market higher for a third straight session. The Dow Jones Industrial Average rose 20.70 points, or 0.2%, to 11559.95, after dropping as much as 110 points early in the day following a dismal reading on consumer confidence. The advance marked the index's sixth gain in seven sessions and highest close since Aug. 3. The Dow has gained 3.7% in the last three trading days., ~~The market got a boost after news that the Feds most potent tool, a third round of asset purchases, was raised as a possibility by some officials at the Aug. 9 meeting.~~ The Standard & Poor's 500-stock index edged up 2.84 points, or 0.2%, to 1212.92, led higher by telecommunication and material stocks.	Stocks rose ~~as minutes of the latest Federal Reserve meeting showed officials discussing another round of bond buying,~~ helping push the market higher for a third straight session. The Dow Jones Industrial Average rose 20.70 points, or 0.2%, to 11559.95, after dropping as much as 110 points early in the day ~~following a dismal reading on consumer confidence.~~ The advance marked the index's sixth gain in seven sessions and highest close since Aug. 3. The Dow has gained 3.7% in the last three trading days. The Standard & Poor's 500-stock index edged up 2.84 points, or 0.2%, to 1212.92, led higher by telecommunication and material stocks.	Stocks market rose higher for a third straight session. The Dow Jones Industrial Average rose 20.70 points, or 0.2%, to 11559.95, after dropping as much as 110 points early in the day. The advance marked the index's sixth gain in seven sessions and highest close since Aug. 3. The Dow has gained 3.7% in the last three trading days. The Standard & Poor's 500-stock index edged up 2.84 points, or 0.2%, to 1212.92, led higher by telecommunication and material stocks.

3.2   Market Summaries Preprocessing

The collected stock market summaries are noisy since a sentence s may not be supported or partially supported by the input features x. In this section, we define a dataset cleaning and annotation task, which consists of the following steps: **(1)** Paragraph Extraction, **(2)** Phrase Deletion, **(3)** Error Correction. Each text processing step is described below with more examples provided in Table 1.

Step 1: Paragraph Extraction. In order to control the quality of the data set, we only select the paragraphs related to the main indexes and their descriptions related to price and market trend of the day. This process is completed by using keyword detection, which involves major indexes such as "U.S. stocks", "Dow" and "S&P 500". Through this process, we significantly eliminate the noise of the articles in our text corpus and set clear boundaries for the paragraph extraction within the scope of study, thus reducing the average article size of 20 paragraphs to just 3.5 paragraphs (88.9 word token).

Step 2: Phrase Deletion. In this step, we manually removes phrases in the sentence unsupported by market prices. This step are restricted such that only phrases deletion operation is allowed, transforming the original sentence $s \rightarrow s_{deletion}$. In Table 1, we remove transform s by removing the two trailing phrases in the end of the sentence. On average, $s_{deletion}$ is different from s for 35% of the sentence in the stock market summaries.

Step 3: Grammar Correction. When performing the phrase deletion described in the previous step, most ending phrases with conjunctions such as "as", "amid" and "after" indicate the existence of external information at the trailing sentence. In this case, it's easier to delete the following phrase without additional corrections. On the other hand, if phrase deletion is performed at the beginning of a sentence, the sentence needs to be rewritten to ensure the fluency of the sentence.

In this step, we fixed the grammatical errors in the sentence to improve the fluency of the sentence. In some cases, it may be necessary to rewrite the sentence to preserve the content to produce the final sentence. Overall, for the transformation of $s_{deletion} \rightarrow s_{final}$, only less than 5% of sentence where $s_{deletion}$ is different than s_{final}.

3.3 Dataset Statistics

The basic statistical information of the stock market summaries is described in Table 2. The three main indexes appear in more than 95% of the stock market summaries, while the small cap index (Russell) and market sectors (S&P 500 sectors) were rarely mentioned. Although intraday related descriptions are often mentioned in this dataset, we do not consider them as part of the scope due to the lack of access to high-quality historical intraday data.

3.4 Generating Input Features

Stock market summaries usually start with an overview of market trends, followed by today's price changes over a number of different time periods (intraday, daily, weekly, monthly, and yearly). They also include expressions of date and time, to indicate the magnitude and extent of price change.

Table 2. Distribution of different entities and its linguistic phenomena in the training dataset.

Types	Percentage
Mention of "Dow"	99.8%
Mention of "S&P 500"	95.8%
Mention of "Nasdaq"	95.7%
Mention of "Russell"	12.9%
Mention of "S&P 500 sectors"	37.5%
Reference to intraday	33.7%
Reference to rare and uncommon features	3.5%
Market speculation	1.6%

Table 3. WSJ dataset statistics.

Property	Value
Training set size	3470
Avg target length (tokens)	88.9
Max target length (tokens)	283
Attributes per entity (Median/Avg/Max)	28/29/52
Avg input length (tokens)	2123
Max input length (tokens)	4965
Development set size	386
Test size size	429

Table 4. Market summaries and the corresponding input specification (right)

Date: Aug. 20, 2018

The Dow Jones Industrial Average rose to its highest level since early February on Monday. The Dow industrials climbed 89.37 points, or 0.3%, to 25758.69 – their highest close since Feb. 1. The S&P 500 added 6.92 points, or 0.2%, to 2857.05, bringing it 0.6% below its January record. The tech-heavy Nasdaq Composite edged up 4.68 points, or less than 0.1%, to 7821.01. The trio of indexes has climbed in three straight sessions. Stocks tied to commodities lifted large indexes, with the materials, energy and industrials sectors ranking as the S&P 500's best performers.

Date	Dow	S&P	Nasdaq
2018-01-26	...	2872.87	...
...	...	...	...
2018-02-01	26186.71	...	...
...	...	...	...
2021-08-17	25669.32	2850.13	7816.33
2018-08-20	25758.69	2857.05	7821.01

(A) Market closing price on August 20, 2018 and past historical data

Attribute	DOW	SPX	NASDAQ
Close	25758.69	2857.05	7821.01
Chg	89.37	6.92	4.68
Chg%	0.35	0.24	0.06
PrevHi	26186.71		
PrevHi.Date	2018-02-01		
Streak	W3	W3	W3
IsRecord	False	False	False
PrevRecord	26616.71	3934.83	14095.47
PrevRecord.Date	2018-01-26	2018-01-26	2018-0725
PrevRecord.%Diff	3.22	0.55	1.4

(B) Input Specification

One of the challenges of this task is to design input features supported by the corresponding market summary. This is because stock market summaries tend to compare changes between today and past historical dates, for example: *"highest level since early February"* and *"0.6% below its January record"*.

To this end, we propose a rule-based heuristic method to create additional attributes or features (as shown in Table 4(B)) to identify prominent data points that are commonly found in the stock-market summaries:

Price Change, Percentage Change. By finding out the difference between today's closing price and the closing price of the previous trading day, we can easily calculate the price change and percentage change of the day.

Winning/Losing Streak. Three types of streak descriptions can be observed in the stock market summaries:

1. Consecutive streak, e.g. *"climbed in three straight sessions"* in Table 4
2. Snapping streak, e.g. *"snapping a three-week streak of losses"* in Fig. 1.
3. Non-consecutive streak, e.g. *"sixth gain in seven sessions."* in Table 1.

For consecutive streak, it can be determined by looking at the previous price change, and classify whether the price changes are positive or negative. In Table 4(B), the attribute `State` = `W3` indicates that three consecutive winning streak have been recorded, including today's changes, while `State` = `L5` represents five consecutive losing streak and vice versa. For snapping streak, it can be identified if `State` = `W1` or `State` = `L1`.

Previous Higher/Lower Attribute. We observed that market summaries often refer to a historical date or duration when the stock market rebounded to its recent high or bottomed to a recent low. Therefore, in Table 4, the description *"highest level since early February"* is represented in the specification as `PrevHi` and its date `PrevHi.Date` for *Dow* entity, which is achieved by finding the latest closing price higher than today's closing price (`Close`).

The last higher attribute is specified only when the observed attribute rose and vice versa (if it fell). Lastly, we add a threshold $t = 10$, in which attributes are specified only when the date difference is at least 10 sessions apart, and the smaller attributes are deleted. (refer to Table 4(B) for strikethrough attributes).

This module is responsible for generating the most additional attributes, including attributes such as Closing Price (`Close`), Price Changes (`Chg`, `Chg%`) and Streak (`State`).

Record Attribute. We create additional attributes to determine if today's closing price has reached a new high (`IsRecord`), and its last recorded closing price (`PrevRecord`), date (`PrevRecord.Date`), and percentage difference from today's closing price (`PrevRecord.%Diff`).

Period Attribute. Consider the last sentence in Fig. 1: *"Nasdaq added 3.1% for the week, snapping a three-week streak of losses."*. We have observed that when the summary is written at the end of the period (Friday), the market summary covered not only the changes of the day, but also market trend of the period (week). Therefore, by using the attribute definition in the previous section, we can derive more attributes by looking up the date, price change, and other related attributes of the period n, where $n \in \{week, month, quarter, year\}$.

By using all the above attribute definitions, we can create up to 32 attributes for each entity. These attributes is served as an input representation to reflect price changes, dates in different periods and the current state of the market (such as winning streak, record breaking).

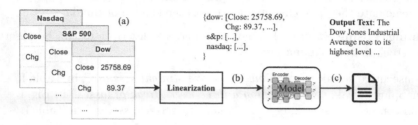

Fig. 2. An overview pipeline of Data-to-Text Generation. (a) Table attributes as input, (b) Linearization from tables and (c) Generated text

3.5 Linearization

In the sequence-to-sequence (seq2seq) model, the input sequence must be "linearized", that is, before it is presented to the seq2seq encoder, it is expressed as a linear sequence of tokens corresponding to the input features and attribute values.

As linearization determines the order of input attribute-value pair, in this study, we employ the "fixed-position" linearization strategy [7], that is, the position of the input sequence is always the same and does not correspond to the output of the generated text sequence.

An example of the linearization step is shown in Fig. 2. In this study, we employed a representation similar to JSON objects. Compared with other linearization strategies (for example, RDF triples in the WebNLG dataset and HTML markup linearization used in Totto), JSON-like sequences are more compact in terms of the sequence length of each entity attribute.

4 Experimental Setup

Datasets. Based on the stock market summaries timestamp, the dataset is divided into three parts: 80% Training (January 2002 – November 2016), 10% Validation (November 2016 – June 2018) and 10% Testing (June 2018 – May 2020). Basic statistics of WSJ dataset are described in Table 3. As the linearized representation resulting in long input sequence (average of 2K tokens), it requires the model that are capable of model long sequences.

Settings. We present baseline results by examining three existing state-of-the-art approaches:

- **Text-To-Text Transfer Transformer (T5)** [15]: The T5 model is based on a Transformer-based encoder-decoder architecture. Finetuning T5 archives state-of-the art results on multiple data-to-text benchmarks, including tables-to-text (ToTTo) [6] and graph-to-text (WebNLG). Compared with conventional Transformer-based pre-training models (such as BERT and BART), the T5 model has no hard limits on the maximum input and output sequence. We choose t5-large variant as our baseline and set the hyperparameters in the fine-tuning processes as follows: batch: 32768 tokens, maximum input length: 2500, learning rate: 1e-4.
- **Longformer** [2]: Longformer encoder-decoder (LED) model is an extension of BART [10], which is also a pretrained Transformer encoder-decoder model that is aim to facilitate modelling long sequences for seq2seq learning, up to 16K tokens. Their results show SOTA performance in summarizing long document scientific datasets. We use the led-base-16384[3] variant as our baseline and set the hyperparameters as follows: maximum sequence length: 2500, learning rate: 3e-5, batch size: 2.
- **Pointer-Generator** [17]: A LSTM Seq2Seq model with attention and copy mechanism. It establishes as the only non-Transformer model and without pre-training. Although originally design for summarization task, it is also commonly used for data-to-text generation task [5]. We train a Bidirectional LSTM with Attention model using OpenNMT [8]. The model hyperparameters are as follows: Number of layers: 2, learning rate: 1e-3, with Adam optimizer. For tokenization, we borrowed the sentencepiece tokenizer for T5 model.

For all the above models, we choose the best performing checkpoint based on validation loss. In order to generate from the model, we use greedy decoding as the preliminary result using beam search (b = 5, 10, 15), thereby reducing the performance of automatic evaluation.

Automatic Evaluation Metrics. The model output is evaluated using two automatic metrics: BLEU [13] and BLEURT [18]. BLEU measure the n-gram overlap between a reference and the generated text, while BLEURT is a metric that employ contextual embeddings and fine-tuned on human ratings for Machine Translation task. The reported results uses the English-only BLEURT-base-512 for BLEURT. Note that for BLEURT, the score is not calibrated like BLEU, therefore the results is not within the range [0,1].

---

[3] We did not attempt to train on the large Longformer-LED model due insufficient GPU computing resources, as the large model cannot be fitted on a single 16 GB GPU.

4.1 Results

Table 5 shows the BLEU and BLEURT scores against different baselines. Both the T5 models perform the best, followed by the Longformer model. The poor performance of Pointer-Generator model indicates that it cannot encode the input of long sequence, which is due to the architectural limitation of recurrent networks such as vanishing gradients and exploding gradients. While the Longformer score is worse than T5, through manual inspection, we found that the difference can largely be attributed to the shorter output sequence generated by Longformer (48.9 tokens vs. 56.3 tokens on average).

4.2 Human Evaluation

For the two best performing models in Table 5, we sampled 100 outputs and perform human evaluation using the following criteria:

- **Correctness** (Precision) – A candidate sentence is considered correct if all the pieces of information are supported by either the input features or the ground-truth reference. Any piece of unsupported information makes the candidates incorrect. For all the identified erroneous sentences, they are divided into two categories: (1) Numerical errors and (2) Incorrect or contradictory descriptions.
- **Fluency** – A candidate sentence is fluent if it is grammatical and natural.
- **Coverage with Respect to Reference** (Recall) – Compared with the reference sentence side by side, we asked whether the candidate sentence contains less information, or equivalent (neutral). If the reference sentence contains factual information that is not mentioned in the candidate, the candidate sentence is considered to be less informative.

4.3 Discussion and and Error Analysis

The results of human evaluation is shown in Table 6. The results showed that although both pretrained models had very high fluency in this task, but did not perform as well in term of correctness. We did not identify any numerical errors generated by the T5 model, but Longformer suffered to decode the correct numerals in 24% of the sentences particularly related to the sector. Overall, we expect T5 to perform better than Longformer due to larger model size.

In terms of factual errors, we observed that both pre-trained models tend to mishandle descriptions related to date differences. For example, the phrase "...with the S&P 500 closing at its highest level in _more than a month_" in Table 7 is imprecise because the more accurate description in the reference is "since the beginning of October", that is, more than five months. This concludes that the pre-training model lacks the ability to perform arithmetic operations related to duration expressions (e.g., more than five months). However, the phrase "Materials shares led the S&P 500 higher" in Table 7 demonstrates that T5 model can perform numerical reasoning, such as calculating argmax between sectors.

Table 5. Automatic evaluation results on the WSJ test set.

Model	BLEU	BLEURT
PointGen	22.0	−0.003
Longformer	27.9	0.045
T5	**32.9**	**0.117**

Table 6. Result of Human Evaluation. For Correctness, we report the percentage of outputs that were completely correct, with the percentage of numerical error (NUM*) and factual error (FACT*). In the last column, it indicates whether the candidate is considered less informative or equivalent (neutral) with respect to the reference sentence.

Model	Correctness (%)			Fluency (%)	Coverage w.r.t. Ref (%)	
	Correct	NUM*	FACT*		Less	Neutral
Longformer	64	24	6	96	98	2
T5	86	0	14	98	74	22

Table 7. Example text generated by the T5 model with error annotations in red, and blue refers to phrases not mentioned in the candidate text.

Date	Reference	Candidate (T5)
Apr 3, 2019	U.S. stocks inched higher Wednesday The S&P 500 closed up 6.16 points, or 0.2%, at 2873.40, posting a fifth consecutive advance, after earlier climbing as much as 0.6%. The index has rebounded 15% so far this year, climbing to its highest level since early October and pulling within 2% of last year's all-time high The Dow Jones Industrial Average added 39.00 points, or 0.1%, to 26218.13. The tech-heavy Nasdaq Composite advanced 46.86 points, or 0.6%, to 7895.55 Materials shares tied to the health of the economy were among the market's best performers, with the S&P 500 materials sector adding 1.3%	U.S. stocks rose Wednesday, with the S&P 500 closing at its highest level in more than a month The Dow Jones Industrial Average rose 39.0 points, or 0.2%, to 26218.13. The S&P 500 rose 6.16 points or 0.2%, to 2873.40, and the Nasdaq Composite Index rose 46.86 points, or 0.6%, to 7895.55 Materials shares led the S&P 500 higher, while energy stocks fell
Nov 14, 2019	The S&P 500 eked out a small gain Thursday to close at a fresh record following a tepid session of trading. The broad index rose in the final hour of trading as shares of real-estate companies and material firms notched gains along with communication and consumer-discretionary stocks The S&P 500 rose 2.59 points, or less than 0.1%, to 3096.63 Thursday. The Dow industrials, meanwhile, fell 1.63 points, or less than 0.1%, to 27781.96, and the Nasdaq Composite declined 3.08 points, or less than 0.1%, to 8479.02	U.S. stocks ended slightly lower Thursday, but the Dow Jones Industrial Average eked out a second straight record close The Dow industrials fell 1.63 points, or less than 0.1%, to 27781.96, while the S&P 500 rose 2.59 points, or 0.1%, to 3096.63. The Nasdaq Composite Index slipped 3.08 points, or less than 0.1%, to 8479.02. The S&P 500's consumer-discretionary sector rose 0.4%, while the energy sector fell 0.3%

From the second examples in Table 7, we also observe factual errors caused by incorrectly named entities (Dow, should be S&P). Nevertheless, we did not find any incorrect usage of verbs (e.g. rise, fall) to describe market trends.

For coverage, we observed that only 22% of candidate sentences had the same amount of information in T5 as the ground truth reference. This shows that although the proposed input feature specification can generate the most accurate description, it is still not comprehensive enough to solve the complexity and diversity of human written summaries. We also observed that in some sentences, model selection did not report certain salient features. For example in Table 7, the generated output did not mention *"the fifth consecutive advance"*.

5   Conclusion

This paper introduces a financial data-to-text task, and proposed a numerical input representation method suitable for general seq2seq model. We identify some writing style characteristics from the stock market summaries, and proposed an input feature specification that represents several key features and descriptions related to market prices. The proposed approach is evaluated using pretrained models and some other baselines.

In future work, we aim to expand the input attribute specification by considering additional market-related features to improve the coverage of the generated output.

References

1. Aoki, T., et al.: Generating market comments referring to external resources. In: Proceedings of the 11th International Conference on Natural Language Generation, pp. 135–139. Association for Computational Linguistics, November 2018
2. Beltagy, I., Peters, M.E., Cohan, A.: Longformer: the long-document transformer. arXiv:2004.05150 (2020)
3. Fan, A., Gardent, C.: Multilingual AMR-to-text generation. In: Proceedings of the 2020 Conference on Empirical Methods in Natural Language Processing (EMNLP), pp. 2889–2901. Association for Computational Linguistics, November 2020
4. Gardent, C., Shimorina, A., Narayan, S., Perez-Beltrachini, L.: The WebNLG challenge: generating text from RDF data. In: Proceedings of the 10th International Conference on Natural Language Generation, pp. 124–133. Association for Computational Linguistics, September 2017
5. Hamazono, Y., Uehara, Y., Noji, H., Miyao, Y., Takamura, H., Kobayashi, I.: Market comment generation from data with noisy alignments. In: Proceedings of the 13th International Conference on Natural Language Generation, pp. 148–157. Association for Computational Linguistics, December 2020
6. Kale, M., Rastogi, A.: Text-to-text pre-training for data-to-text tasks. In: Proceedings of the 13th International Conference on Natural Language Generation, pp. 97–102. Association for Computational Linguistics, December 2020
7. Kedzie, C., McKeown, K.: Controllable meaning representation to text generation: linearization and data augmentation strategies. In: Proceedings of the 2020 Conference on Empirical Methods in Natural Language Processing (EMNLP), pp. 5160–5185. Association for Computational Linguistics, November 2020

8. Klein, G., Kim, Y., Deng, Y., Senellart, J., Rush, A.: OpenNMT: open-source toolkit for neural machine translation. In: Proceedings of ACL 2017, System Demonstrations, pp. 67–72. Association for Computational Linguistics, July 2017

9. Konstas, I., Lapata, M.: Inducing document plans for concept-to-text generation. In: Proceedings of the 2013 Conference on Empirical Methods in Natural Language Processing, pp. 1503–1514. Association for Computational Linguistics, October 2013

10. Lewis, M., et al.: BART: denoising sequence-to-sequence pre-training for natural language generation, translation, and comprehension. In: Proceedings of the 58th Annual Meeting of the Association for Computational Linguistics, pp. 7871–7880. Association for Computational Linguistics, July 2020

11. Murakami, S., et al.: Learning to generate market comments from stock prices. In: Proceedings of the 55th Annual Meeting of the Association for Computational Linguistics, pp. 1374–1384. Association for Computational Linguistics, July 2017

12. Novikova, J., Dušek, O., Rieser, V.: The E2E dataset: new challenges for end-to-end generation. In: Proceedings of the 18th Annual SIGdial Meeting on Discourse and Dialogue, pp. 201–206. Association for Computational Linguistics, August 2017

13. Papineni, K., Roukos, S., Ward, T., Zhu, W.J.: BLEU: a method for automatic evaluation of machine translation, pp. 311–318. Association for Computational Linguistics, July 2002

14. Parikh, A., et al.: ToTTo: a controlled table-to-text generation dataset. In: Proceedings of the 2020 Conference on Empirical Methods in Natural Language Processing (EMNLP), pp. 1173–1186. Association for Computational Linguistics, November 2020

15. Raffel, C., et al.: Exploring the limits of transfer learning with a unified text-to-text transformer. J. Mach. Learn. Res. **21**(140), 1–67 (2020)

16. Reiter, E., Dale, R.: Building Natural Language Generation Systems. Cambridge University Press, Cambridge (2000)

17. See, A., Liu, P.J., Manning, C.D.: Get to the point: summarization with pointer-generator networks. In: Proceedings of the 55th Annual Meeting of the Association for Computational Linguistics, pp. 1073–1083. Association for Computational Linguistics, July 2017

18. Sellam, T., Das, D., Parikh, A.: BLEURT: learning robust metrics for text generation. In: Proceedings of the 58th Annual Meeting of the Association for Computational Linguistics, pp. 7881–7892. ACL, July 2020

19. Uehara, Y., et al.: Learning with contrastive examples for data-to-text generation. In: Proceedings of the 28th International Conference on Computational Linguistics, pp. 2352–2362. International Committee on Computational Linguistics, December 2020

20. Wiseman, S., Shieber, S., Rush, A.: Challenges in data-to-document generation. In: Proceedings of the 2017 Conference on Empirical Methods in Natural Language Processing, pp. 2253–2263. Association for Computational Linguistics, September 2017

A Comparative of a New Hybrid Based on Neural Networks and SARIMA Models for Time Series Forecasting

Chalermrat Nontapa[1(✉)], Chainarong Kesamoon[1], Nicha Kaewhawong[1], and Peerasak Intrapaiboon[2]

[1] Department of Mathematics and Statistics, Faculty of Science and Technology, Thammasat University, Pathum Thani 12120, Thailand
chalermrat.non@dome.tu.ac.th, {chainarong,nicha}@mathstat.sci.tu.ac.th
[2] Corporate Innovation Office, Siam Cement Group, Bangkok 10800, Thailand
peerasai@scg.com

Abstract. In this paper, we present a new hybrid forecasting model using decomposition method with SARIMA model and Artificial Neural Network (ANN). The proposed model has combined linear and non-linear models such as decomposition method with SARIMA model and ANN. The new hybrid model is compared to RBF, ANN, SARIMA, decomposition method with SARIMA models and RBF. We applied the new hybrid forecasting model to real monthly data sets such that the electricity consumption in the provincial area of Thailand and the SET index. The result shows that the new hybrid forecasting using decomposition method with SARIMA model and ANN can perform well. The best hybrid model has reduced average error rate for 3 months, 12 months and 24 months lead time forecasting of 93.3763%, 81.3731% and 74.3962%, respectively. In addition, the new hybrid forecasting model between decomposition method with SARIMA models and ANN has the lowest average MAPE of 0.1419% for 3 months, 0.4472% for 12 months and 1.7600% for 24 months lead time forecasting, respectively. The best forecasting model has been checked by using residual analysis. We conclude that the combined model is an effective way to improve more accurate forecasting than a single forecasting method.

Keywords: Decomposition method · SARIMA · Artificial neural network · Radial basis function · Hybrid model

1 Introduction

Improving the forecasting accuracy has become vital for decision makers and managers in various fields of science especially time series forecasting. Many researchers believe that combining different models or using hybrid models can be an effective solution to improve forecasting accuracy and to overcome limitations of single models. Theoretical, as well as, empirical evidences in the literature suggest that by combining in homogeneous models, the hybrid models will

© Springer Nature Switzerland AG 2021
P. Chomphuwiset et al. (Eds.): MIWAI 2021, LNAI 12832, pp. 94–105, 2021.
https://doi.org/10.1007/978-3-030-80253-0_9

have lower generalization variance or error. On the other hand, the main aim of combined models is to reduce the risk of failure and obtain results that are more accurate [1].

Many researchers have been devoted to develop and improve the hybrid time series models, since the early work of Reid [2], Bates and Granger [3]. In pioneering work on combined forecasts, Bates and Granger showed that a linear combination of forecasts would give a smaller error variance than any of the individual methods. Since then, the studies on this topic have expanded dramatically. Combining linear and nonlinear models are one of the most popular and widely used hybrid models, which have been proposed and applied in order to overcome the limitations of each component and improve forecasting accuracy. Chen and Wang [4] constructed a combination model incorporating SARIMA model and SVMs for seasonal time series forecasting. Khashei et al. [5] presented a hybrid autoregressive integrated moving average and feedforward neural network to time series forecasting in incomplete data situations, using the fuzzy logic. Pai and Lin [6] proposed a hybrid method to exploit the unique strength of ARIMA models and SVMs for stock prices forecasting.

In this paper, we present the performance of a new series hybrid models for time series using decomposition method with SARIMA model and ANN model. The main aim of this paper is to determine the relative predictive capabilities of the decomposition method with SARIMA-ANN models. On the other hand, this paper aims to conclude that which sequence of decomposition method with SARIMA and ANN is better for constructing series hybrid models for time series forecasting of the electricity consumption in provincial area of Thailand and the SET index. The rest of this paper is organized as follows: In the following section, we review the decomposition method, SARIMA, ANN, RBF and proposed method. Section 3 explains data preparation and model evaluation criteria, which use to experiment in this research. Results for comparing the forecasting techniques from two monthly real data sets are illustrated in Sect. 4. The final section provides the conclusion and future research.

2   Methodology

2.1   Decomposition Method

An important goal in time series analysis is the decomposition of a series into a set of non-observables components that can be associated to different types of temporal variations such as trend, seasonal, cycle and irregular. The most common forms are known as additive and multiplicative decompositions, which are expressed in Eqs. (1) and (2), respectively.

$$y_t = (T_t + S_t + C_t + I_t) + \varepsilon_t \tag{1}$$

$$y_t = (T_t \times S_t \times C_t \times I_t) + \varepsilon_t \tag{2}$$

2.2 Seasonal Autoregressive Integrated Moving Average (SARIMA) Model

Seasonal Autoregressive Integrated Moving Average (SARIMA) Model is an extension of ARIMA that explicitly supports univariate time series data with a seasonal component. It adds three new hyperparameters to specify the autoregression (AR), differencing (I) and moving average (MA) for the seasonal component of the series, as well as an additional parameter for the period of the seasonality [7].

SARIMA$(p, d, q) (P, D, Q)_s$ model:

$$\phi_p (B) \Phi_P (B^S) (1 - B)^d (1 - B^S)^D y_t = \theta_q (B) \Theta_Q (B^S) \varepsilon_t \tag{3}$$

$$\left(1 - \sum_{i=1}^{p} \phi_i B^i\right) \left(1 - \sum_{k=1}^{P} \Phi_k B^{kS}\right) z_t = \left(1 - \sum_{j=1}^{q} \theta_j B^j\right) \left(1 - \sum_{l=1}^{Q} \Theta_l B^{lS}\right) \varepsilon_t \tag{4}$$

2.3 Artificial Neural Network (ANN)

Artificial Neural Network is computing algorithms that can solve complex problems, that consist of artificial neurons or nodes, which are information processing units arranged in layers and interconnected by synaptic weights (connections). Neurons can filter and transmit information in a supervised fashion in order to build a predictive model that classifies data stored in memory. ANN model is a three-layered network of interconnected nodes: the input layer, the hidden layer, and the output layer [8]. The nodes between input and output layers can form one or more hidden layers. Every neuron in one layer has a link to every other neuron in the next layer, but neurons belonging to the same layer have no connections between them (see Fig. 1(a)).

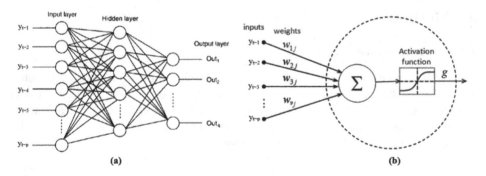

Fig. 1. Architecture of artificial neural network and active node. (**a**) Artificial neural network architecture; (**b**) Artificial neural network active node.

Input layer phase: The input layer receives information from the outside world, the hidden layer performs the information processing and the output layer produces the class label or predicts continuous values. For the time series problems, an ANN is fitted with past lagged value of actual data $(y_{t-1}, y_{t-2}, y_{t-3}, ..., y_{t-p})$ as an input vector. Therefore, input layer is composed of p nodes that are connected to the hidden layer.

Hidden layer phase: The hidden layer is an interface between input and output layers. The ANN model which are designed in this paper have two hidden layer with q nodes. In this step, one of the important tasks is determining the type of activation function g(y) which is identifying the relationship between input and output layer (see Fig. 1(b)). Artificial neural networks support a wide range of activation function such as linear, quadratic, tanh and logistic. In this research tanh function is used as the hidden layer activation function that is shown in Eq. (5).

$$g(y) = \frac{e^y - e^{-y}}{e^y + e^{-y}} \tag{5}$$

Output layer phase: In this step, by selecting an activation transfer function and the appropriate number of nodes, the output of artificial neural network is used to predict the future values of time series. In this paper, output layer designed by artificial neural network contains one node because the one–step-ahead forecasting is considered. Also, the linear function as a non-linear activation function is introduced for the output layer. The formula of relationship between input and output layer is shown in Equation (6).

$$y_t = w_0 + \sum_{j=1}^{q} w_j \cdot g \left[w_{0,j} + \sum_{i=1}^{p} w_{i,j} \cdot y_{t-i} \right] + \varepsilon_t \tag{6}$$

where, $w_{i,j}(i = 0, 1, ..., p \quad and \quad j = 1, 2, ..., q)$ and $w_j(j = 0, 1, ..., q)$ are referred as an connection weights. It should be noted that deciding the number of neurons in hidden layer (q) and the number of lagged observations, (p) and the dimension of the input vector in input layer are vital parts of artificial neural network architectures, but no methodical rule exists in order to selecting theses parameters and the only possible way to choose an optimal number of p and q is trial and error [5].

2.4   Radial Basis Function (RBF)

Radial Basis Function Network [9] form a special class of artificial neural networks, which consist of three layers. The first layer corresponds to the inputs of the network, the second is a hidden layer consisting of a number of RBF non-linear activation units, and the last one corresponds to the final output of the network. Activation functions in RBFNs are conventionally implemented as Gaussian functions (see Fig. 2(b)). Figure 2(a)) shows an example of the RBFN structure.

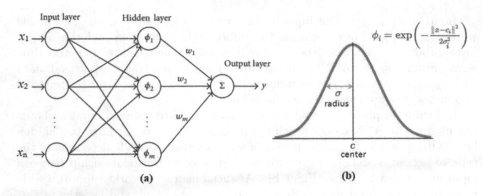

Fig. 2. Architecture of radial basis function and active node. (a) Radial basis function network architecture; (b) Gaussian activation functions.

The output of the ith activation function ϕ_i in the hidden layer of the network can be calculated using Eq. (7) based on the distance between the input pattern x and the center i.

$$\phi_i(x, c_i) = exp\left(-\frac{\|x - c_i\|^2}{2\sigma_i^2}\right) \tag{7}$$

Here, $\| \cdot \|$ is the Euclidean norm, c_i and σ_i are the center and width of the hidden neuron i, respectively. Then, the output layer of the network can be calculated using the Eq. (8).

$$y_t = \sum_{i=1}^{m} w_i \phi_i(x, c_i) + \varepsilon_t \tag{8}$$

2.5   Proposed Method

We proposed the new hybrid methodologies combining linear model such as decomposition method with SARIMA model and non-linear model such as artificial neural network. This method includes three steps as follows (see Fig. 3). It must be the first noted that, in the Zhang's hybrid model [10] is the additive linear combination model shown in Eq. (9).

$$y_t = L_t + N_t + \varepsilon_t \tag{9}$$

where, y_t is the observation at time t, L_t denotes the linear component at time t and N_t denotes the non-linear component at time t, ε_t is a random error at time t and t is a unit of time ($t = 1, 2, ..., n$). These two components have to be estimated from the data. The first step, linear component is estimated by the decomposition with SARIMA model. The decomposition with SARIMA start by decomposing in time series data into four parts such that irregular (I), trend-cycle (TC), trend-cycle-irregular (TCI) and seasonality (S) components by using multiplicative decomposition. SARIMA is applied to the trend-cycle-irregular part to find model that the best describes it. After that, each of SARIMA trend-cycle-irregular is then combined with seasonal index to make series of forecast values. Let e_t denote the residual of the DEC-SARIMA model at time t:

$$e_t = y_t - \hat{L}_t \tag{10}$$

The second step, an artificial neural network is used to model the residuals from the decomposition with SARIMA. For p input nodes, the ANN model for the residuals will be:

$$e_t = f\left(e_{t-1}, e_{t-2}, e_{t-3}, ..., e_{t-p}\right) + \varepsilon_t \tag{11}$$

$$e_t = w_0 + \sum_{j=1}^{q} w_j \cdot g\left[w_{0,j} + \sum_{i=1}^{p} w_{i,j} \cdot e_{t-i}\right] + \varepsilon_t \tag{12}$$

The third step, to calculate the combined forecast value as shown in Eq. (13). The proposed hybrid model consists of two steps. In the first step, DEC-SARIMA is used to analyze the linear part of the problem. In the second step, ANN is developed to model the residuals from DEC-SARIMA.

$$\hat{y}_t = \hat{L}_t + \hat{N}_t \tag{13}$$

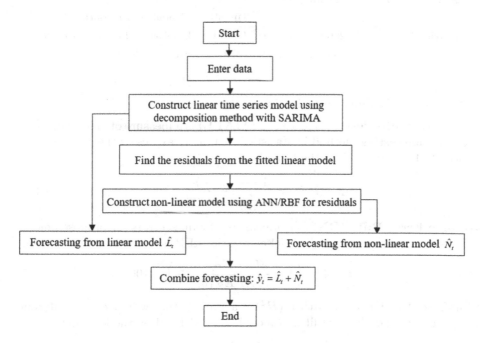

Fig. 3. Hybrid model chart between DEC-SARIMA model and ANN/RBF.

3   Data Preparation and Model Evaluation Criteria

3.1   Data Descriptions and Data Preparation

In this paper, we have two real monthly data sets, which are used to demonstrate the effective of proposed methods such that the electricity consumption in the provincial area of Thailand and the SET index.

To assess the forecasting performance of different models, each data set is divided into two samples of training and testing. The training data is used exclusively for model development and then, the test sample for 3 months, 12 months and 24 months are used to evaluate the established model. The data compositions for the two data sets such that the electricity consumption in provincial area of Thailand [11] and the SET index [12] are given in Table 1.

The electricity consumption in provincial area of Thailand from January 2002 to December 2020 shows a seasonal pattern and fluctuations, giving a total of 228 observations.

The SET index contains the monthly time series data from January 1998 to December 2020 shows a trend pattern which has a change in fluctuations, giving total of 276 observations.

Table 1. Details of the time series data sets.

Series	Sample size	Training set	Test set		
			3 months	12 months	24 months
Electric	228	2002–2018 (204)	Jan–Mar	Jan–Dec	Jan 2019–Dec 2020
SET	276	1998–2018 (252)	2019	2019	

3.2   Model Evaluation Criteria

Mean Absolute Percentage Error (MAPE) is a measure of prediction accuracy of a forecasting method in statistics. It usually expresses the accuracy as a ratio. MAPE is defined by the formula:

$$MAPE\% = \frac{1}{n} \sum_{t=1}^{n} \left| \frac{y_t - \hat{y}_t}{y_t} \right| \times 100 \qquad (14)$$

Reduce Error Rate (RER) is a measure of reduce errors for proposed model when compares with original model as a ratio. RER is defined by the formula:

$$RER\% = \left(1 - \frac{MAPE_{Proposed}}{MAPE_{SARIMA}} \right) \times 100 \qquad (15)$$

Coefficient of Determination (R^2) is a statistic that will give some information about the goodness of fit of a model. R^2 is defined by the formula:

$$R^2\% = \left(1 - \frac{SSE}{SST} \right) \times 100 \qquad (16)$$

where, SSE is the sum of squares error and SST is the sum of squares total.

4   Results and Discussion

The results for two real monthly data sets using RBF, ANN, SARIMA, the decomposition method with SARIMA models, the hybrid model between the decomposition method with SARIMA and RBF model and the hybrid model between the decomposition method with SARIMA and ANN model for 3 months, 12 months and 24 months lead time forecasting were showed in Table 2. We have conducted experiments on RStudio and SPSS package.

Tables 2 show MAPE of six time series forecasting methods for 3 months, 12 months and 24 months lead time forecasting, respectively. It found that hybrid model between the decomposition method with SARIMA model and ANN has the lowest MAPE for two data sets and average MAPE of 0.1419%, 0.4472%, 1.7600% for 3 months, 12 months and 24 months lead time forecasting, respectively.

Moreover, the hybrid model between the decomposition method with SARIMA model and ANN fitting was adequate for two real monthly data sets with the Portmanteau Statistic Q of Box-Ljung. This model has been checked by using residual analysis. We conclude that the random errors are normally distributed, no autocorrelated, zero mean and constant variance.

Table 2. MAPE of two data sets.

Time forecasting	Models	Electric	SET
3 months	RBF	7.5704	3.6439
	ANN	2.9710	3.6414
	SARIMA	2.0102	4.3900
	DEC-SARIMA	1.2399	3.3090
	Hybrid (DEC-SARIMA-RBF)	0.4200	0.8981
	Hybrid (DEC-SARIMA-ANN)	**0.2516**	**0.0321**
12 months	RBF	5.4968	3.9165
	ANN	3.1642	2.2118
	SARIMA	2.3067	3.7751
	DEC-SARIMA	2.1757	3.5516
	Hybrid (DEC-SARIMA-RBF)	0.9892	0.5055
	Hybrid (DEC-SARIMA-ANN)	**0.8044**	**0.0899**
24 months	RBF	4.5973	4.9229
	ANN	2.7136	5.3100
	SARIMA	3.5504	14.2754
	DEC-SARIMA	3.9763	13.4812
	Hybrid (DEC-SARIMA-RBF)	1.2638	4.7182
	Hybrid (DEC-SARIMA-ANN)	**1.2547**	**2.2652**

Table 3. RER% for 3 months, 12 months and 24 months lead time forecasting of two data sets using hybrid model between the decomposition method with SARIMA model and ANN.

RER%	Electric	SET
3 months	87.4838	99.2688
12 months	65.1277	97.6186
24 months	64.6603	84.1321

Table 3 shows Reduce Error Rates (RER%) of hybrid model between the decomposition method with SARIMA model and ANN for two real monthly data sets in 3 months, 12 months and 24 months lead time forecasting. It found that the proposed model has average RER of 93.3763%, 81.3731% and 74.3962%, respectively. Moreover, the proposed model for 3 months lead time forecasting is more accurate than for 12 months and 24 months lead time forecasting, respectively.

Hybrid model between the decomposition method with SARIMA model and ANN for two monthly data sets are expressed as follows:

1. Electric: Hybrid model ($R^2\% = 99.4747$)

DEC-SARIMA$(1,2,3,4,13,15,17),1,(11,47))(0,0,0)_{12} - ANN(12 \times 100 \times 100 \times 1)$

DEC-SARIMA$(1,2,3,4,13,15,17),1,(11,47))(0,0,0)_{12}$

$L_t = [\theta_0 + \phi_1\omega_{t-1} + \phi_2\omega_{t-2} + \phi_3\omega_{t-3} + \phi_4\omega_{t-4} + \phi_{13}\omega_{t-13} + \phi_{15}\omega_{t-15} + \phi_{17}\omega_{t-17} - \theta_{11}\varepsilon_{t-11} - \theta_{47}\varepsilon_{t-47} + \varepsilon_t] \times S_t + \varepsilon'_t$

$\hat{L}_t = [30.9247 - 0.1344\omega_{t-1} - 0.3593\omega_{t-2} - 0.2355\omega_{t-3} - 0.2505\omega_{t-4} - 0.2104\omega_{t-13} - 0.2260\omega_{t-15} - 0.1513\omega_{t-17} - 0.1538\varepsilon_{t-11} - 0.2387\varepsilon_{t-47}] \times \hat{S}_t$

$\hat{N}_t = ANN(12 \times 100 \times 100 \times 1)$ with 12 input nodes $(e_{t-1}, e_{t-2}, e_{t-3}, ..., e_{t-12})$ 100 nodes in the first hidden layer, 100 nodes in the second hidden layer and 1 output node.

2. SET: Hybrid model ($R^2\% = 99.3883$)

DEC-SARIMA$((33),0,(1))(0,0,0)_{12} - ANN(14 \times 100 \times 100 \times 1)$
SARIMA$((33),0,(1))(0,0,0)_{12}$

$L_t = [\phi_{33}\omega_{t-33} - \theta_1\varepsilon_{t-1} + \varepsilon_t] \times S_t + \varepsilon'_t$

$\hat{L}_t = [-0.1578\omega_{t-33} - 0.9974\varepsilon_{t-33}] \times \hat{S}_t$

$\hat{N}_t = ANN(14 \times 100 \times 100 \times 1)$ with 14 input nodes $(e_{t-1}, e_{t-2}, e_{t-3}, ..., e_{t-14})$, 100 nodes in the first hidden layer, 100 nodes in the second hidden layer and 1 output node.

In Fig. 4 shows that the sequence chart between the actual value (blue line) and forecast value (red line) for two real monthly data sets (a) Electric and (b) SET index using hybrid model between the decomposition method with SARIMA model and ANN.

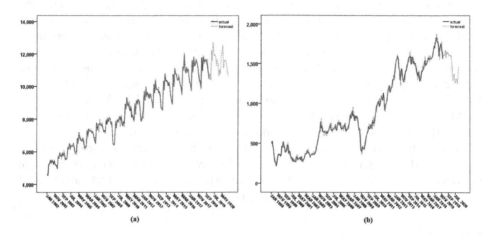

Fig. 4. The time plots of actual value (blue line) and forecast value (red line) for two real monthly data sets: (a) Electric and (b) SET index using hybrid model between the decomposition method with SARIMA model and ANN.

The non-linear component from the hybrid model is trained with the modifications of conventional backpropagation algorithm (Levenberg-Marquardt algorithm) over the training set and then tested over the testing set. The convergence criteria used for training is MSE less than or equal to 0.001 or a maximum of 1000 iterations. The experiment was repeated 10 times and searched for the best non-linear model under number input of 1 to 15 nodes, hidden nodes of 1 to 120 in each the first and the second hidden layers and 1 output node for forecasting performance of artificial neural network. The best model of artificial neural network of residual structures were delimited as $12 \times 100 \times 100 \times 1$ for the electricity consumption in provincial area of Thailand and $14 \times 100 \times 100 \times 1$ for the SET Index.

The proposed methodology can be a more effective way in order to combine linear and non-linear models together than another models in this research such as RBF, ANN, SARIMA, decomposition method with SARIMA models and RBF. Therefore, it can be applied as an appropriate alternative methodology for hybridization in time series forecasting field, especially when higher forecasting accuracy is needed. The proposed hybrid model has the lowest average MAPE of 0.7830% for 3 periods of lead time forecasting. Therefore, the proposed hybrid model can yield more accurate result than the ARIMA-MLP hybrid model was presented by Khashei and Hajirahimi [13].

5 Conclusion and Future Research

5.1 Conclusion

Time series forecasting is one of the very demanding subjects over the last few decades, since can be applied for financial, economics, engineering and scientific modeling. The standard statistical technique from the literature, namely decomposition method and Box-Jenkins method are well known for many researchers. The aim of this research are prefer new hybrid method, namely decomposition method with SARIMA-ANN model with application to two real monthly data sets such that the electricity consumption in the provincial area of Thailand and the SET index. The proposed methods are compared to RBF, ANN, SARIMA, the decomposition with SARIMA and the decomposition method with SARIMA and RBF. The performance evaluation results indicated that the decomposition method with SARIMA and ANN can perform well. In additions, the decomposition method with SARIMA and ANN model have average reduced error rate of 93.3763%, 81.3731% and 74.3962% for 3 months, 12 months and 24 months lead time forecasting, respectively which are compared to SARIMA model.

5.2 Future Research

We can try to use trend-cycle-irregular (TCI) in Exponential Smoothing method or Holt-Winters method by applying this technique to some other problems and big data sets with various numbers of features.

Acknowledgments. This research was supported by the Government of Canada, Canada-ASEAN Scholarships and Educational Exchanges for Development (SEED 2019–2020).

References

1. Hibon, M., Evgeniou, T.: To combine or not to combine: selecting among forecasts and their combinations. Int. J. Forecast. **21**, 15–24 (2005)
2. Reid, M.J.: Combining three estimates of gross domestic product. Economica **35**, 431–444 (1968)
3. Bates, J.M., Granger, C.W.J.: Combination of forecasts. Oper. Res. **4**, 451–468 (1969)
4. Chen, K.Y., Wang, C.H.: A hybrid SARIMA and support vector machines in forecasting the production values of the machinery industry in Taiwan. Expert Syst. Appl. **32**, 254–264 (2007)
5. Khashei, M., Bijari, M., Raissi, G.A.: Improvement of auto-regressive integrated moving average models using fuzzy logic and artificial neural networks. Neurocomputing **72**, 956–967 (2009)
6. Pai, P.F., Lin, C.S.: A hybrid ARIMA and support vector machines model in stock price forecasting. Omega **33**, 497–505 (2009)
7. Brownlee, J. https://machinelearningmastery.com/sarima-for-time-series-forecasting-in-python/. Accessed 10 Dec 2020

8. Dalffa, M.A.: ANN for Tic-Tac-Toe learning. Int. J. Eng. Inf. Syst. **3**(2), 9–17 (2019)
9. Friedhelm, S., Kestler, H.A., Günther, P.: Three learning phases for radial-basis-function networks. Neural Netw. **14**, 439–458 (2001)
10. Zhang, P.G.: Time series forecasting using a hybrid ARIMA and neural network model. Neurocomputing **50**, 159–175 (2003)
11. Energy Policy and Planning office (EPPO): Ministry of Energy, electricity consumption in the provincial area of Thailand. http://www.eppo.go.th/index.php/en/en-energystatistics/electricity-statistic. Accessed 10 Jan 2021
12. Stock Exchange of Thailand, the SET index. https://www.set.or.th/en/market/market_statistics.html. Accessed 15 Jan 2021
13. Khashei, M., Hajirahimi, Z.: A comparative study of series ARIMA/MLP hybrid models for stock price forecasting. Commun. Stat. Simul. Comput. **48**(9), 2625–2640 (2019)

Cartpole Problem with PDL and GP Using Multi-objective Fitness Functions Differing in a Priori Knowledge

Peter David Shannon[1,2(✉)], Chrystopher L. Nehaniv[1,3,4],
and Somnuk Phon-Amnuaisuk[5]

[1] Adaptive Systems Research Group, Centre for Computer Science & Informatics Research,
University of Hertfordshire, Hatfield, UK
`CNehaniv@uwaterloo.ca`
[2] Laksmana College of Business, Bandar Seri Begawan, Negara Brunei Darussalam
[3] Department of Systems Design Engineering, University of Waterloo, Waterloo, ON, Canada
[4] Department of Electrical & Computer Engineering, University of Waterloo, Waterloo,
ON, Canada
[5] School of Computing and Informatics, Universiti of Teknologi Brunei,
Bandar Seri Begawan, Brunei
`isuk@utb.edu.bn`

Abstract. We present a study looking at the effect of a priori domain knowledge on an EA fitness function. Our experiment has two aims: (1) applying an existing NSGA-II framework for GP with PDL to the cartpole problem—applying GP & PDL to cartpole and a purely behavioral problem for the first time—and (2) contrasting two multi-objective fitness functions: one with high and the other with low a priori domain knowledge. In our experiment we created two populations with an EA, varying in the number of objectives use for the fitness function, 2 objective criteria to represent low a priori knowledge and 3 to represent high. With fitness functions tailored to find specifically prescribed solutions we expect greater discriminating power and more feedback to an evolutionary process. This comes at the cost of excluding some unexpected solutions from the evolutionary process and placing a greater burden on the designer. We address the question: how large is the disadvantage for the low a priori fitness function in a worst-case scenario, where innovative solutions will not enhance performance. This question is interesting because we would prefer to guide EA with simple, easy to create and understand, objective criteria rather than complex and highly specific criteria. Understanding any associated penalty for using simple, easy to create fitness functions, is crucial in assessing how much effort and should be put into designing objective criteria.

Keywords: Programming · Process description language · PDL · Fitness functions · Cartpole · EA · MO criteria · NSGA-II

© Springer Nature Switzerland AG 2021
P. Chomphuwiset et al. (Eds.): MIWAI 2021, LNAI 12832, pp. 106–117, 2021.
https://doi.org/10.1007/978-3-030-80253-0_10

1 Introduction

The Process Description Language (PDL) [1] is a formalism for defining dynamical robot behavior. We are using a form of Evolutionary Algorithm (EA), a form of meta-heuristic search, which we guide using a Multiple Objective (MO) pareto optimization approach is closely based on Nondominated Sorting Genetic Algorithm-II (NSGA-II) together with Genetic Programming (GP). Previous work used PDL and GP on a modified tractor-trailer truck problem [4], to find how to parallel park a car embodied in a physics simulation [2, 3]. The work used a fitness function with low a priori knowledge [5] to simultaneously solve planning and behavioral problems. PDL has no equivalent to subsumption's layered behavior selection mechanism [6] or states and policies of Reinforcement Learning (RL) [7]. Complex emergent behavior comes about through the interaction and cumulative effects of multiple processes influencing behavior in parallel (we will generally refer to processes as *behaviors*, although technically each process has a behavior). The cartpole problem, the structure of PDL and how PDL interacts with robots is summarized in Fig. 1.

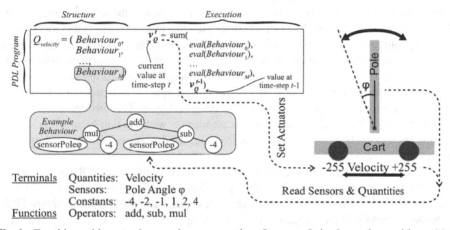

Fig. 1. For this problem we have only one quantity, $Q_{velocity}$. It is shown here with multiple behaviors $0...M$. The behaviors, small programs structured as trees, can access the current value of sensors and quantities via terminals. Each behavior is evaluated to produce a positive or negative number, its influence. The influences of each behavior are summed with the previous quantity value to produce the new quantity value for the current time-step (v_Q^t) and the actuator is set. Quantities and sensors, like velocity and the pole angle, are restricted to the range 0 ± 255 and in addition to constants form the set of available terminals; operators are the available as functions.

In our discussion we make considerable use of the term a priori, we shall take a moment to explain what we mean by it here. We use a simple definition: knowledge which is: reasoned from understanding or theory. We can, in general terms contrast it with *a posteriori* knowledge which is: derived from experience—measurement or observation. Incorporating knowledge into algorithms is necessary to solve specific problems but we believe that adding complex knowledge makes algorithms less useful, less a meta-heuristic and more a heuristic. So, here we examine how a control fitness function, with low a priori knowledge, composed of two criteria, compares to an experimental fitness function, with higher a priori knowledge, composed of the same two criteria augmented with an additional moderately complex criterion. Restating for clarity, the control fitness function uses 2 objective criteria and the experiment uses 3. We draw conclusions on how to balance generality and simplicity against specificity and complexity. The functions were designed in this way so that they might be as similar as possible but one is more specific than the other. We created two populations, one using the experimental fitness function and the other the control.[1] In order to compare the two populations quantitively, we reevaluated the control population against the additional criterion the used in experimental fitness function. Such a comparison may ordinarily be questionable but we consider it valid in this case. The fitness functions are designed to be as similar as possible with the experimental function providing a stronger signal to search for almost the same thing. A second way we evaluate the populations is by observing the behavior of individuals in the final generation, classifying their pole balancing strategy types— by hand, so to speak—as upright, inclining in direction of travel (generally referred to as inclining from now on) or declining in direction of travel (generally referred to as declining from now on) and tallying the occurrences.

PDL is a relatively simple formalism which is intrinsically modular having an individual's behavior determined by an array of simple programs. We expect this modularity can be exploited to improve exploration and exploitation in the solution space. Potential ideas for further investigation include: correlation of behavior influences to automatically define groupings (modules) of behaviors to be preserved during crossover; and discovery of behaviors which have little impact on an episode and are likely to be safe to remove (de-bloat). Complex behaviors demonstrated by PDL controlled robots [8, 9] has shown PDL to be a viable alternative to approaches with explicit behavior selection mechanisms and we hope to see such complex behavior discovered with an evolutionary approach.

The essential objective of our overarching research is to assess PDL as a program representation for GP by testing its viability against a number of benchmark problems. Here we detail an experiment based on the classic RL cartpole control problem [10]. The basic cartpole problem is relatively simple long since solved using an evolutionary process [11]. This problem was selected to evaluate the performance of GP with PDL against a standard benchmark which has purely reactive (behavioral) solutions. We do not try to improve on the performance of pervious research but merely show our approach— the PDL program representation and a fitness function which makes few assumptions about how the problem should be solved—can be applied successfully to this problem.

We continue with: Sect. 2 discussing how PDL and GP has been used to solve the cartpole problem, Sect. 3 provides experimental results and finally, a conclusion and discussion of further research is given in Sect. 4.

---

[1] A video of the representatives from both groups is available at https://youtu.be/99S11Kr9vRs.

2 Cartpole Problem with Pdl

Parts of this section are adapted from [3]. Steels, describes PDL as: "Control programs viewed as dynamical systems which establish a continuous relation between the time varying data coming out of sensors and a stream of values going to the actuators [1]." It is a cooperative architecture in which behaviors operate in parallel accessing sensor information and asserting an influence on quantities. PDL has no selection mechanism, such as subsumption or activation thresholds; all behaviors are active at all times. Typically, each actuator is associated with a quantity; the quantity's value is used to set its actuator at each time-step. Here, the robot controllers only manipulate one quantity, $Q_{velocity}$ (the velocity quantity), which controls wheel motors. This differs from the typical implementation of the cartpole problem in which forces are applied directly to the cart. Each behavior in our implementation of PDL is a small tree, e.g., for a very simple behavior, such as $1 + 5$, the root would be an addition operator with two operands, 1 and 5.

A PDL program P could be formally defined as a tuple of quantities where quantity Q could be defined as a tuple of behaviors:

$$P = (Q_0, \ldots, Q_N) \tag{1}$$

$$Q = (B_0, \ldots, B_M) \tag{2}$$

Each quantity also has a value, which changes each time-step, and is normally linked to an actuator, the value of the quantity is used to set the control signal to the actuator.

The value of Q, v_Q, can be determined for a given timestep by summing all the previous the changes of v_Q at each time-step. Quantity values are restricted such that $v_Q \in \{-255, \cdots, 255\}$. If t stands for the current time-step and T the set of all time-steps in an episode, we can define v_Q at the current time-step, v_Q^t:

$$v_Q^t = \sum_{t=0}^{T} \delta\left(Q_n^t\right) \tag{3}$$

$\delta\left(Q_n^t\right)$ is the change in v_Q from $t - 1$ to t. $\delta\left(Q_n^t\right)$ can be determined by evaluating of each of Q's behaviors and summing the results. Each of Q's behavior, $B_{0...M}$, is a small depth limited program and is evaluated, accessing sensor information, to determine its influence:

$$\delta\left(Q_n^t\right) = \sum_{m=0}^{M} eval\left(B_m^t\right) \tag{4}$$

To illustrate the continuous relationship between behaviors and their quantity of a breakdown of how $Q_{velocity}$ is calculated (for a controller whose listing is shown in Fig. 3) is shown in Table 1. The next value of $Q_{velocity}$ is determined by adding the previous value of $Q_{velocity}$ to the result of evaluating its behaviors. The numbers in the *Next Value* column were read from the angular velocity of the cart's wheel joints. The control signal from the program may not be fully expressed in the robot's behavior if the quantity value changes quickly (the simulated bodies have inertia and take time to accelerate and decelerate and the motors have limited power), so the next values does not in practice always equal the previous value plus the influence of the behaviors.

Table 1. Quantity value and behavior influence by time-step. B_1 dominates the value of the quantity, as it inverts so does the quantity, see Fig. 4 for a complete graph of this episode.

Time-step	Eval (B_1)	Eval (B_2)	Next value
0	−6	−10	−16
1	−25	−9	−49
2	−111	−8	−172
3	−432	−6	−255
	...		
21	108	−56	−218
22	374	−60	105
23	1221	−67	255

Table 2. Parameters for selecting a reproduction method.

Method	Rate
Crossover (one-point crossover with 80% leaf bias)	25%
Crossover-copy (copies a whole syntax tree)	25%
Mutation (node replacement uniform mutation)	15%
Mutation-add (adds a randomly created syntax tree)	5%
Mutation-subtract (deletes a randomly selected syntax tree)	30%

2.1 PDL and Genetic Programming

Most GP systems represent programs as trees, although several other representations are used. In this case programs are represented as several tuples of syntax trees, one tuple for each quantity. Basic GP operators, which work on a single tree, crossover and mutation, are implemented using Distributed Evolutionary Algorithms in Python, DEAP [12]. We add to these operators which work on a tuple of trees. Behaviors can be copied from one tuple to another, or removed, without any concern the resulting PDL program will crash. The rate at which these operators are used is given in Table 2. These new operators are designed to afford manipulations at a modular level. In this way we might consider each behavior to be a module and each quantity tuple a super-module.

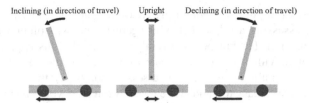

Inclining (in direction of travel)   Upright   Declining (in direction of travel)

Fig. 2. Left: an inclining robot will make larger forward and backward movements to act on the pole in response to it overbalancing and correct. **Middle**: an upright cartpole robot will remain almost still, making small movements, forward and back, to keep the pole balanced. **Right**: a declining robot will not move in response to the pole or move insufficiently and, unlike the first two strategies, will not maintain balance.

2.2 Experiment & Fitness Function Design

The cartpole problem is embodied in a 3D virtual environment[2] and a physics simulation.[3] Our objective is to find programs which balance an inverted pendulum on a self-propelling cart. If the pendulum (pole) tips over more than 30° or the episode exceeds a fixed number of time-steps the episode is terminated.

As different criteria are not compared against each other with NSGA-II—and selection probability is not weighted as with roulette wheel selection—ensuring a given fitness value for one is equivalently good for the same value of another criterion is unnecessary. Experimental group 1 uses all three criteria but control group 2 only uses two criteria for their fitness functions. All three criteria are normalized (1 is best, 0 is worst). The first criterion, *time* score is given in Eq. 5 and is how long the pole was balanced. It is a crude measure of how well a controller works, a time limit is imposed though as we expect to find controllers which will balance the pole indefinitely.

$$Time\ score = \frac{runtime}{\max\ runtime} \tag{5}$$

The next criterion, *distance* score given in Eq. 6, is the distance traveled from the starting point at the end of the episode. Again crudely, it measures how much space the controller used to balance the pole. We consider these criteria both to be low a priori as they are derived from simple reasoning about performance.

$$Distance\ score = \frac{1}{1 + distance\ travelled\ from\ starting\ point} \tag{6}$$

The final high a priori knowledge criteria is φ *change*, given in Eq. 7, measures how much the pole angle changes over an episode. Again T is the set of all time-steps in an episode, $t \in T$ and φt is the pole angle at t.

$$\varphi\ change\ score = \frac{1}{1 + \left(\left(\sum_{t=1}^{T} |\varphi_t - \varphi_{t-1}|\right)\middle/ runtime\right)} \tag{7}$$

---

[2] https://www.panda3d.org/.

[3] https://www.ode.org/.

Using a priori knowledge (known through reasoning or a posteriori, learned through experience) and assessing a robots behavior against a known solution provides very positive feedback to an EA but poses several issues: firstly, this approach cannot be applied to a problem with unknown solutions; secondly, a designer must have technical expertise to create a suitably invasive tests to assess the solution as the episode progresses; thirdly, it may be just as easy to hand-write the solution as it would be to write the test; and finally, the EA will not find innovative solutions which the designer did not expect. Ideally, we would like to avoid assumptions about how problems should be solved.

```
Qvelocity(
    B₀(
        add(
            sub(sub(mul(velocity, 4.0),
                    sub(-1.0, -4.0)),
                sub(mul(1.0, -4.0), add(1.0, pole))),
            mul(mul(mul(-4.0, pole), mul(-4.0, 2.0)),
                add(add(-1.0, 4.0),
                    sub(sub(pole, 0.0), pole)))
        )
    )
    B₁(
        add(mul(4.0, -2.0), mul(mul(pole, 2.0), -4.0))
    )
))
```

Fig. 3. An example of an upright controller program found by the EA, from the control group. $Q_{velocity}$ here has 2 behaviors (B_0 & B_1). This program is representative of those found in control group 2, it is discussed further below. The relationship between φ, the pole angle, and $Q_{velocity}$ for this individual is shown in Fig. 4 and labelled control.

We have two objectives: firstly, show GP & PDL can find good solutions for a simple standard benchmark; and secondly, to what degree, if any, an EA using a fitness function with more a priori knowledge performs better. Our experiment consists of to groups: group 1 using all 3 criteria (see above Eqs. 5, 6 and 7) and group 2 using only the first two criteria (Eqs. 5 and 6). In order to compare like for like, individuals in group 2 were reevaluated with the extra high a priori knowledge criteria (φ change score) and the results recorded for later analysis.

The high a priori knowledge, group 1, uses an additional criterion, φ change score defined in Eq. 7. It is the sum of how much the pole angle, φ, has changed at each time-step throughout the episode. We maintain that the other two criteria measure essentially the same thing but φ change gives a much stronger signal for how much the cart moves during a simulated episode. It is conceptually more complex and more complex to implement and therefore uses more a priori knowledge. We consider the criteria to be partially conflicting, for example, the time and distance criteria (Eqs. 5 and 6) are certainly in conflict, the easiest way to cover the shortest distance would be to remain stationary but then the pole would fall and the episode would halt immediately (Tables 3 and 4).

Table 3. Balancing strategy of individuals

Group No.		Upright	Inclining (in direction of travel)	Declining (in direction of travel)
1	Experiment	21%	13%	66%
2	Control	10%	38%	52%

Table 4. Experimental parameters.

Group No.		A priori Knowledge	MO Criteria	Individuals per generation	Generations per run	Run repetitions
1	Experiment	High	Equations 5, 6 and 7	30	30	100
2	Control	Low	Equations 5 and 6	30	30	100

3 Results

Group 1 is indicated to perform better than control group 2. Figure 5 shows some of those differences although but does not indicate clear superiority: group 1 is shown on average to have higher φ change and distance scores but lower time scores. Classifying controllers—by hand using the simple definition given in Fig. 2—selected for reproduction (by NSGA-II) in the final generation of runs does indicate group 1 yields better results, more upright controllers are found. However, it also finds fewer inclining controllers and more declining controllers. This analysis, based on the first five runs completed, group 1 has approximately twice as many upright controllers and a quarter more declining controllers. More details are given in Table 5.

In Fig. 4 we look in detail at representatives of the two groups. Both have the same mean criterion score but typify differences between the two groups. Group 1 representative is an example of an upright controller (based on the balancing strategy in Fig. 2) whose $v_{Q_{velocity}}$ remains in the range 0 ± 5 and φ pole angle varies almost as little. In contrast the control group 2 controller is of the inclining type, it far less stable, $v_{Q_{velocity}}$ and φ pole angle fluctuate wildly in the ranges 0 ± 2500 and $0 \pm 20°$ respectively. However, it still maintains balance as it rushes from side to side correcting for the overbalancing pole.

Table 5. Analysis of mean of objective criteria

Group No.		Starting criterion μ	Ending criterion μ	Criterion μ change	Sample size	p Value	t Value
1	Experiment	0.51	0.67	31%	3000	2.03×10^{-18}	8.78
2	Control	0.52	0.64	23%	3000		

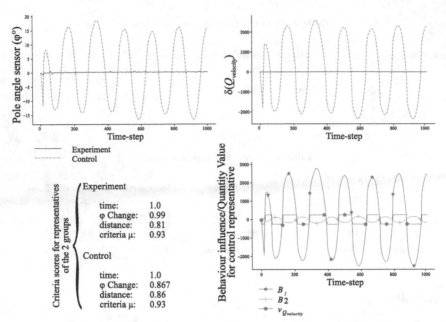

Fig. 4. As readers of this paper will not necessarily be able to observe the cartpole robot running (a link to a video showing running robots is given earlier), we include three graphs which show how actuator output changes in response to sensor input. The first two graphs show two of the best individuals representative of the most common types of behaviors found in the two groups. The group 1 control program is shown in Fig. 3, during simulation it moves forward and back in response to the pole tilting; by contrast the group 2 experiment individual balances the pole but is almost motionless. **Top Left:** the angle φ of the pole at each time-step. **Top Right:** $\delta(Q^t_{velocity})$ is the change in $Q_{velocity}$ from one time-step to the next, see Eq. 4. Most of the controller's output at each time-step is discarded as the value of any quantity must be $\in \{-255, \cdots, 255\}$. **Bottom Left:** the criteria score and mean for each individual. **Bottom Right:** An overview of the relationship between behaviors B_1 and B_2. The value of the $Q_{velocity}$ is dominated by B_1; B_2 only has a very marginal impact on the quantity value (v_Q). The definition of the behaviors is given in Fig. 3.

Table 5 also shows a simple statistical analysis of a composite of the fitness scores, the mean of the three objectives of an individual, *criterion* μ. For the first three columns samples were the aggregated from the first and last generation of individuals created in each run show how much criterion μ changed on average across all 100 runs for each group. The last three columns show the results of a t-test. Our null hypothesis is *the solutions found in group 1 are not different to those found in group 2*. Again, the sample was of criterion μ, aggregated from the final generation of each run. The p-value and t-value indicate we should strongly reject our null hypothesis: the two samples are not from the same population.

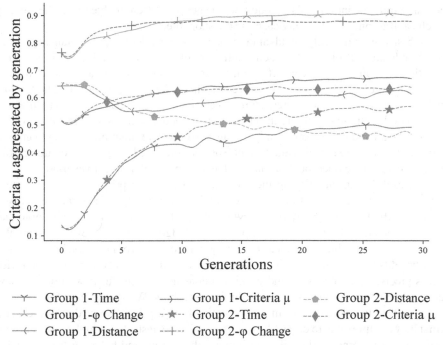

Fig. 5. The average of each criterion aggregated by generation for both groups. Here we show 4 pairs of plots; to make reading it a little easier, each group 1 plot is solid and each group 2 plot is dashed, we have also ensured marks do not overlap. Although there are differences between the same criterion for each group, considering how clearly different the two groups appear to be when we watch them balance the pole, the differences are surprisingly small for time, φ change and criteria μ. For three of the four criteria the change is only about 10% and the distance scores actually go down, indicating the partial conflict we mentioned earlier. We should also note that the individual scores only matter relative to each other as NSGA-II uses binary tournaments fitness in one criterion is not compared to fitness in another.

4 Conclusions and Future Work

We show, for the first time, (i) PDL and GP can be used to solve the classic RL Cartpole problem and (ii) offer simple advice on whether or not to implement high a priori fitness criteria.

Starting this work, we posed a simple question: how large is the disadvantage for the low a priori fitness function in a worst-case scenario, where innovative solutions will not enhance performance? We partially answer this question by looking to statistics and balancing strategy. The balancing strategy of controllers found in final generations, in Fig. 2, and the analysis in Table 5, both indicate that group 1 finds better solutions than group 2; 8% better if with look at the difference in criterion μ change (the change in mean average of all criteria). However, while this is indicative, as we note earlier directly comparing values of different criterion fitness values does not make much sense. No effort was made to calibrate criteria so equal fitness values for different criteria does not necessarily indicate individuals are equivalently good at different objectives; the validity of such calibration would, in any case, be questionable.

The best way to quantify an advantage may be to consider the pole balancing strategies (as indicated in Fig. 2) for each controller selected for reproduction in the final generation of each run. Some effort was made to do this here but an automated method would be desirable to check every run. Breaking from the general theme here that high a priori knowledge criteria are better, group 2 had better time objective scores than group 1. As noted, this did not translate into finding more better individual in this experiment which can be attributed to group 2 only having two objective functions leading to greater emphasis on searching for individuals which balance the pole longer and, stemming from this, differences developed population emphasizing particular objectives more.

More useful than quantifying the advantage of a high a priori knowledge fitness function maybe the confirmation that it is significant for purely behavioral problems— at least with the PDL & NSGA-II framework and problem used here. We also note that useful solutions were found using low a priori knowledge criteria but they were generally less upright, more inclining and less declining individuals. From our results we should expect benefits from complex objective tests when we desire exacting precise behavior but less precise tests may still find good solutions and are useful if we do not know or care to predetermine the exact behavior for our robots. We should therefore balance how much benefit we expect from incorporating high a priori knowledge into criteria against how complex it is to create the requisite objective tests. So, if high a priori fitness criteria can be incorporated easily and better indicate required behavior then we have little reason not to and can expect better performance. These conclusions are, in general, in line with our expectations when designing this study but we are encouraged to note that the low a priori group also found good individuals too but performed at a lower level.

Our continuing research priority is to create new testbed problems to gauge the generality of using GP and PDL to search for robot controllers and to explore appropriate uses for the technique. Delineating capabilities of PDL & GP would be useful. From our work so far, it is clear that PDL and GP are effective for finding solutions for simple control problems, like cartpole, and can stretch to find solutions to more complex control problems, which overlay behaviors, and solve multi-phase problems—as for the parallel parking problem [2]—but it is unclear where the limitations lie and what the sweet-spot is for applying these ideas. Finding these bounds would assist in understanding the general applicability of our approach.

References

1. Steels, L.: Mathematical analysis of behavior systems. In: Proceedings of PerAc '94. From Perception to Action, pp. 88–95. IEEE Computer Society Press (1994)
2. Shannon, P., Nehaniv, C L.: Evolving robot controllers in PDL using genetic programming. In: 2011 IEEE Symposium on Artificial Life (IEEE ALIFE), pp. 92–99. IEEE (2011)
3. Shannon, P.D., Nehaniv, C.L., Phon-Amnuaisuk, S.: Enhancing exploration and exploitation of NSGA-II with GP and PDL. In: Tan, Y., Takagi, H., Shi, Y. (eds.) ICSI 2017. LNCS, vol. 10385, pp. 349–361. Springer, Cham (2017). https://doi.org/10.1007/978-3-319-61824-1_38

4. Koza, J.R.: Genetic Programming: on the Programming of Computers by Means of Natural Selection. MIT Press, Cambridge (1992)
5. Nelson, A.L., et al.: Fitness functions in evolutionary robotics: a survey and analysis. Robot. Auton. Syst. **57**(4), 345–370 (2009)
6. Brooks, R.: A robust layered control system for a mobile robot. IEEE J. Robot. Autom. **2**(1), 14–23 (1986)
7. Sutton, R.S., Barto, A.G.: Reinforcement Learning: An Introduction. MIT Press, Cambridge (2011)
8. Schlottmann, E., et al.: A modular design approach towards behaviour oriented robotics (1997)
9. Birk, A., et al.: Programming with behavior-processes. Robot. Auton. Syst. **39**(3–4), 115–127 (2002)
10. Barto, A.G., et al.: Neuronlike adaptive elements that can solve difficult learning control problems. In: IEEE Transactions on Systems, Man, and Cybernetics 5, pp. 834–846 (1983)
11. Koza, J.R., Keane, M.A.: Genetic breeding of non-linear optimal control strategies for broom balancing. In: Bensoussan, A., Lions, J.L. (eds.) Analysis and Optimization of Systes, pp. 47–56. Springer, Berlin (1990). https://doi.org/10.1007/BFb0120027
12. Fortin, F.-A., et al.: DEAP: evolutionary algorithms made easy. J. Mach. Learn. Res. **13**(1), 2171–2175 (2012)

Learning Robot Arm Controls Using Augmented Random Search in Simulated Environments

Somnuk Phon-Amnuaisuk[1]([⊠]) [iD], Peter David Shannon[2], and Saiful Omar[1]

[1] Universiti Teknologi Brunei, Gadong, Brunei
{somnuk.phonamnuaisuk,saiful.omar}@utb.edu.bn
[2] University of Hertfordshire, Hartfield, UK

Abstract. We investigate the learning of continuous action policy for controlling a six-axes robot arm. Traditional tabular Q-Learning can handle discrete actions well but less so for continuous actions since the tabular approach is constrained by the size of the state-value table. Recent advances in *deep reinforcement learning* and *policy gradient* learning abstract the look-up table using function approximators such as *artificial neural networks*. Artificial neural networks abstract loop-up policy tables as policy networks that can predict discrete actions as well as continuous actions. However, deep reinforcement learning and policy gradient learning were criticized for their complexity. It was reported in recent works that *Augmented Random Search* (ARS) has a better sample efficiency and a simpler hyper-parameter tuning. This motivates us to apply the technique to our robot-arm reaching tasks. We constructed a custom simulated robot arm environment using *Unity Machine Learning Agents* game engine, then designed three robot-arm reaching tasks. Twelve models were trained using ARS techniques. Another four models were trained using the state-of-the-art PG learning technique i.e., *proximal policy optimization* (PPO). Results from models trained using PPO provide a baseline from the policy gradient technique. Empirical results of models trained using ARS and PPO were analyzed and discussed.

Keywords: Augmented Random Search · Robot arm controls · Reinforcement learning

1 Introduction

Learning a stochastic policy function $\pi_\theta : \mathcal{S} \mapsto \mathcal{A}$ (that maps states $s \in \mathcal{S}$ to actions $a \in \mathcal{A}$) using parameters θ may be achieved using policy gradient techniques. In the past decades, the policy gradient approach has received a lot of attention from the community and many tactics have been devised to improve learning effectiveness, for examples, *experience replay* in *deep Q-Learning* [1], trust-region, and importance sampling in *Trust Region Policy Optimization*

© Springer Nature Switzerland AG 2021
P. Chomphuwiset et al. (Eds.): MIWAI 2021, LNAI 12832, pp. 118–128, 2021.
https://doi.org/10.1007/978-3-030-80253-0_11

(TRPO) [2]. These tactics enhance performances and improve the sample efficiency issue. However, these tactics also introduce many hyper-parameters into the learning process and result in hyper-parameter sensitivity [3].

A recent study using Augmented Random Search (ARS) by [4] demonstrated improved performance over policy gradient techniques in terms of *sample efficiency* and simple *hyper-parameters* tuning. Sample efficiency implies fewer training samples. Thus fewer training steps are required. The linear policy search using ARS also has fewer hyper-parameters. These plus points motivate us to investigate the ARS technique in the robot arm controlling tasks.

Our contributions in this paper are in the following activities: (i) constructing a custom simulated robot arm environment using Unity ML-Agents game engine [5], and (ii) investigating ARS in the learning of continuous control policy in the simulated environment as well as benchmarking the results with the PPO [6] which is a state-of-the-art policy gradient technique. We report the empirical results from using ARS to approximate a stochastic policy in controlling a 6DoF robot arm, and a comparison with the PPO technique. The rest of the paper is organized into the following sections: Sect. 2 discusses the background of policy gradient-based optimization and policy gradient search; Sect. 3 discusses our approach and gives the details of the experimental setup; Sect. 4 provides the experimental results and provides a critical discussion of the output; and finally, the conclusion and further research are presented in Sect. 5.

2   Estimating Policy Using Random Search

Follow [7], *Markov Decision Process (MDP)* is a tuple of $(\mathcal{S}, \mathcal{A}, \mathcal{P}_{ss'}^a, \mathcal{R}_s^a)$. Let $t \in \{0, 1, 2, ...\}$ denote a discrete time step, $s_t \in \mathcal{S}$ and $a_t \in \mathcal{A}$ denote a state and an action at time step t respectively. Let $\mathcal{P}_{ss'}^a$ be a state transition probability representing the action policy of an agent, $\mathcal{P}_{ss'}^a$ can be approximated through a value function, or directly using an independent function approximator with its own parameters θ, such as neural network weights.

The Policy Gradient approach has been explored since the early stage of reinforcement learning research [8]. In recent years, many variations of Policy Gradient approach have re-emerged as a popular gradient-based RL techniques. The basics of Policy Gradient technique can be summarized as follow: let θ denote a vector representing policy parameters and ρ representing the performance of the policy. A policy gradient method approximates the near optimal policy by adjusting the policy based on gradient computing from $\Delta\theta \approx \alpha \frac{\partial \rho}{\partial \theta}$, where α is the step size and $\frac{\partial \rho}{\partial \theta}$ can be expressed as:

$$\frac{\partial \rho}{\partial \theta} = \sum_s d^\pi(s) \sum_a \frac{\partial \pi(s, a)}{\partial \theta} Q^\pi(s, a) \tag{1}$$

where $d^\pi(s)$ is the stationary distribution of states, and $Q^\pi(s, a)$ is the value of a state-action pair under π.

Many improvement of the standard policy gradient given in Eq. 1 have been reported in recent years. Deterministic Policy Gradient (DPG) [9] and Deep

Deterministic Policy Gradient (DDPG) [10] extend a discrete control to a continuous control. Trust Region Policy Optimization (TRPO) improves training stability by curbing the update of new untrusted regions [2]. PPO further simplifies TPRO by using a clipped surrogate objective while retaining similar performance, further improving sample efficiency [6].

As the policy gradient methods become sophisticated, their hyper-parameters become complex and their performance too becomes sensitive to the hyper-parameters tuning [3]. The authors of [4] employed ARS to train linear policies and able to achieve state-of-the-art sample efficiency on the *Multi-Joint dynamics with Contact (MuJoCo)* which is a proprietary physics engine for locomotion tasks. ARS performs *policy space search* based on the *finite-difference* technique which will be explained in the next section.

2.1 Policy Space Search Using Augmented Random Search

All search techniques are designed to exploit the search landscape's gradient information. The goal is to find effective policies to explore the search space. This is commonly achieved by tracking and exploiting information obtained from the agents' search experiences. For example, the state-action value i.e., $Q(s, a)$ evaluation in reinforcement learning [11]; the concepts of *Global-best particle* and *Local-best particle* in the *Particle Swarm Optimization* could be seen as providing a means to calculate the gradient relative to other particles in the swarm [12].

A pure random policy decides its next action from all possible actions. Although a random search does not have a clear notion of gradient, it is possible to approximate local gradient information to guide the search. A random search can inspect the local landscape before deciding on its next action i.e., estimate its local gradient. Exploiting extra information often improves its performance. Two variations of the random search techniques are discussed in the following sections.

A Basic Random Search (BRS). In [4], the authors exploit gradient information in the policy parameter space θ by perturbing θ in the positive and negative directions i.e., $\theta + \nu\delta$ and $\theta - \nu\delta$ where $\nu < 1$ is the noise, δ is random numbers sampled from a normal distribution, and δ has the same dimension as the policy parameter θ.

This positive-negative perturbation approach is known as *finite-differences* technique. In brief, let $r(\theta + \nu\delta, \mathbf{x})$ and $r(\theta - \nu\delta, \mathbf{x})$ be the rewards obtained from input $\mathbf{x}$ following the perturbed policy parameters θ in positive and negative directions. If N random moves are sampled by perturbing the policy parameters θ_t (at step t) N times, then a local gradient can be expressed as:

$$\Delta_t = \frac{1}{N} \sum_{n=1}^{N} \delta_n [r(\theta - \nu\delta, \mathbf{x}) - r(\theta - \nu\delta, \mathbf{x})]_n \qquad (2)$$

and the policy parameters θ_t can be updated

$$\theta_{t+1} = \theta_t + \alpha\Delta_t \qquad (3)$$

where α is the learning rate.

Augmented Random Search (ARS). In brief, ARS augments BRS in the following areas: (i) normalize the states, $x = \frac{x-\mu}{\sigma_x}$, (ii) scaling by the standard deviation σ_R, where σ_R is computed from rewards of all perturbations and (iii) using top performing b directions (see the update section in the Alg. 1). ARS algorithm is included below for readers' convenience. Readers are invited to read detailed discussion in the original paper by [4].

Algorithm 1. Augmented Random Search (ARS)

Let ν a positive constant < 1, let α be the learning rate > 0, let N the number of perturbations, and b be the number of top-performing perturbations, $b < N$.
Let $|A| = p$ be the desired number of actions, let θ and be a $p \times n$ matrix representing the parameters of the policy π, and let δ_k be a $p \times n$ matrix representing the kth perturbation. The ARS can be expressed as follow:

initialize: $\theta_0 = 0 \in R^{p \times n}, \mu_0 = 0 \in R^{p \times n}, \Sigma_0 = I \in R^{p \times n}$, and $j = 0$.
while end condition not satisfied **do**:

    Generate N perturbations δ_k from a normal distribution.
    Generate 2N episodes and their 2N rewards using π_{k+} and π_{k-}
        Normalize $\pi_{j,k,+} = (\theta_j + \nu\delta_k)\text{diag}(\Sigma_j)^{-1/2}(\mathbf{x} - \mu_j)$ and
        Normalize $\pi_{j,k,-} = (\theta_j - \nu\delta_k)\text{diag}(\Sigma_j)^{-1/2}(\mathbf{x} - \mu_j)$
    Collect the rewards $r(\pi_{j,k,+})$ and $r(\pi_{j,k,+})$ for each perturbation.
    Sort all δ_k by $max(r(\pi_{j,k,+}), r(\pi_{j,k,+}))$
    Update
$$\theta_{j+1} = \theta_j + \frac{\alpha}{b\sigma_R} \sum_{k=1}^{b} [r(\pi_{j,k,+}) - r(\pi_{j,k,+})]\delta_k$$
    $j \leftarrow j + 1$
end while

---

3   Empirical Set up Using Robot Arm Domain

In our implementation, we use a free robot arm asset for Unity shared by Lukasz-Konopacki.[1] We construct a custom task domain for evaluation using the Unity Machine Learning Agents Toolkit (Unity ML-Agents).[2] The task domain here is to train a six degree of freedom robot arm (6DoF) to reach a cube randomly spawned on a bench.

3.1   Designing Robot Arm-Reaching Tasks

Fig. 1 shows the three tasks carried out in this report. The robot learns to reach the cube on the left hand side for the task 1 (top-left), on the right hand side for the task 2 (middle-left) and on both sides for the task 3 (bottom-left).

---

[1] https://unitylist.com/p/w03/Robot-Simulator-Unity.
[2] https://github.com/Unity-Technologies/ml-agents.

From the set up, the complexity of the task 1 and task 2 should be at the same level and the complexity of task 3 should be higher than the task 1 and 2.

It is our intention to design the three tasks to be closely related in order to see the behaviors of linear policy learning using ARS. Upon inspecting the task domain, a human would quickly realize that the main distinction between task 1 and task 2 is the rotation of the base axis, while skills learned for moving other arm joints are the same. However, the ARS (as well as other contemporary policy gradient techniques) will not be able to infer this since it involves meta-level reasoning about the domain.

3.2   State Representations

The robot arm has six axes. These six axes are controlled by stepping motors in the actual physical robot. These axes serve the following purposes: (i) turning the base (1st axis) between $[-180, 180]$ degrees, (ii) rotating the 2nd arm axis between $[-60, 140]$ degrees, (iii) rotating the 3rd arm axis between $[-72, 185]$ degrees, (iv) turning the 4th arm axis between $[-180, 180]$ degrees, (v) rotating the effector (5th axis) between $[-120, 120]$ degrees, and (vi) turning the effector (6th axis) between $[-180, 180]$ degrees. Variations in the rotating degrees result from the physical dimension of the robot arm model.

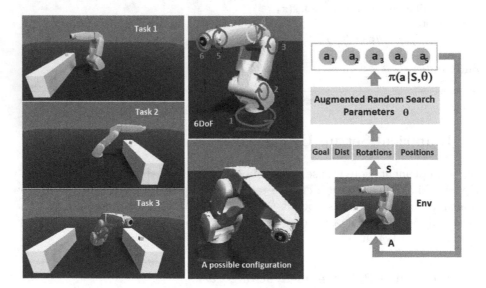

Fig. 1. This figure illustrates the three tasks carried out in our experiments, task 1, task 2, and task 3 (from top-left to bottom-left, respectively). The robot learns to move its effector to the cube with minimum time steps by moving its joints. The middle pane shows information regarding the 6DoF axes. The right pane presents a graphical summary of the environment

Observations and Actions. In our experiment, it was decided to articulate the robot arm with five actions, each for controlling one axis. This was because turning an effector (the 6th axis) would not affect the distance between the effector to the goal. Hence, articulating five axes are sufficient for our robot-arm reaching tasks. Therefore, the output vector has the space size of 5 values.

Let $\mathbf{x}$ denote an observation at any time step, the vector $\mathbf{x}$ captures the following information: (i) the position of the goal (i.e., (x, y, z) coordinate of the cube), (ii) the distance (dx, dy, dz) between the effector and the goal, (iii) the rotations of all arm axes in quaternion $(a + bi + cj + dk)$, and (iv) the position of all arm axes (x, y, z). Hence the observation vector has the space size of 48 values which should be sufficient and appropriate to represent the state space of our task domain.

3.3   Training a Robot Arm Using ARS

The training process was given an initial parameter θ. The Unity ML-Agents environment randomly spawned the goal on the bench and randomly configured the robots starting position. The benches ($D \times W \times H = 0.2 \times 1.0 \times 0.3$) were placed at the following coordinates. The bench on the right: depth was 0.55 to 0.75 units, width was -0.5 to 0.5 units and height was 0.3 units. The bench on the left: depth was -0.55 to -0.75 units, width was -0.5 to 0.5 units and height was 0.3 units.

Observation and Action. The robot-arm agent collected observations and corresponding actions were generated using the policy parameter θ. In our setup, each episode is limited to 64 steps (it was set to 64 steps because we observed that after successful learning, the arm can move from an arbitrary starting point to an arbitrary goal position within 64 steps). The agent received a positive reward signal if it moved closer to the goal and received a negative reward signal if it moved further from the goal. The episode is terminated and the negative reward signal is fed-back to the learning algorithm if the robot arm moved into an impossible *physical configuration*, such as: moving into the ground, hitting the bench, or crashing its joints. This is achieved by implementing *collision detection* for the robot arms. The learning of parameters θ has been described in the Sect. 2. In the training phase, rewards are logged and used as the learning indicator.

Evaluation Criteria. The performance of the trained model was measured using the final distance between the effector and the goal (in this implementation, the episode is terminated if the distance was less than or equal to 0.05 unit, or the episode reaches 64 steps). In this report, after the models were trained, they were tested using randomly generated goals for 200 trials, each trial was also limited with 64 steps. For each trial, the final distance between the effector and the goal was recorded. Comparing histogram plots among different models revealed their performances.

Table 1. Parameters employed in our ARS experiments

	Learning rate α	Constant ν	Perturb N	Top performing	Episode steps	Training steps	Evaluation episodes
All tasks	0.02	0.03	24	12	64	800	200

Parameters Setting. We started our experiments by running task 1 nine times based on combinations of the following learning rate, $lr \in \{0.05, 0.01, 0.005\}$ and perturbation $N \in \{16, 24, 32\}$. Each run was limited to only 300 time steps. We inspected the results and found that too low a learning rate and too many perturbations may not be desirable. Table 1 summarizes the parameters employed in our experiments.

4   Empirical Results and Discussion

A total of twelve trained models were created for the evaluation of ARS, four models for each task. Figure 2 (left pane) summarises the rewards obtained during the training phase. We limited the training to 800 time-steps, then saved the models.

Each model was then tested with 200 random goal positions (the choice of 200 is arbitrary). The final distances between the effector and the goal were recorded and their histograms are plotted on the right pane of Fig. 2. It is observed that ARS could learn task 1 and task 2 better than task 3.

For task 1 and 2, the robot learned to locate the goal successfully. It could, most of the time, reach the goal within 0.05 units within 64 steps. Task 3 is, however, less successful. It is observed that the robot performed well on one of the benches while performing poorly on the other bench. This could be contributed to the linear policy parameters θ.

Comparing with Results from Proximal Policy Optimization. PPO is the current state of the art policy gradient method. In comparison to ARS, PPO requires more training samples. Since PPO employs neural network which gives non-linear policy parameters. We decided to train the three tasks using PPO for 1.2 million steps and compared results from both techniques.

The density plots of final distances obtained from PPO are superimposed with results from ARS (see Fig. 3). The performance from ARS and PPO are comparable. We would comment that PPO offers a slightly better output quality as the density plots are slightly shifted to the left. This implies that the distance to the goal is slightly nearer than ARS method. PPO appears to deliver a better

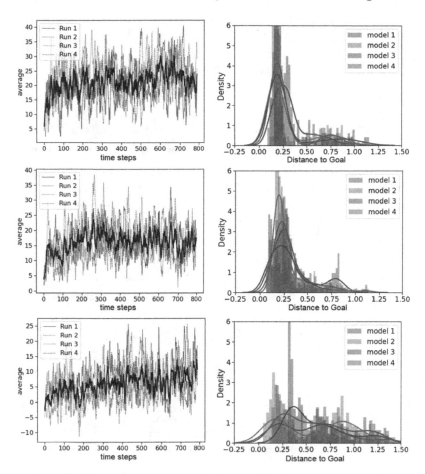

Fig. 2. Top row: The training rewards from task 1 (left pane). The x-axis shows the training steps and the y-axis shows the reward. The black line is the average reward from the four runs. The evaluation of the four models based on the final distance between the effector to the goal is shown on the right pane. Second and third rows: Rewards and evaluations of task 2 and task 3, respectively.

performance in task 3 as well which could be from its non-linear policy (see Fig. 3 and Table 2). Finally, ARS technique possesses a much better sample efficiency than PPO.

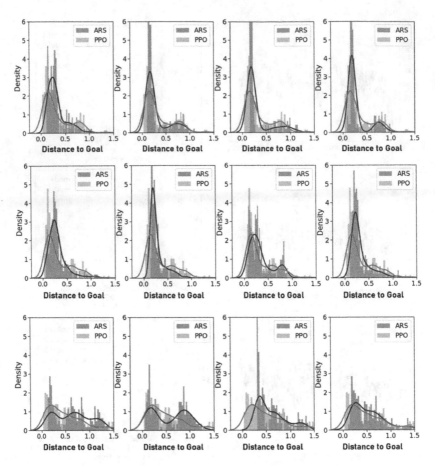

Fig. 3. This figure provides graphical comparison between ARS and PPO. The density plot of task 1, 2 and 3 from PPO are superimposed on the density plots from ARS. Top row. second row and third rows show the output of task 1, task 2 and task 3, respectively.

Table 2. This table summarizes the minimum distance (min), the mean (avr) distance and the standard deviation from two hundred tests of the three tasks. Each episode was limited to 64 steps and the distance was measured at the end of each episode.

	Task 1			Task 2			Task3		
	min	avr	std	min	avr	std	min	avr	std
ARS	0.08	**0.28**	**0.21**	0.06	**0.30**	**0.19**	0.03	0.51	**0.31**
PPO	**0.03**	0.33	0.28	**0.03**	0.32	0.27	**0.02**	**0.47**	0.35

5 Conclusion

We investigated the application of augmented random search (ARS) in training robot-arm reaching tasks. Three tasks were set up for the 6DoF robot arm to reach a randomly spawned cube on a bench. The empirical results confirm previous results by [4] that ARS requires fewer samples in the training process (i.e., sample efficiency). We believe that policy learning based on a linear policy may be one of the reasons behind its sample efficiency property. We speculate that the performance of a linear policy approach should be inferior to a non-linear policy approach. Hence, the three tasks were also benchmarked with the current state-of-the-art proximal policy optimization (PPO) which employed non-linear policy parameters θ. From the empirical results, PPO exhibits a slightly better performance than ARS from all test runs.

In future works, we are interested in exploring the skill transfer between tasks. Transferring skills learned in performing one task to another relevant task without retraining (or with a short training session) will mitigate issues related to training effectiveness in deep RL such as the sample efficiency issue, the long training time issue.

Acknowledgments. We wish to thank anonymous reviewers for their comments that have helped improve this paper. We would like to thank CPD, Universiti Teknologi Brunei for their financial support given to this research.

References

1. Mnih, V., et al.: Human-level control through deep reinforcement learning. Nature **518**(7540), 529 (2015)
2. Schulman, J., Levine, S., Moritz, P., Jordan, M.I., Abbeel, P.: Trust region policy optimization. arXiv:1502.05477 (2015)
3. Islam, R., Henderson, P., Gomrokchi, M., Precup, D.: Reproducibility of benchmarked deep reinforcement learning tasks for continuous control. arXiv preprint arXiv:1708.04133 (2017)
4. Mania, H., Guy, A., Recht, B.: Simple random search of static linear policies is competitive for reinforcement learning. In: Advances in Neural Information Processing Systems, pp. 1800–1809 (2018)
5. Juliani, A., et al.: Unity: a general platform for intelligent agents. arXiv preprint arXiv:1809.02627. https://github.com/Unity-Technologies/ml_agents (2020)
6. Schulman, J., Wolski, F., Dhariwal, P., Radford, A., Klimov, O.: Proximal policy optimization algorithms. arXiv:1707.06347 (2017)
7. Sutton, R., McAllester, D., Singh, S., Mansour, Y.: Policy gradient methods for reinforcement learning with function approximation. In: Advances in Neural Information Processing Systems, pp. 1057–1063 (1999)
8. Tesaruo, G.: Neurogammon wins computer Olympiad. Neural Comput. **1**, 321–323 (1989)
9. Silver, D., et al.: Deterministic policy gradient algorithms. In: Proceedings of the 31st International Conference on Machine Learning (ICML), Beijing, China, June 2014 (2014). http://proceedings.mlr.press/v32/silver14.html. [hal-00938992]

10. Lillicrap, T.P., et al.: Continuous control with deep reinforcement learning. arXiv:1509.02971 (2019)
11. Phon-Amnuaisuk, S.: Generating tonal counterpoint using reinforcement learning. In: Proceedings of the 16th International Conference on Neural Information Processing, pp. 580–589 (2009)
12. Atyabi, A., Phon-Amnuaisuk, S., Ho, C.K.: Applying area extension PSO in robotic swarm. J. Intell. Robot. Syst. **58**(3), 253–285 (2010)

An Analytical Evaluation of a Deep Learning Model to Detect Network Intrusion

Md Al-Imran, Kazi Jahidur Rahaman, Mohammad Rasel,
and Shamim H. Ripon[✉]

Department of Computer Science and Engineering, East West University,
Dhaka, Bangladesh
{2020-1-96-011,2015-3-60-012,2020-1-96-013}@std.ewubd.edu, dshr@ewubd.edu

Abstract. Widespread use of internet connected devices results in a flow of data among the connected devices. This has led to creating these network systems prone to different type of cyber attacks among which network intrusion is one of a kind. To detect network intrusion, an intrusion detection system (IDS) is placed in the system. The previous works in this field classify the attack mainly with traditional machine learning algorithm based models. This experiment proposes Long Short Term Memory (LSTM) based neural network model along with two other machine learning models i.e. Support Vector Machine (SVM), K-Nearest Neighbor (KNN), which shows significant improved performance in intrusion detection. The performance of the model is proved to be effective comparing to the previous works and also deployable in real life environments which is validated by using explainable AI. For this experiment, Kyoto University Honeypot log dataset has been used to build and evaluate the performances of the IDS model.

Keywords: Intrusion detection · LSTM · SVM · LIME · Class imbalance

1 Introduction

The successive improvement of networking technologies have been actively contributing to connecting a wide range of businesses, organizations, and industries [1]. Through these connections, data, also labeled as "The New Oil" by some experts and professionals [2], is continuously being transmitted. As a result, the data sources and connections have turned into a popular target of cyberattacks. Different policies have been introduced to protect the network from cyberattack such as, the authors of [3] developed Intrusion Detection System (IDS) using Kohonen Self-Organizing map. Claiming every algorithm has pros and cons, some experts believe supervised learning algorithms can help to solve network intrusion [4]. Through the significant works on IDS, researchers previously suggested algorithms like Non-Dominated Genetic Algorithm [5], Support Vector Machine (SVM) with Softmax or rbf models, Naïve Bayes, and so on. Therefore,

© Springer Nature Switzerland AG 2021
P. Chomphuwiset et al. (Eds.): MIWAI 2021, LNAI 12832, pp. 129–140, 2021.
https://doi.org/10.1007/978-3-030-80253-0_12

we have attempted to develop the IDS using the deep learning and machine learning (ML) approach with help of Kyoto University Honeypot dataset [6].

This experiment builds three different IDS models by using Long Short Term Memory (LSTM) Neural Network, SVM, and K-Nearest Neighbor (KNN), and compares the results with existing works. The experiment contributes in evaluation of deep learning model with the implementation of effective machine learning models. The proposed models require authentication of deployment, so we validate one of the IDS models with an explainable artificial intelligence [7]. The paper is organized as follows: Sect. 2 presents a literature review on the subject, Sect. 3 details the data used in the experiments, which are described in Sect. 4. Details about the settings and results are described in Sect. 5 and Sect. 6 highlights the main conclusions.

2   Literature Review

Marzia Zaman *et al.* [8] implemented SVM, Naïve Bayes, KNN, Fuzzy C-Means, Radial Basis Function, and Ensemble Methods. The accuracies recorded as 94.26%, 97.54% and 96.72% for SVM, KNN, and Ensemble method respectively. The authors developed IDS models on Kyoto 2006+ dataset.

Abien Fred [9] developed a deep learning model on Kyoto 2013 dataset. The author demonstrated the accuracy of 70.75% for Gated Recurrent Unit Softmax classifier and 84.15% accuracy for Gated Recurrent Unit SVM (GRU SVM).

Ravi Vinayakumar *et al.* [10] proposed a deep neural network model and used various network intrusion dataset including Kyoto 2015 dataset, where they reported 88.5% accuracy and 0.964 recall value.

Ahmad Javaid *et al.* [11] experimented on NSL-KDD dataset to detect network intrusion through the implementation of Self-Taught Learning (STL) approach. The authors recorded STL accuracy as 98%.

A survey is developed under certain parameters to assess the impact of dataset in IDS field by Markus Ring *et al.* [12]. The authors used many datasets, some of them are- AWID focused on 802.11 networks, CIDDS-001, CIDDS-002, DARPA, DDoS2016, KDD Cup 99, NSL-KDD, and UNSN-NB15.

Random Forest, and Decision Tree classifiers were implemented on KDD dataset by the authors of [13] to detect network intrusion. The authors listed the accuracies as 93.77% for Random Forest, and 92.44% for Decision Tree.

NSL-KDD datset was used by the authors of [4] to develop an intrusion detection system through applying four supervised learning algorithm. The authors listed 75% accuracy in SVM, and 99% accuracy in Random Forest.

3   Dataset Overview

The Kyoto 2013 dataset [6] is comprised of both network packet based and flow based data having satisfied the requirement of quality dataset such as findability, and reliability [12]. The relevancy of the dataset to intrusion detection increased, as the dataset is originally constructed from real honeypot network traffic log of Kyoto University [14] excluding the use of Servers, Routers, or any kind of BoTs.

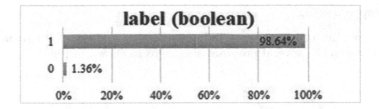

Fig. 1. Class distribution

The dataset consists of 15 continuous and 9 categorical features whose details can be found in [6]. Figure 1 shows the class distribution of the Kyoto Data set where 1 refers to attack at a rate of 98.64% while 0 to normal at a rate of 1.36% signifies class imbalance problem. Hence dataset balancing is inevitable task before training the model. Additionally, constant feature problem exists which will be solved in later section.

4 Research Methodology

The dataset preprocessing is given exclusive emphasis, as it has significant impact on generalization performance of ML algorithms [15]. Later on, the dataset is undertaken feature selection and class imbalance handling processes before input into the model.

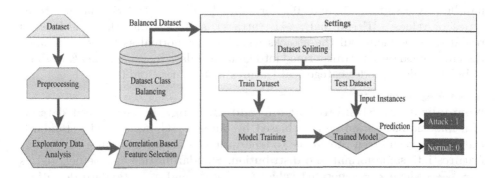

Fig. 2. Workflow diagram

The schematic workflow diagram of the proposed model is illustrated in Fig. 2. After preprocessing of the collected dataset, insights have been created which pave the way to select impactful features applying feature selection technique. Then the class imbalance problem is solved before splitting the dataset into train and test sets. The training dataset is fed into classifiers to train the models. Finally, performance of the trained models is evaluated through prediction with the test instances.

4.1   Preprocessing

Since the presence of inconsistent and noisy data may lead to fatal error [16], it is taken through the several preprocessing steps as shown in Fig. 3.

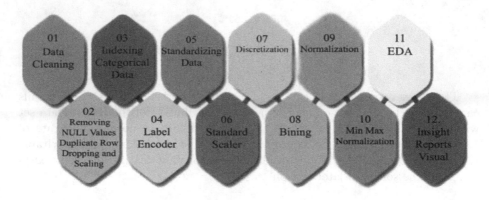

Fig. 3. Different preprocessing phases

Data Cleaning, Scaling, and Label Encoding. Pandas library contains `dataframe.isna.any()` which identifies and removes the duplicate instances from the dataset. Since some features contain string data, these features are handled by assigning '1' and '0'. For example, the label of the dataset three types of values −'1' (normal), '−1' (attack), and '−2' (attack). The label is rescaled by replacing all the attacks with '1', and normal as '0'. Additionally, the categorical data is transformed into numerical data by using Label Encoding. Label Encoder encodes categorical features with values from 0 to n−1.

Normalization, Standardization, and Binning. In imbalanced dataset, Min-max normalization can be biased by outliers [16]. As a result, standardization has been given preference to transform continuous and quasi continuous features into same format and distribution. Standardization can be denoted as $z = \frac{x-\mu}{\sigma}$, where z = generated value, μ = mean, and σ = standard deviation. After balancing the dataset, Min Max normalization is applied to transform values of features into range of 0 to 1. Therefore, the equation is $x_{new} = \frac{x-x_{min}}{x_{max}-x_{min}}$. Following that decile qcut binning is applied to tackle probable skewness and exponential distribution errors such that performance of model is preserved.

4.2   Feature Selection

Feature Selection in a particular dataset is typically performed either manually or with the help of algorithms to impart the most important features by removing redundant features without hampering actual data pattern [17].

The src_ip_add and dest_ip_add were processed multiple times during the construction of the dataset by the authors of [14] where the processing included converting public IPs into private or local IPs due to security concerns [6]. Since the actual source and destination IPs are unknown, these two features lack importance. Hence, the dataset has 22 features after removing those two features manually. Then Correlation based feature Selection is applied on 22 features to measure how two features are associated with each other [18].

Fig. 4. Pearson's correlation matrix

The Fig. 4 shows the correlation values of the features which indicating that dest_bytes and src_bytes are highly associated with correlation coefficient of $\rho = 0.8253$, hence, dest_bytes is dropped from the dataset. The pandas_profiling identified two constant features which were also removed.

4.3   Class Imbalance Handling

During the effort to solve the class imbalance problem, the under sampling technique may cause loss of information because of actual data size reduction. On contrary, oversampling can lead to overfitting as well. Keeping both risks in mind we applied the SMOTETomek resampling algorithm [19], which reduces the disadvantage of oversampling and undersampling method.

4.4 Long Short Term Memory (LSTM)

Deep learning has been used by the researchers to solve audio signal processing [20], and image processing [21] problems. Recurrent Neural Network (RNN) is prone to vanishing and exploding gradient problems [22] which was addressed in LSTM algorithm. The authors in [23] developed LSTM containing Input Gate layer, Output Gate layer, and Forget Gate layer. These gates are robust to eliminate problems occurred in RNN.

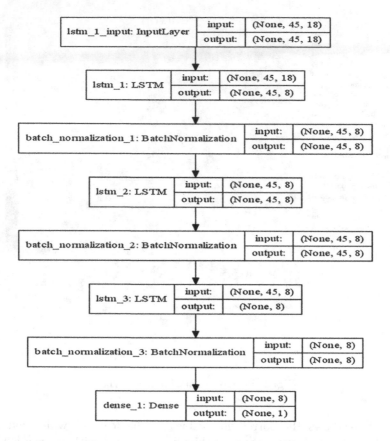

Fig. 5. Proposed LSTM IDS architecture

The proposed LSTM model is illustrated in Fig. 5, which consists of input layer, 3 LSTM layers, 3 Batch Normalization layers, and output layer. The proposed model is implemented through `Keras` for achieving the best outcome. The Batch Normalization Layer is used to stabilize and fasten the network. To bring the weights of inputs with biases in range from 0 to 1, we have considered both soft sigmoid $\phi(z) = \frac{1}{e^{-z}}$ and hard sigmoid $\phi(z) = max(0, min(1, \frac{z+1}{2}))$ activation functions among which the later one is given preference because of its less computational complexity with improved performance [24].

4.5   Machine Learning Models

We have chosen Support Vector Machine, and K-Nearest Neighbor (KNN) algorithm influenced by existing works to convey performance comparison.

SVM: SVM is a supervised learning classifier with two linearly separable vectors which are divided by hyperplane. Since the hyperplane and margin classify a new class as either positive or negative, the probability of misclassification remains [25]. Since the dataset is a binary classification problem, the set of possible predictions are 'Attack': '1', 'Normal': '0'. But theoretically, there are either positive support vectors or negative support vectors in the SVM model. So, we denoted label classes by $\{+1, -1\}$ and consider the predictor of the form $f : \mathbb{R}^D \mapsto \{+1, -1\}$ Where each data point $x_n \epsilon \mathbb{R}^D$ and labels $y_n \epsilon \{+1, -1\}$ where D is the corresponding input real feature vector.

KNN: KNN computes existing proximity between data points. The distance between points is calculated using several distance computation methods and highly suitable for large training data [26].

5   Results and Discussions

Experimental Settings: The population data is chunked into 10 equal-shaped datasets to choose a sample from those. Then resampling algorithm is applied to that dataset. After that, the resampled dataset is split up into the train, test data with a ratio of 7:3. The test split is further divided equally into test and validation datasets. Finally, the models are trained using the training dataset, followed by the performance evaluation based on validation and test dataset using the following formula from 1 to 4 [26].

$$Accuracy = \frac{TP + TN}{Total observations} \tag{1}$$

$$Precision = \frac{TP}{TP + FP} \tag{2}$$

$$Recall = \frac{TP}{TP + FN} \tag{3}$$

$$F1Score = 2 \times \frac{Precision \times Recall}{Precision + Recall} \tag{4}$$

Neural Network Performance: The performance of the LSTM model on 100 epochs in Table 1 shows the accuracy is 96.78%. The credibility of such accuracy is further justified by the Precision, Recall, and F1 Score, all being the same of 97.0%. Thus, it is to say, the system is drawing significant reliability. Figure 6 contains Epoch vs Accuracy and Epoch vs Loss curve. It is demonstrating that in between 80 to 100 epochs, there is almost 97% accuracy for both training and validation, and no fluctuation between the curves; the validation loss is not completely 0 either. However, despite enabling early stopping callback, the training stopped with an optimum loss of above 10% on hundredth epoch.

Table 1. Neural network and machine learning model performances

NN, ML Algorithm	Accuracy %		Recall	Precision	F1 Score
	Test	Train			
LSTM	96.78	96.85	97.00	97.00	97.00
SVM	96.89	96.87	94.87	95.78	95.86
KNN	98.11	98.52	96.39	99.83	97.44

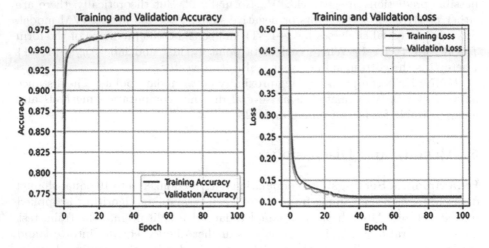

Fig. 6. Accuracy and loss curve of LSTM

Machine Learning Model Performance: Table 1 summerizes the performances of our developed SVM and KNN models. It can be seen that the SVM model showed 96.89% accuracy with precision and recall of 97.8% and 94.87% respectively. The relevancy of these values in terms of FP and FN predictions is justified by the F1 Score of 95.8%. In terms of KNN the model demonstrated 98.11% accuracy on our test dataset. The accuracy of the same model on the training dataset was 98.52%. So, it can be implied that the model neither underfitted nor overfitted. The precision shows that it predicted 99.83% of relevent TP classes. However, 96.39% recall indicates that it make more of FN predictions.

IDS Performance Assessment: Figure 7 represents the summary of the the performances of NN and ML IDS models. From the chart it is observed that LSTM model has the highest recall, hence can be said that, it made less false negative classifications. The SVM model also provided significant performance. Although, overall 97.44% F1 Score indicates KNN to be better than LSTM, and SVM. But in terms of getting balanced performance in detecting TP attacks, LSTM based model is the most efficient among three models.

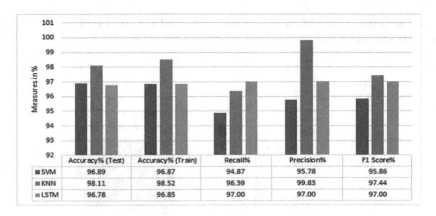

	Accuracy% (Test)	Accuracy% (Train)	Recall%	Precision%	F1 Score%
■ SVM	96.89	96.87	94.87	95.78	95.86
■ KNN	98.11	98.52	96.39	99.83	97.44
■ LSTM	96.78	96.85	97.00	97.00	97.00

Fig. 7. IDS model performance assessment

Table 2. Comparison with existing literature

Works	Method	Dataset domain	Accuracy
Marzia *et al.* [8]	SVM	Kyoto	94.26%
	KNN		97.54%
Ravi *et al.* [10]	Neural Network	Kyoto	88.15%
	KNN		85.61%
	SVM rbf		89.50%
Proposed models	**SVM**	Kyoto	**96.89%**
	KNN		**98.11%**
	LSTM		**96.36%**

Comparison with Existing Works: Our proposed SVM and KNN model outstrips the accuracies of the models of Marzia *et al.* [8], listed in Table 2, by 2.63% and 0.57%, respectively. Due to thorough preprocessing steps and appropriate class balancing, the proposed KNN is slightly performed better than others. However, they did not mention whether they balanced the dataset or not. Unbalanced dataset may provide higher accuracy while predicting wrong class. The SVM and KNN outperform the same of [10] by 13.28% and 7.30%. The proposed LSTM IDS model which is not considered in any literature of this dataset also shows significantly improved accuracy.

Machine Learning Interpretation with LIME: As ML models contain intricate computational operations, a person hardly understands its mechanism. Claiming that LIME [27] interprets the machine learning models to validate reliability [28] of IDS model deployment. Therefore, LIME provides the required computation which can be applied to authenticate the proposed models. So SVM among the three proposed models, and X_test dataset are provided as input to lime_tabular module.

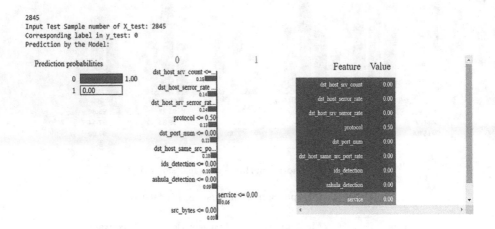

Fig. 8. LIME interpretation

From Fig. 8, it is observed that LIME is predicting class as per the input instances which resembles actual class.

Table 3. Five random instances and LIME prediction

Instance number (k)	Actual label	LIME interpret
2845	0	0 (Normal)
5690	0	0 (Normal)
6828	1	1 (Attack)
18208	0	0 (Normal)
19915	1	1 (Attack)

The deployability is further authenticated by comparing the actual and predicted labels of five random instances, shown in Table 3. For all input instances of X_test.iloc[k], the LIME demonstrates label as shown in Fig. 8; i.e. for X_test.iloc[2845] from Table 3, the LIME interprets the instance as label '1'='Attack' same as actual class which validates the aforementioned claim of trustworthiness.

6 Conclusion

Application of LSTM model in intrusion detection is rarely found in the literature. This paper proposes IDS models with LSTM that demonstrate a significant improvement of performances over the state of the art. The improved efficiency, and the LIME interpretation strengthen our claim that the proposed IDS model can be deployed for such a network environment. It is to mention that, due to limited hardware capacity, only a limited part of the dataset is considered in our experiment. Our future plan includes conducting experiments over the whole dataset. In addition, we are also keen to conduct experiments by using L2 SVM and then perform a comparative analysis of multiple network datasets.

References

1. Beqiri, E.: The implications of information networking at the pace of business development. KNOWLEDGE - Int. J. **27**(1), 17–22 (2018)
2. Nolin, J.M.: Data as oil, infrastructure or asset? three metaphors of data as economic value. J. Inf. Commun. Ethics Soc. **18**(1), 28–43 (2020)
3. Rhodes, B.C., Mahaffey, J.A., Cannady, J.D.: Multiple self-organizing maps for intrusion detection. In: Proceedings of the 23rd National Information Systems Security Conference, pp. 16–19 (2000)
4. Belavagi, M.C., Muniyal, B.: Performance evaluation of supervised machine learning algorithms for intrusion detection. Procedia Comput. Sci. **89**, 117–123 (2016)
5. Suman, C., Tripathy, S., Saha, S.: Building an effective intrusion detection system using unsupervised feature selection in multi-objective optimization framework. arXiv preprint arXiv:1905.06562 (2019)
6. Song, J., Takakura, H., Okabe, Y.: Description of kyoto university benchmark data (2006). http://www.takakura.com/Kyoto_data/BenchmarkData-Description-v5. pdf. Accessed 15 March 2016
7. Rai, A.: Explainable AI: from black box to glass box. J. Acad. Mark. Sci. **48**(1), 137–141 (2020)
8. Zaman, M., Lung, C.-H.: Evaluation of machine learning techniques for network intrusion detection. In: NOMS 2018–2018 IEEE/IFIP Network Operations and Management Symposium, pp. 1–5. IEEE (2018)
9. Agarap, A.F.M.: A neural network architecture combining gated recurrent unit (GRU) and support vector machine (SVM) for intrusion detection in network traffic data. In: Proceedings of the 2018 10th International Conference on Machine Learning and Computing, pp. 26–30 (2018)
10. Vinayakumar, R., Alazab, M., Soman, K.P., Poornachandran, P., Al-Nemrat, A., Venkatraman, S.: Deep learning approach for intelligent intrusion detection system. IEEE Access **7**, 41525–41550 (2019)
11. Javaid, A., Niyaz, Q., Sun, W., Alam, M.: A deep learning approach for network intrusion detection system. In: Proceedings of the 9th EAI International Conference on Bio-inspired Information and Communications Technologies (formerly BIONETICS), pp. 21–26 (2016)
12. Ring, M., Wunderlich, S., Scheuring, D., Landes, D., Hotho, A.: A survey of network-based intrusion detection data sets. Comput. Secur. **86**, 147–167 (2019)

13. Almseidin, M., Maen, A., Kovacs, S., Alkasassbeh, M.: Evaluation of machine learning algorithms for intrusion detection system. In: 2017 IEEE 15th International Symposium on Intelligent Systems and Informatics (SISY), pp. 000277–000282. IEEE (2017)
14. Song, J., Takakura, H., Okabe, Y.: Cooperation of intelligent honeypots to detect unknown malicious codes. In: 2008 WOMBAT Workshop on Information Security Threats Data Collection and Sharing, pp. 31–39. IEEE (2008)
15. Teng, C.M.:. Correcting noisy data. In: ICML, pp. 239–248. Citeseer (1999)
16. García, S., Luengo, J., Francisco, H.: Data Preprocessing in Data Mining, vol. 72. Springer (2015)
17. Tsai, C-F., Hsu, Y-F., Lin, C-Y., Lin, W-Y.: Intrusion detection by machine learning: a review. Expert Syst. Appl. $36(10)$, 11994–12000 (2009)
18. Liu, Y., Mu, Y., Chen, K., Li, Y., Guo, J.: Daily activity feature selection in smart homes based on pearson correlation coefficient. Neural Process. Lett. pp. 1–17 (2020)
19. Wang, Z., Chunhua, W., Zheng, K., Niu, X., Wang, X.: Smotetomek-based resampling for personality recognition. IEEE Access 7, 129678–129689 (2019)
20. Purwins, H., Li, B., Virtanen, T., Schlüter, J., Chang, S.-Y., Sainath, T.: Deep learning for audio signal processing. IEEE J. Select. Top. Sign. Process. $13(2)$, 206–219 (2019)
21. Gal, Y., Islam, R., Ghahramani, Z.: Deep Bayesian active learning with image data. In: International Conference on Machine Learning, pp. 1183–1192. PMLR (2017)
22. Alhagry, S., Fahmy, A.A., El-Khoribi, R.A.: Emotion recognition based on EEG using LSTM recurrent neural network. Emotion $8(10)$, 355–358 (2017)
23. Hochreiter, S., Schmidhuber, J.: Long short-term memory. Neural Comput. $9(8)$, 1735–1780 (1997)
24. Courbariaux, M., Bengio, Y., David, J-P.: Binaryconnect: Training deep neural networks with binary weights during propagations. arXiv preprint arXiv:1511.00363 (2015)
25. Ikram Sumaiya Thaseen and Cherukuri Aswani Kumar: Intrusion detection model using fusion of chi-square feature selection and multi class SVM. J. King Saud Univ. Comput. Inf. Sci. $29(4)$, 462–472 (2017)
26. Rezvi, M.A., Moontaha, S., Trisha, K.A., Cynthia, S.T., Ripon, S.: Data mining approach to analyzing intrusion detection of wireless sensor network. Indonesian J. Electric. Eng. Comput. Sci. $21(1)$, 516–523 (2021)
27. Ribeiro, M.T., Singh, S., Guestrin, C.: Why should i trust you? explaining the predictions of any classifier. In: Proceedings of the 22nd ACM SIGKDD International Conference on Knowledge Discovery and Data Mining, pp. 1135–1144 (2016)
28. Visani, G., Bagli, E., Chesani, F., Poluzzi, A., Capuzzo, D.: Statistical stability indices for lime: obtaining reliable explanations for machine learning models. arXiv preprint arXiv:2001.11757 (2020)

Application of Machine Learning Techniques to Predict Breast Cancer Survival

Jaree Thomgkam[1]([✉]), Vatinee Sukmak[2], and Papidchaya Klangnok[3]

[1] Faculty of Informatics, Mahasarakham University, Maha Sarakham 44150, Thailand
jaree.t@msu.ac.th
[2] Faculty of Nursing, Mahasarakham University, Maha Sarakham 44150, Thailand
[3] Faculty of Sports and Health Science, National Sports University Sisaket Campus,
Mueang Nuea 33000, Sisaket, Thailand

Abstract. Despite recent significant advances in big data analytics, there is substantial evidence of machine learning techniques that perform poorly when building prediction models. This research aimed to investigate the performance and effectiveness of machine learning techniques including Naive Bayes (NB), PART, Random Forest (RF), Support Vector Machine (SVM), Adaboost, and Bagging in order to advance existing understandings of model behavior with big data. A large dataset of hospital-based breast cancer from the SEER data file with diagnostic information was used from 2005 to 2014. To address outliers and imbalance issues, we used C4.5 and Synthetic Minority Oversampling TEchnique (SMOTE) to eliminate outliers and balance the dataset. Stratified 10-fold cross-validation was used to divide the dataset to reduce bias and variance of experimental results. Accuracy, G-mean (G), F-measure, and Matthews correlation coefficient (MCC) are employed as criteria to present the overall performance of the models. Moreover, sensitivity, specificity, and precision are utilized as criteria to show the insightful performance of the models. The experimental results indicate that RF is superior to Naive Bayes (NB), PART, Support Vector Machine (SVM), Adaboost, and Bagging in all criteria. Also, models generated from datasets with few outliers and balanced data outperform the original dataset in terms of insight and overall performances.

Keywords: Breast cancer survival models · Machine learning techniques · Random forest

1 Introduction

Breast cancer is one of the most common diseases and the leading cause of death in women worldwide. In January 2021, more than 3.8 million women in the United States had a history of breast cancer [1]. More than 280,000 new cases of metastatic disease, along with 49,290 new cases of in situ breast cancer, are expected to be diagnosed in 2021 [2]. Furthermore, it was the fifth leading cause of cancer mortality globally in 2020, accounting for 685,000 deaths [3] and nearly 43,600 women will die from breast cancer in the United States in 2021 [1].

© Springer Nature Switzerland AG 2021
P. Chomphuwiset et al. (Eds.): MIWAI 2021, LNAI 12832, pp. 141–151, 2021.
https://doi.org/10.1007/978-3-030-80253-0_13

Early detection with mammography screening and better treatment have significantly increased survival rates, but the cost of treating breast cancer is greater than that of any other cancer [4]. Breast cancer medical costs are predicted to exceed $16.5 billion, surpassing colorectal cancer ($14 billion) in 2020 [5]. However, the risk for breast cancer is caused by a combination of factors, including being a woman and getting older, especially in women over the age of 50 [6]. The classification of women based on breast cancer risk factors will help improve risk-free procedures and design targeted breast cancer screening programs [7]. As a result, it is necessary to identify the various factors that affect breast cancer patients' survival rate.

Statistical and data mining techniques can help in the identification of factor patterns and relationships between variables, as well as the prediction of disease outcomes. For example, Alica et al. [8] used the Kaplan-Meier survival analysis to predict local relapse and survival in patients treated with surgery for breast cancer using demographic, treatment, grade, size, and metastasis stage factors. According to the findings, there was no significant difference in recurrence from surgery and the subsequent presence of metastatic disease. Tapak et al. [9] created breast cancer survival and metastases prediction models from 550 records using NB, RF, AdaBoost, SVM, Least-square SVM (LSSVM), Adabag, Logistic Regression (LR), and Linear Discriminant Analysis (LDA). Their results revealed that SVM and LDA have the highest accuracy (93.00%).

Machine learning approaches such as Naïve Bayes (NB), Partial Decision Tree (called PART), Random Forest (RF), support vector machine (SVM) are now widely used. Naive Bayes (NB) is a well-known classification technique that using numeric estimator class precision values to classify based on training data interpretation. This technique is a simple way to build a model [10]. In the text mining classification of large datasets, Naive Bayes provides high performance. It can also be used to reduce training and testing times in large datasets [11, 12]. Several studies have attempted to enhance the performance of the Naive Bayes model. Sun et al. [12], for example, developed lossless pruned Naive Bayes from building 7,205 instances of text prediction models. The results showed that a lossless pruned Naive Bayes model can be built seven times faster than normal a conventional Naïve Bayes model.

PART is a rule-based technique that is used for classification tasks [13]. It used a separate-and-conquer strategy to build a partial decision tree for each iteration and then select the best leaf in the rule. It is recognized that PART is ideal for real-world datasets. Exarchos et al. [14] showed that PART can generate rules for predicting symptoms with an accuracy of up to 77.4%. In datasets such as audiology, balance-scale, and waveform-noise, Frank and Witten [13] demonstrated that the PART outperforms C4.5. Chang et al. [15], on the other hand, pointed out that the decision tree rule has poor sensitivity.

SVM [16] is extensively used for classification and regression tasks. Sequential implementations of support vector machines, however, are usually unable to solve a large dataset. SVM is an effective technique for classifying linear classification in a dataset of 88,772 records, according to Zou and Jin [17], but it requires a considerable amount of memory to build the models.

RF is a classification and regression ensemble learning method. Its trees are built based on the variables selected by Gini and the mean accuracy needed to achieve the best accuracy. Ganggayah et al. [18] used a RF technique to build prediction models to predict breast cancer survival in Malaysia with 8,066 records. The result showed that this technique outperformed the decision tree technique in terms of accuracy.

Adaboost and Bagging are ensemble techniques in machine learning that combine a large number of weak classifiers into a single strong classifier to generate highly accurate prediction models [19, 20]. Selvathi and Selvaraj [21] used Adaboost to improve the performance of random forests from 30 images of glioma patients. Moreover, Wu et al. [20] demonstrated that Adaboost outperforms Bagging in terms of decision tree performance.

Many survival prediction experiments have conducted using statistical and artificial neural network approaches. However, there were only a few studies on medical diagnosis, and the dataset was incredibly limited, with only 88,772 records [18]. Also, most techniques face many challenges when it comes to developing high-performance models from big data, such as low predicting accuracy, heavy memory use, and time-consuming training and testing datasets.

In this study, the authors developed cancer survival prediction models with a large dataset of more than 100,000 records using NB, PART, RF, and SVM techniques to determine which approach works best. Furthermore, Adaboost and Bagging, both of which have high classification accuracy, are used to compare the performance of the base models. Stratified 10-fold cross-validation is used to reduce the bay and variance of experimental outcomes. Accuracy, G, F-measure, and MCC are performance measures for the overall evaluation of the models, while sensitivity, specificity, precision are used to conduct insight into the performance of the models.

2   Material and Method

In this section, machine learning techniques are briefly illustrated. The methods are then thoroughly outlined in the paper.

2.1   Machine Learning Techniques

In this article, cancer survival prediction models were built using NB, PART, RF, SVM, Adaboost, and Bagging to evaluate which approach performs better in a large dataset. NB [10], a classification technique that uses precision values of numeric estimator classes to classify data based on an analysis of the training dataset, while PART [13] is a rule-based technique that is built from a decision tree. Aside from the PART, RF is a forest of trees that were constructed at random. It builds a tree forest by randomly selecting data from the dataset with replacement. SVM [16] employs the featured space to form hyperplanes with the minimum support for classification and regression problems.

Adaboost and Bagging are also ensemble techniques used to improve base learners such as decision stump and REPTree. Adaboost selects instances using boosting concepts while Bagging selects instances using bootstrap to decrease the variance in the prediction [19]. The Adaboost technique employs a decision stump to build the decision tree models. The Bagging technique, on the other hand, utilizes REP Tree to build decision tree models [20].

2.2 Methods

This section describes the methods for large dataset analysis. There are three steps including data preparation, data pre-processing, and experimental design.

Data Preparation. To evaluate the performance and effectiveness of the selected techniques, we used the SEER database at the National Cancer Institute of the United States for the year 2014. The estimated number of breast cancer cases was 199,269, with 86 attributes. However, some attribute values were missing or had unknown values. This may be that the diagnostic systems have changed over time. Therefore, attributes were chosen as important prognostic factors identified in most studies [18]. The primary site feature contains the origin of breast cancer which is related to patient survival periods.

There are two classes in the class attribute: 'Dead' and 'Alive'. The 'Dead' class refers to patients who died within five years after diagnosis. In contrast, the 'Alive' class refers to patients who have survived for more than five years after diagnosis. As a consequence, the total number of instances totals is 193,053 records which is divided into 109,799 records for the 'Dead' class and 83,254 records for the 'Alive' Class. The dataset is displayed in Table 1 for nominal attributes and Table 2 for integer attributes.

Table 1. Nominal attributes.

No.	Description	Numbers of value
1	Marital status	7
2	Race	4
3	Primary site	9
4	Lateral	2
5	Cancer grade	4
6	Stage	5
7	Surgery of primary site	5

Table 2. Numeric attributes.

No.	Descriptions	Min	Max	Mean	SD
1	Age at diagnosis	7	100	62.57	13.5
2	Tumor size	1.00	9.97	25.82	88.92

Data Pre-processing. The data pre-processing step in data mining is used to improve data quality by eliminating outliers, balancing classes, and selecting attributes [22]. In this data pre-processing step, the data on breast cancer was compiled into four datasets. The first dataset (called dataset1) is an original dataset that has been cleaned up of duplicate data. After cleaning dataset1, we found that the model performance is low. In order to improve data quality, the misclassification method was used to identify outliers in the dataset1 [23]. The C4.5 technique was then used to extract the effect of outliers from dataset1 with a 10% threshold error and a 25% confidence factor for tree pruning. As a result, the first dataset from which the outliers were removed was called dataset2. However, we found an issue with an imbalanced dataset as well as a smaller number of data in both the majority and minority classes. To address a disparity in data, the SMOTE was used to increase the amount of data in the minority class to nearly equal to that in the majority class, referred to as dataset3. Also, the SMOTE was used to deal with a lower number of data by calculating the ratio between the majority class ('Dead' class) in dataset2 (74,717), and the average number in dataset1 (77,604), and subtracting it by 1. This allows the majority class to have up to 3.80% of the majority class in dataset2 and then increases the minority class to almost equal the majority class, referred to as dataset4. The result of the four datasets is illustrated in Table 3.

Table 3. All datasets used in the experiment.

Datasets	'Dead' Class	'Alive' Class	'Dead' Class Ratio	'Alive' Class Ratio
Dataset1	88,762	66,446	57.19%	42.81%
Dataset2	74,717	17,440	81.08%	18.92%
Dataset3	74,717	74,643	50.02%	49.98%
Dataset4	77,556	77,590	49.99%	50.01%

Table 3 shows the four datasets that will be used to evaluate the performance and effectiveness of the techniques used in this paper. Dataset1 and dataset2 have some problems: dataset1 contains nearly 59% outliers and dataset 2 has an imbalanced class problem. On the contrary, dataset3 and dataset4 have no outlier or imbalance problems, with dataset3 being smaller than dataset4.

Experimental Design. The experimental design is the start of four datasets used to evaluate the performance and effectiveness of data mining techniques. These four datasets are then divided into training and testing sets using stratified 10-fold cross-validation to prevent over-fitting of training data, which is common in classification problems. Only the training set is used for the building of NB, PART, RF, SVM, Adaboost, and Bagging models. The testing set is used to evaluate the performance and effectiveness of the models. Performance criteria, including accuracy, F-measure, G-mean (G), and MCC, are used to present the overall performance of the models.

Also, sensitivity, specificity, and recall are used to demonstrate the insightful performance of the models. Accuracy and F-measure are widely used criteria for measuring the performance of prediction models, while G-mean is the geometric mean of sensitivity and specificity [20, 21]. Since G parameters are not given in the application, G-mean is rarely used. However, it is sufficient to evaluate models that have imbalance class problems. Besides, Matthews Correlation Coefficient (MCC) is a method for assessing the quality of a binary classification. It has a value of -1 to 1, with -1 indicating a completely incorrect binary classifier and 1 indicating a completely correct binary classifier. The experimental design is shown in Fig. 1.

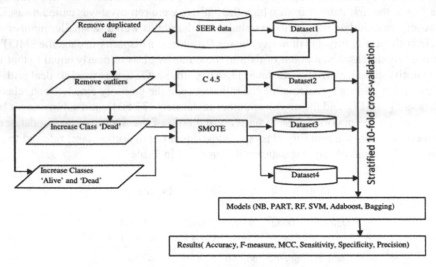

Fig. 1. Experimental design.

The evaluation metrics are defined in Eq. 1 through Eq. 7, which is derived from the elements of the confusion matrix.

$$Acc = \frac{TP + TN}{TP + FP + TN + FN} \times 100 \tag{1}$$

$$G = \sqrt{\left(\frac{TP}{TP + FN}\right) \times \left(\frac{TN}{TN + FP}\right)} \times 100 \tag{2}$$

$$F - measure = \frac{2TP}{2TP + FP + FN} \times 100 \tag{3}$$

$$MCC = \frac{(TP * TN) - (FP * FN)}{\sqrt{[(TP + FP)(TP + FN)(TN + FP)(TN + FN)]}} \times 100 \tag{4}$$

$$Sensitivity = \frac{TP}{TP + FN} \times 100 \tag{5}$$

$$Specificity = \frac{TN}{TN + FP} \times 100 \tag{6}$$

$$Precision = \frac{TP}{TP + FP} \times 100 \tag{7}$$

Where TP denotes the amount of correctly classify non-survival (true positive), TN denotes the number of correctly classify survival (true negative). The results of the evaluation will be reported in percentage terms.

3 Experiment Results

Accuracy, G, F-measure, MCC, sensitivity, specificity, and precision were used in this study to compare the prediction performance and effectiveness of the NB, PART, RF, SVM, Adaboost, and Bagging techniques, with the dataset divided into training and test sets by stratifies 10-fold cross-validation (VEcv) values. The insight of each model and overall performance are displayed in Sect. 3.1 and Sect. 3.2, respectively.

3.1 Insight Model Performance

Performance models used stratified 10-fold cross-validation to divide the dataset into training and testing datasets equally. Sensitivity, specificity, and precision are used to demonstrate the insightful performance of the models. The results are shown in Table 4.

Table 4. Insight model performance.

Dataset	Models	Sensitivity	Specificity	Precision
Dataset1	NB	91.15 ± 0.86	14.12 ± 1.20	58.64 ± 0.18
	PART	76.76 ± 5.12	28.56 ± 5.68	58.96 ± 0.46
	RF	55.01 ± 0.58	30.79 ± 0.40	51.50 ± 0.30
	SVM	92.52 ± 0.59	12.19 ± 0.60	58.47 ± 0.15
	Adaboost	100.00	0.00	57.19 ± 0.00
	Bagging	65.70 ± 0.42	30.91 ± 0.50	55.95 ± 0.17
Average		80.19 ± 1.26	19.43 ± 1.40	56.79 ± 0.21
Dataset2	NB	93.76 ± 0.29	58.10 ± 1.30	90.55 ± 0.26
	PART	99.35 ± 0.08	97.06 ± 0.49	99.31 ± 0.11
	RF	99.70 ± 0.04	97.57 ± 0.32	99.44 ± 0.07
	SVM	97.59 ± 0.23	71.53 ± 1.09	93.63 ± 0.22
	Adaboost	94.65 ± 2.56	54.67 ± 22.44	90.23 ± 3.83
	Bagging	99.21 ± 0.10	96.40 ± 0.59	99.16 ± 0.14
Average		97.38 ± 0.55	79.22 ± 4.37	95.39 ± 0.77
Dataset3	NB	77.44 ± 0.58	92.58 ± 0.27	91.27 ± 0.29
	PART	97.48 ± 0.25	98.02 ± 0.13	98.01 ± 0.13
	RF	98.53 ± 0.08	99.32 ± 0.14	99.32 ± 0.14
	SVM	93.34 ± 0.22	94.13 ± 0.13	94.09 ± 0.13
	Adaboost	74.87 ± 0.44	92.54 ± 0.33	90.95 ± 0.35
	Bagging	97.98 ± 0.17	97.62 ± 0.23	97.63 ± 0.22
Average		89.94 ± 0.29	95.70 ± 0.21	95.21 ± 0.21
Dataset4	NB	77.27 ± 0.55	92.66 ± 0.25	91.32 ± 0.29
	PART	97.43 ± 0.29	98.05 ± 0.27	98.04 ± 0.26
	RF	98.56 ± 0.10	99.29 ± 0.10	99.29 ± 0.1
	SVM	93.46 ± 0.28	94.20 ± 0.23	94.16 ± 0.21
	Adaboost	73.4 ± 1.73	93.36 ± 0.79	91.72 ± 0.79
	Bagging	97.89 ± 0.09	97.78 ± 0.20	97.78 ± 0.2
Average		89.67 ± 0.51	95.89 ± 0.31	95.39 ± 0.31

Table 4 shows the performance of the NB, PART, RF, SVM, Adaboost, and Bagging models in predicting 5-year breast cancer survival. The results show that RF models outperform NB, PART, SVM Adaboost, and Bagging in terms of average sensitivity, specificity, and precision. The experimental results of the models have four dimensions as follows:

Firstly, dataset models, except for RF, have shown high sensitivity but low specificity values. RF, on the other hand, has similar sensitivity, specificity, and precision values, implying that RF can predict dead and alive classes, whereas others can only predict the majority class. Secondly, dataset2 models based on NB, PART, RF, SVM, Adaboost, and Bagging have extremely high sensitivity and precision. Besides, NB and Adaboost are unable to build models well in the imbalanced dataset. Thirdly, for dataset3 and dataset4, which have no imbalance problems, NB, PART, RF, SVM, Adaboost, and Bagging have very high sensitivity, specificity, and precision. Finally, average values of sensitivity, specificity, and precision values from all datasets show that PART has the highest sensitivity and precision, while RF has the highest specificity.

3.2 Overall Model Performance

The results of the overall model performance, accuracy, G, F-measures, and MCC for evaluating the effectiveness of the six techniques for building breast cancer survival models from large datasets are shown in Table 5.

Table 5. Overall model performance.

Dataset	Models	Accuracy	G	F-measure	MCC
Dataset1	NB	58.17 ± 0.27	35.84 ± 1.37	71.37 ± 0.25	8.31 ± 0.87
	PART	56.12 ± 0.62	46.46 ± 2.30	66.60 ± 1.93	6.08 ± 0.92
	RF	44.64 ± 0.37	41.15 ± 0.35	53.20 ± 0.42	−14.41 ± 0.71
	SVM	58.13 ± 0.28	33.58 ± 0.77	71.65 ± 0.24	7.98 ± 0.95
	Adaboost	57.19 ± 0.00	–	72.76 ± 0.00	-
	Bagging	50.81 ± 0.23	45.06 ± 0.32	60.44 ± 0.24	-3.57 ± 0.50
Average		54.18 ± 0.30	33.68 ± 0.85	66.00 ± 0.51	0.73 ± 0.66
Dataset2	NB	87.01 ± 0.30	73.80 ± 0.81	92.13 ± 0.18	55.34 ± 1.08
	PART	98.91 ± 0.11	98.20 ± 0.25	99.33 ± 0.07	96.45 ± 0.36
	RF	99.30 ± 0.07	98.63 ± 0.16	99.57 ± 0.04	97.72 ± 0.23
	SVM	92.66 ± 0.17	83.55 ± 0.58	95.57 ± 0.10	74.84 ± 0.61
	Adaboost	87.09 ± 2.19	69.01 ± 18.87	92.28 ± 0.97	53.80 ± 13.73
	Bagging	98.68 ± 0.16	97.80±0.32	99.19 ± 0.10	95.70 ± 0.52
Average		93.94 ± 0.50	86.83 ± 3.50	96.34 ± 0.24	78.97 ± 2.75
Dataset3	NB	85.01 ± 0.31	84.67 ± 0.33	83.79 ± 0.37	70.84 ± 0.58
	PART	97.75 ± 0.14	97.75 ± 0.14	97.74 ± 0.14	95.50 ± 0.27
	RF	98.93 ± 0.08	98.93 ± 0.08	98.92 ± 0.08	97.86 ± 0.16
	SVM	93.74 ± 0.13	93.74 ± 0.13	93.72 ± 0.14	87.48 ± 0.26

(continued)

Table 5. (*continued*)

Dataset	Models	Accuracy	G	F-measure	MCC
	Adaboost	83.70±0.21	83.24 ± 0.23	82.13 ± 0.26	68.48 ± 0.42
	Bagging	97.80 ± 0.15	97.80 ± 0.15	97.80 ± 0.15	95.59 ± 0.29
Average		92.82 ± 0.17	92.69 ± 0.17	92.35 ± 0.19	85.96 ± 0.33
Dataset4	NB	84.97 ± 0.32	84.61 ± 0.34	83.71 ± 0.38	70.77 ± 0.60
	PART	97.74 ± 0.18	97.74 ± 0.18	97.73 ± 0.18	95.49 ± 0.36
	RF	98.93 ± 0.06	98.93 ± 0.06	98.92 ± 0.06	97.86 ± 0.13
	SVM	93.83 ± 0.15	93.83 ± 0.15	93.81 ± 0.15	87.67 ± 0.30
	Adaboost	83.38 ± 0.66	82.77 ± 0.78	81.53 ± 0.93	68.15 ± 1.12
	Bagging	97.84 ± 0.12	97.84 ± 0.12	97.84 ± 0.11	95.67 ± 0.23
Average		92.78 ± 0.25	92.62 ± 0.27	92.26 ± 0.30	85.94 ± 0.46

Table 5 shows the performance and effectiveness of the breast cancer prediction models using accuracy, G, F-measure, and MCC. The results reveal that most techniques are unable to generate high performance and effective models from dataset1 due to outliers. In contrast, dataset 2, which used C4.5 to filter out the outliers, improved RF performance by up to 112.13% when evaluated with MCC. Adaboost improved the least, improving up to 19.52%. The G of RF improved marginally in dataset 3 relative to dataset 2, while the Accuracy of RF decreased. The performance of Adaboost improved to 14.68% as measured by precision, F-measure, G, and MCC. The results for datasets 3 and 4 revealed that dataset 4 did not improve effectiveness over dataset 3.

4   Discussion and Conclusion

This study aims to investigate the performance and effectiveness of NB, PART, RF, SVM, Adaboost, and Bagging in a large dataset of hospital-based breast cancer patients from the SEER data file which was used between 2005 and 2014. To limit bias and variance in experimental outcomes, the stratified 10-fold cross-validation was employed to evaluate models. Moreover, the overall evaluation metrics which includes accuracy, G-mean (G), F-measure, and, MCC and the insightful performance criterion which includes sensitivity, specificity, and precision, are used to measure model effectiveness. The experimental results show that RF outperforms NB, PART, SVM, Adaboost, and Bagging in all criteria. Similarly, the result in predicting breast cancer survival showed that RF is better than SVM [18]. On the other hand, previous research has shown that SVM outperforms RF in predicting survival and metastasis in breast cancer patients [9]. This may be because their dataset is small. Moreover, models generated from dataset3 and dataset4 which contain few outliers and more balanced data can provide better specificity and precision than dataset2. This may be because most classification models have weakness in imbalanced datasets which lead to overfitting problem. Also, the G and MCC criteria are better criteria for imbalanced datasets. Despite the fact that C4.5 was used to remove the outlier, it reduced the overfitting problem in the raw dataset by pruning a tree. Our results are consistent with what Trabelsi et al. [24] reported in that the pruning method can be used to prevent the overfitting problem in their data.

Acknowledgments. This research was financially supported by the faculty of Informatics, Mahasarakham University (Grant year 2019). The researchers would like to thanks the SEER website for providing the data used for analyzing the survival model of patients with breast cancer.

References

1. Current year estimates for breast cancer. https://www.cancer.org/cancer/breast-cancer/about/how-common-is-breast-cancer.html. Accessed 18 Jan 2021
2. U.S. Breast cancer statistics. https://www.breastcancer.org/symptoms/understand_bc /statistics. Accessed 04 Feb 2021
3. Bray, F., Ferlay J., Soerjomataram I., Siegel R.L., Torre L.A., Jemal, A.: Global cancer statistics 2018: GLOBOCAN estimates of incidence and mortality worldwide for 36 cancers in 185 countries. CA: Cancer J. clin. **68**(6), 394–424 (2018)
4. Ekwueme, D.U., Guy, G.P., Rim, S.H., White, A., Hall, I.J., Fairley, T.L., et al.: Health and economic impact of breast cancer mortality in young woman. Am. J. Prev. Med. **46**(1), 71–79 (2014)
5. The financial burden of breast cancer. https://www.forbes.com/sites/nextavenue/2020/01/21 /the-financial-burden-of-breast-cancer/?sh=13f53854d217. Accessed 12 Feb 2021
6. What are the risk factors for breast cancer?. https://www.cdc.gov/cancer/breast/basic_info /risk_factors.htm. Accessed 12 Jan 2021
7. Momenimovahed, Z., Salehiniya, H.: Epidemiological characteristics of and risk factors for breast cancer in the world. Breast Cancer (Dove Med Press). **11**, 151–164 (2019)
8. Tejera Hernández, A.A., Vega, B.V., M., Rocca Cardenas J.C., Gutiérrez Giner M.I., Díaz Chico J.C., Hernández Hernández J.R.: Factors predicting local relapse and survival in patients treated with surgery for breast cancer. Asian J. Surg. **42**(7), 755–760 (2018)
9. Tapak, L., Shirmohammadi-Khorram, N., Amini, P., Alafchi, B., Hamidi, O., Poorolajal, J.: Prediction of survival and metastasis in breast cancer patients using machine learning classifiers. Clin. Epidemiol. Glob. Health. **7**(3), 293–299 (2019)
10. John, G.H., Langley, P.: Estimating continuous distributions in bayesian classifiers. In: Eleventh Conference on Uncertainty in Artificial Intelligence, pp. 338–45 (1995)
11. Liu, B., Blasch E., Chen Y., Shen D., Chen G.: Scalable sentiment classification for big data analysis using Naïve Bayes classifier. In: 2013 IEEE International Conference on Big Data, pp. 99–104. (2013)
12. Sun, N., Sun, B., Lin, J., Wu, M.Y.-C.: Lossless pruned naive Bayes for big data classifications. Big Data Res. **14**, 27–36 (2018)
13. Frank, E., Witten, I.H.: Generating accurate rule sets without global optimization. In: 5th International Conference on Machine Learning, pp. 144–51 (1998)
14. Exarchos, T.P., Tzallas, A.T., Baga, D., Chaloglou, D., Fotiadis, D.I., Tsouli, S., et al.: Using partial decision trees to predict Parkinson's symptoms: a new approach for diagnosis and therapy in patients suffering from Parkinson's disease. Comput. Biol. Med. **42**(2), 195–204 (2012)
15. Chang, C., Lai, C., Wu, R.: Decision tree rules for insulation condition assessment of pre-molded power cable joints with artificial defects. IEEE Trans. Dielectr. Electr. Insul. **26**(5), 1636–1644 (2019)
16. Fan, R.-E., Chen, P.-H., Lin, C.-J.: Working set selection using second order information for training SVM. Mach. Learn. Res. **6**, 1889–1918 (2005)
17. Zou, H., Jin Z.: Comparative study of big data classification algorithm based on SVM. In: 2018 Cross Strait Quad-Regional Radio Science and Wireless Technology Conference (CSQRWC), pp. 1–3 (2018)

18. Ganggayah, M.D., Taib, N.A., Har, Y.C., Lio, P., Dhillon, S.K.: Predicting factors for survival of breast cancer patients using machine learning techniques. BMC Med. Inform. Decis. Mak. **19**(48), 1–17 (2019)
19. Wu, Z., Li, N., Peng, J., Cui, H., Liu, P., Li, H., et al.: Using an ensemble machine learning methodology-Bagging to predict occupants' thermal comfort in buildings. Energy Build. **173**, 117–127 (2018)
20. Wu, Y., Ke Y., Chen Z., Liang S., Zhao H., Hong H.: Application of alternating decision tree with AdaBoost and bagging ensembles for landslide susceptibility mapping. CATENA. **187**, 104396 (2020)
21. Selvathi, D., Selvaraj H.: Segmentation of brain tumor tissues in MR images using multiresolution transforms and random forest classifiers with Adaboost technique. In: 2018 26th International Conference on Systems Engineering (ICSEng), pp. 1–7 (2018)
22. Jia, W., Xia, H., Jia, L., Deng, Y., Liu, X.: The selection of wart treatment method based on synthetic minority over-sampling technique and axiomatic fuzzy set theory. Biocybern. Biomed. Eng. (2020)
23. Baldomero-Naranjo, M., Martínez-Merino, L.I., Rodríguez-Chía, A.M.: A robust SVM-based approach with feature selection and outliers detection for classification problems. Expert Syst. Appl. **178**, 115017 (2021)
24. Trabelsi, S., Elouedi, Z., Mellouli, K.: Pruning belief decision tree methods in averaging and conjunctive approaches. Int. J. Approximate Reasoning **46**(3), 568–595 (2007)

Thai Handwritten Recognition on BEST2019 Datasets Using Deep Learning

Rapeeporn Chamchong$^{(\boxtimes)}$ ⓘ, Umaporn Saisangchan, and Pornntiwa Pawara ⓘ

POLAR Lab, Faculty of Informatics, Mahasarakham University,
Kantarawichai, Maha Sarakham 44150, Thailand
`{rapeeporn.c,umaporn}@msu.ac.th`

Abstract. Handwritten recognition is a difficult task. The conventional technique relies on the character segmentation, feature extraction, and classification process. The segmentation is a tremendous challenge when there are variation of character patterns and alignments in a sentence, such as linking segments between characters in the Thai language. Promising segmentation outcome is favorable but not applicable in most applications. This work proposes a methodology for Thai handwritten recognition by applying Convolutional Neural Networks (CNNs) and Recurrent Neural Networks (RNNs). The first step is text localization before feeding to the network. CNN extracts the abstract features before they are fed to RNN to learn the sequence of characters in an image. The optimization is performed with an integrated Connectionist Temporal Classification (CTC) module (to arrange the final results). A standard Thai handwritten dataset (BEST2019) and more collection are used in this study. for training and test sets. The experimental results show that the integration of CNN and RNN provides promising results of the test set with a Character Error Rate (CER) of 1.58%. For testing with the seen and unseen dataset of the final round of BEST2019 competition, the CER is at 24.53%.

Keywords: Deep learning · Convolutional Neural Network · Recurrent Neural Network · Handwritten recognition

1 Introduction

In the past, most of the manuscripts in Thailand were written by hand to record invaluable knowledge. By digitizing the image manuscripts, the content can be preserved and made widely available to the interested community via electronic media. Handwritten recognition has become an inherent part of the processing to extract relevant information from these document images efficiently. Although some researchers proposed promising Thai print Optical Character Recognition (OCR) techniques such as ThaiOCR and ArnThai [1], a few research can be used for Thai handwritten recognition.

The original version of this chapter was revised: Errors have been corrected in section 4.3 and Table 3. The correction to this chapter is available at
https://doi.org/10.1007/978-3-030-80253-0_17

© Springer Nature Switzerland AG 2021, corrected publication 2021
P. Chomphuwiset et al. (Eds.): MIWAI 2021, LNAI 12832, pp. 152–163, 2021.
https://doi.org/10.1007/978-3-030-80253-0_14

Most researches on Thai handwritten recognition are focused on the feature extraction and recognition model. While feature extraction problems still need solutions, there are three main obstacles related to Thai words and character segmentation. (i) There is no stop word, like a full stop in English, (ii) there is no white space between each word, making it difficult to separate characters, words, or sentences, and (iii) the Thai characters can be located on one of the three levels; main text line, above, and under the main text line.

A deep neural network has recently been proposed to learn feature hierarchies ranging from higher levels by the composition of lower-level features. This learning process can be applied in computer vision and image processing by input all pixels of the image without feature extraction from the image processing. Convolutional Neural Network (CNN) [2] is deep learning that emerged as a powerful class of models for recognizing printed and handwritten texts. CNN can achieve high accuracies, surpassing those of previously reported results such as in [2–5]. However, CNN has been mostly used for character-based recognition (feeding an image of a single character to CNN to perform a classification). There is still a need for character segmentation. As a result of this study, it is difficult to separate Thai handwriting characters. Other deep learning techniques such as Recurrent Neural Networks (RNNs) are well suited to learning such sequences of characters. OCRopus [6] and Tesseract 4.0 [7] use Long Short-Term Memory (LSTM) to recognize handwritten characters of multiple languages.

Recently, Benchmark for Enhancing the Standard for Thai language processing (BEST) [8] was established and organized by NECTEC (National Electronics and Computer Technology Center) in 2009. In March 2019, there was a competition of Handwritten Recognition in the 18th Thailand IT Contest Festival. The benchmark dataset of Thai handwriting for the competition has been distributed, called "BEST2019". This competition aims to apply and modify the technique for Thai handwritten recognition.

In this study, the BEST2019 dataset has been used to evaluate the model. Instead of processing the recognition on a single character, this work considers the sequences of character scripts and uses them for the final prediction. There are two main steps in this work, (i) preprocessing and text localization, and (ii) model generation. The arrangement of the rest sections of this paper is as follows. Section 2 describes related works and is followed by the detail of the datasets in Sect. 3. Section 4 is the methodology of Thai handwritten recognition. The evaluation result is reported in Sect. 5. Finally, a conclusion is drawn in Sect. 6.

2 Related Works

2.1 Thai Language Property

Thai alphabet set [9] consists of 44 consonants, 18 vowels, four voice tones, five special symbols, and ten numerals, as shown in Table 1.

Thai writing starts from left to right and from top to bottom. There is no space between words. The sentences can be either separated by spaces or no separate. There are four writing levels: the tone, upper vowel, body, and lower vowel levels, as shown in Fig. 1.

Table 1. Thai alphabet set.

Type	Member
Consonants	ก ข ฃ ค ฅ ฆ ง จ ฉ ช ซ ฌ ญ ฎ ฏ ฐ ฑ ฒ ณ ด ต ถ ท ธ น บ ป ผ ฝ พ ฟ ภ ม ย ร ล ว ศ ษ ส ห ฬ อ ฮ
Vowels	ะ า อิ อี อึ อื อุ อู เอ แอ ใอ โอ ไอ ๅ ฤ ฦ
Tones	อ่ อ้ อ๊ อ๋
Special symbols	อ็ อ์ ๆ ฯ
Numerals	๐ ๑ ๒ ๓ ๔ ๕ ๖ ๗ ๘ ๙

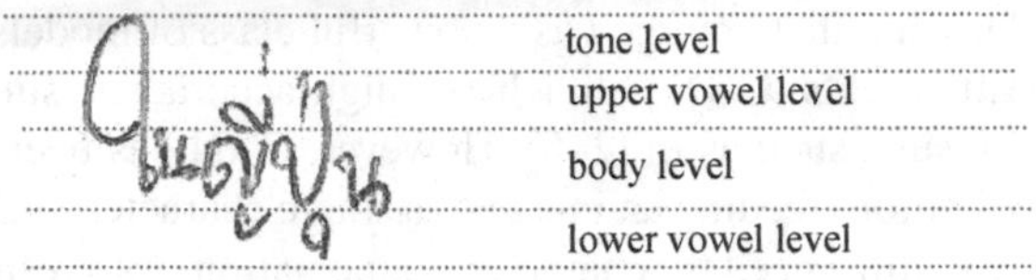

tone level
upper vowel level
body level
lower vowel level

Fig. 1. Four levels of Thai writing.

2.2 Thai Handwritten Recognition

Character morphology is one of the pioneer methods that have been applied to recognize Thai characters [10]. However, morphology features such as shapes with perfect segmentation are not practical and poor outcomes in the classification step. Word formation is a refinement step integrating contextual information of word construction and patterns to improve the recognition results. A stroke-based technique is also proposed to recognize Thai handwritten characters [11]. Character features are generated using the vertical stroke detection method, which determines the shapes of each character. The classification is then performed using Artificial Neural Network. The work reports promising results on the pre-segmented characters in the images. Vertical stroke detection, horizontal stroke, zigzag stroke, tail stokes, and loop detection are applied to describe the characters' characteristics. However, in the classification step, a genetic algorithm is applied. Although some researchers have reported promising results in Thai character recognition, most of the work assumes pre-segmented character images.

(manual and semi-automated), which provides a good segmentation. In contrast to this work, all characters in images will be learned and recognized without character segmentation.

3   The Datasets

In this work, the standard data comes from the Benchmark for Enhancing the Standard of Thai Language Processing (BEST) [8]. In 2019, the competition of handwritten recognition was established, which is called "BEST2019". The dataset was used in the training stage that collected handwritten from different people using collection forms. The dataset comprises three subsets of data, i.e.

1. 68PersonBmp: the majority of images in this set are single Arabic numbers and blocks of numbers. The images in the collection contain the handwriting of Arabic numerals from different people. The example of images in the set is demonstrated in Fig. 2(a),
2. WD200–200: the images in this set are the handwriting of words from multiple people. Besides, the collection contains some short sentences. An example of the dataset is shown in Fig. 2(b), and
3. ST200–200: this set comprises the handwriting of long sentences (multiline). An example is depicted in Fig. 2(c).

In this study, the authors collected more handwriting from 50 people filled in the form, and these sentences were used in the first round of the BEST2019 competition (Fig. 2 (d)). Moreover, the words and sentences from Benchmark for Enhancing the Standard of Thai language processing (BEST I corpus) [12] that most often occur in the corpus are collected by generating automatic handwriting and writing by humans, as shown in (Fig. 2(e) and (f)).

Although BEST2019 has provided formatted forms for handwriting recognition practice, it needs to extract as a text line or word from them. Text line extraction is proceeded by using text localization and projection profile and detection line that explains in Sect. 4.

After text line separation, the ground truth was prepared by typed text appearing in the forms. The summary of the dataset is shown in Table 2.

In this study, the datasets on A and B were used for the model evaluation. The dataset was separated into two categories: a training set of 80% and a test set of 20%.

Furthermore, the model was tested with dataset C with seen and unseen texts.

Table 2. The summary of the datasets.

Dataset	The number of text images
A. Handwriting by a human for training model	**15,878**
A.1 BEST2019 (68PersonBMP, WD200–200, ST200–200)	3,413
A.2 Additional handwritten text line based on BEST2019 (50 people)	6,130
A.3 Additional handwritten text block based on BEST2019 (50 people)	6,335
B. Artificial handwriting for training model	**151,390**
B.1 Word from BEST I corpus (Selected by high frequency)	56,389
B.2 Text line from BEST I corpus	95,001
Total A and B	**167,268**
C. Words and text lines of final round competition of BEST2019 (Seen text and unseen text)	**3,550**

(a) Example of 68PersonsBmp set

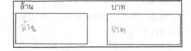

(b) Example of WD200-2 set

(c) Example of ST200-2 set

เป็นมนุษย์สุดประเสริฐเลิศคุณค่า กว่าบรรดาฝูงสัตว์เดรัจฉาน

จงฝ่าฟันพัฒนาวิชาการ อย่าล้างผลาญฆ่าฟันเข่นฆ่าบีฑาใคร

(d) Example of the competitor form

(e) Example of the words

(f) Example of generic handwriting

Fig. 2. Sample images of datasets for the training process.

4 Methodology of Thai Handwritten Recognition

This section provides the details of the proposed methods for recognizing Thai hand-writing. Instead of processing the recognition on a single character, this work considers the sequences of character strings and uses them for final prediction. There are two main steps in this works, (i) text localization and (ii) model generation.

4.1 Text Localization

In the preprocessing, an image is converted to a grayscale image. Then, noise removal is performed using a Gaussian blur method before text localization is carried out. Considering WD200–2 and ST200–2, an image in the dataset may contain multiple lines of handwritten. However, in this work's training strategy, a single text line of handwriting will be fed to the model generation step. Therefore, text localization can be applied to select text lines for training purposes.

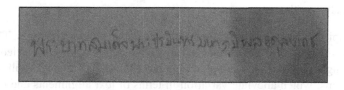

(a) Example of original image 1

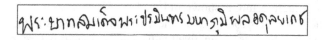

(b) Output image 1 of text localization

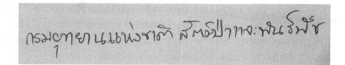

(c) Example of original image 2

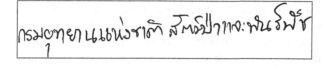

(d) Output image 2 of text localization

Fig. 3. Example of text localization.

This step tries to eradicate some of the image background areas and crop precisely the image's text regions, as shown in Fig. 3. The text region localization step is described below.

1. Input the RGB image and split it into R, G, and B planes.
2. Dilate the image in each plane with a 7×7 square structure element.
3. Blur image using Median Filtering in each plane with 21×21 kernel size.
4. Find the difference between the input image and blur image in each plane.
5. Merge the R, G, and B results from step 4.
6. Binarize the image from step 5.
7. Dilate the binary image from 6 with a square structure element.
8. Find horizontal histogram (vertical projection profile) to detect the top and bottom line by a minimum of the histogram, and find vertical histogram (horizontal projection profile to detect left and right text line by a minimum of the histogram.
9. Bounding box text line (single line)

4.2 Model Generation

This work applies a deep learning technique to recognize input text images. The training images are resized (320×128 pixels) before image augmentation is carried out. Only image zooming is applied in the augmentation process as the dataset was collected by the collection forms, which alleviate variation in terms of text alignments and orientation, but not scales. This work implements the integration of CNN and RNN networks to train the text images for predicting a sequence of characters in the unobserved image. The proposed network architecture is shown in Fig. 4.

In CNN, the model has four layers. The convolutional layers in the CNN play an essential role in extracting discriminative features in the images before the prediction is performed. Therefore, as opposed to the conventional architecture, the dense layer in the CNN is dropped. The extracted image features are then connected and feed to the RNN network. This network is two layers of Bidirectional Gate Recurrent Unit (BiGRU). The loss is calculated from a Connectionist Temporal Classification (CTC) 14, and the optimization is performed using Stochastic Gradient Descents (SGD) and RMSprop. The CTC processing explains in the following sub-section.

4.3 Connectionist Temporal Classification (CTC)

CTC is a loss function that allows the RNN to generate output. The CTC loss function is fed by an output from RNN and the ground truth labels. The "blank" symbol is introduced in CTC without translating into any characters. It is used to separate the individual characters so the blank symbol can separate that duplicate characters. For instance, when the words "พร"and "พรร"are decoded, "-" is used for blank symbol so "พร"can be decoded as "---พพพพรรรร", "-พ-ร-", or "พร"while "พรร"an be decoded as "---พพพพร-ร", "-พ-ร-ร-", or "พร-ร"but not "พรร".

Input image (320 x 128)
Convolution size 32 (kernel 3x3, activation reLU)   Max Pooling(2,2), stride 2, dropout 0.2   Output layer (160 x 64 x 32)
Convolution size 32 (kernel 3x3, activation reLU)   Max Pooling(2,2), stride 2, dropout 0.2   Output layer (80 x 32 x 32)
Convolution size 32 (kernel 3x3, activation reLU)   Max Pooling(1,1), stride 2, dropout 0.2   Output layer (80 x 32 x 32)
Convolution size 32 (kernel 3x3, activation reLU)   Max Pooling(1,1), stride 2, dropout 0.2   Output layer (80 x 32 x 32)
Reshape (80 x 1024)
Input layer (80x64)   Bidirectional GRU   (hidden size 256, time steps 64,dropout 0.2 and weigh decay 0.001)   Output layer (80 x 256)
Bidirectional GRU   (hidden size 256, time steps 64,dropout 0.2 and weigh decay 0.001)   Output layer (80 x 512)
SoftMax   Output layer (80 x 94)
CTC
Output

Fig. 4. Integration of CNN and RNN network for Thai handwritten recognition model.

4.4 Character Error Rate (CER)

The CER is calculated by counting the minimum number of edit operations required to transfer the recognized text into the ground truth labels. This research uses the Levenshtein edit-distance [16] to compute the CER, as shown in Eq. (1).

$$CER = \frac{\#insertions + \#deletions + \#substitutions}{length(Ground\ truth\ label)} \tag{1}$$

5 Experiment and Results

The previous sections explain the dataset and the network architecture for recognizing a sequence of Thai characters in the images. There are 93 alphabets in this study that were encoded from the dataset. The experiment is conducted to validate and determine the performance of the proposed technique. In the training process, there are the model parameters that are required to initiate. Optimization of the first model is SGD and the second model is RMSprop. The number of epochs is 50. The training process is carried out using Keras [17] and run on a PC with Core I7–3.70 GHz-CPU, 16GB-RAM, GTX1080Ti-GPU, and WINDOWS10 64bit-OS. There are 167,268 text line images for the training process from datasets A and B in the performance evaluation. It is separated into 80% of training and 20% test set.

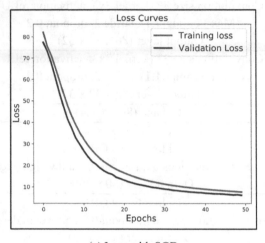

(a) Loss with SGD

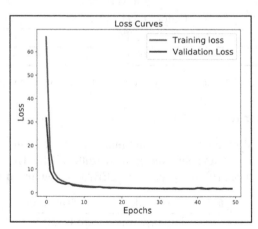

(b) Loss with RMSprop

Fig. 5. Training outcome: training and validation loss.

The loss graphs' training error, as shown in Fig. 5, indicate that the SGD can slightly decrease error loss while RMSprop can rapidly decrease error loss. The evaluation results indicate the CER with the test set (20%) of SGD and RMSprop at 6.88% and 1.58%,

Table 3. Examples of prediction results of dataset C

Description	Image/ Ground truth/ Prediction	CER (%)
Image 1 (set A)	เป็นมนุษย์สุดประเสริฐเลิศคุณค่า กว่าบรรดาฝูงสัตว์เดรัจฉาน	
Ground truth	เป็นมนุษย์สุดประสริฐเลิศคุณค่า กว่าบรรดาฝูงสัตว์เดรัจฉาน	
Result-SGD	เห็พมทุมจปราเปรินาจทุกรา เมหออามูรนรแ๕นง	73.68
Result-RMSprop	เป็นมุษย์สัดประเสริสเดคุณค่า กว่าบรรดาฝูงสิาว์เดกรัอฉาน	17.54
Image 2 (set B)	ผู้ชายที่ดูดีกว่าพี่อาร์มมากๆ	
Ground truth	ผู้ชายที่ดูดีกว่าพี่อาร์มมากๆ	
Result-SGD	ผู้ชายที่ดูดีกว่าพี่อาร์มมากๆ	0.00
Result-RMSprop	ผู้ชายที่ดูดีกว่าพี่อาร์มมากๆ	0.00
Image 3 (set C-seen)	บุรีรัมย์	
Ground truth	บุรีรัมย์	
Result-SGD	หุรีรมม์	33.33
Result-RMSprop	บุรีรัมย์	0.00
Image 4 (set C-seen)	กรุงเทพฯ	
Ground truth	กรุงเทพฯ	
Result-SGD	ทรุมทพบฯ	62.50
Result-RMSprop	กรุงมเทพฯ	12.50
Image 5 (set C-seen)	ปฏิบัติประพฤติกฎกำหนดใจ พูดจาให้จ๊ะๆ จ๋า น่าฟังเอยฯ	
Ground truth	ปฏิบัติประพฤติกฎกำหนดใจ พูดจาให้จ๊ะๆ จ๋า น่าฟังเอยฯ	
Result-SGD	หิรินระทคิกๆกำบเดใจ พูดาในจีย จ๋า น่าเป็อยก	50.98
Result-RMSprop	ปฏิบัติประพฤติกฎกำหนดใจ พูดจาให้จ๊ะๆ จ๋า น่าฟังเอยฯ	1.96
Image 6 (set C-unseen)	ทุกสิ่งที่เกิดขึ้นมักมีเหตุผลเสมอ	
Ground truth	ทุกสิ่งที่เกิดขึ้นมักมีเหตุผลเสมอ	
Result-SGD	ทุกสิ่งที่เทิดชื่นม่กม่เงพตุมลงเสมอ	33.33
Result-RMSprop	ทุกสิ่งที่คิดขึ้นม่กมีเหตุผลเสมอ	15.15
Image 7 (set C-unseen)	จุลชีววิทยาเฟิร์น	
Ground truth	จุลชีววิทยาเฟิร์น	
Result-SGD	จุตชัวิทยาแมิด่น	35.29
Result-RMSprop	จุลชื่อ วิทยาเมิ ชัน	35.29
Image 8 (set C-unseen)	สมเด็จพระเจ้าบรมวงศ์เธอกรมพระยาดำรงราชานุภาพ	
Ground truth	สมเด็จพระเจ้าบรมวงศ์เธอกรมพระยาดำรงราชานุภาพ	
Result-SGD	สตสดมมเ๋ามมอจ๋ตอกรมหรษาดำมงหฯฺจพนย	70.45
Result-RMSprop	สมดังพมเจ๋ามเมองห์หอกรมกรยาดำราราชุงกะป	54.55

respectively. When this model was applied with dataset C (seen and unseen dataset of the final round of BEST2019 competition), the CER of SGD and RMSprop is 58.45% and 24.53%, respectively. Table 3 demonstrates the results obtained from the prediction of test set and dataset C. The example results show the performance of seen data shows outperform compared to unseen data, and RMSprop gives higher CER than SGD. If the images come from mobile or RGB, image 7 and 8 affect the CER result. Image 4 shows a higher result than image 3 that may cause by a few data of this word image in the training set.

6 Conclusion

Recognition of handwritten is a difficult task. This work presents an approach for Thai handwritten recognition. The proposed method applies deep learning to perform a prediction on a single text line image. Noise in the image is removed, and the image is processed to resize before feeding to the network. Also, image augmentation is carried out to expand the scale and increase the variation of the training set. The CNN extracts the abstract features before they are feed to the RNN. The optimization is performed with an integrated CTC module (to arrange the final results). Image data were collected from a standard dataset (BEST2019) and additional collection. The experiments were conducted, and the results demonstrate that the proposed method provides promising results achieving CER 1.58%. This model was also applied with the seen and unseen dataset from the final round of BEST2019's competition. The result showed CER at 24.53%.

The future work is designated to improve the result's performance by applying beam search to integrate the language model and the dictionary-based approach. Fine-tuning the model CNN and RNN will be applied. Moreover, the equality of each word or sentence image data set should be considered.

References

1. NECTEC.: OCR ArnThai service, http://arnthai.nectec.or.th/. Accessed 28 Feb 2015
2. LeCun, Y., Kavukcuoglu, K., Farabet, C.: Convolutional networks and applications in vision. In: Proceedings of 2010 IEEE International Symposium on Circuits and Systems (ISCAS), pp. 253–256 (2010)
3. Bouchain, D.: Character recognition using convolutional neural networks. In: Institute for Neural Information Processing (2007)
4. Simard, P. Y., Steinkraus, D., Platt, J.C.: Best practices for convolutional neural networks applied to visual document analysis. In: Proceedings of the 7th International Conference on Document Analysis and Recognition, pp. 958–963. (2003)
5. Lauer, F., Suen, C.Y., Bloch, G.: A trainable feature extractor for handwritten digit recognition. Pattern Recogn. **40**(6), 1816–1824 (2007)

6. Breuel, T., Frinken V., Liwicki, M.: High-performance OCR for printed English and Fraktur using LSTM networks. In: Proceedings of the 12th International Conference on Document Analysis and Recognition (ICDAR), pp. 683–687.(2013)
7. Smith, R.: Tesseract-ocr/docs, https://github.com/tesseract-ocr/docs/tree/master/das_tutorial2016. Accessed 22 Dec 2017
8. Sinthupinyo, W.: Benchmark for Enhancing the Standard Thai Language Processing (BEST). https://thailang.nectec.or.th/best/best2019-handwrittenrecognition-objective/. Accessed 15 May 2019
9. Chamchong, R., Fung, C.C.: Text line extraction using adaptive partial projection for palm leaf manuscripts from Thailand. In: Proceeding of 2012 International Conference on Frontiers in Handwriting Recognition (ICFHR), pp. 588–593 (2012)
10. Karnchanapusakij, C., Suwannakat, P., Rakprasertsuk W., Dejdumrong, N.: Online handwriting thai character recognition. In: The 6th International Conference on Computer Graphics, Imaging and Visualization, Tianjin, pp. 323–328 (2009)
11. Methasate, I., Sae-tang, S.: The clustering technique for thai handwritten recognition. In: Proceeding of International Workshop on Frontiers in Handwriting Recognition, Japan, pp. 450–454. (2004)
12. NECTEC, NSTDA, https://aiforthai.in.th/index.php. Accessed 20 Dec 2019
13. Simonyan, K., Zisserman, A.: Very deep convolutional networks for large-scale image recognition. In: International Conference on Learning Representations, pp. 730–734 (2015)
14. Graves, A., Fernández, S., Gomez, F., Schmidhuber, J.: Connectionist temporal classification: labelling unsegmented sequence data with recurrent neural networks. In: Proceedings of the 23rd International Conference on Machine learning, pp. 369–376. ACM (2006)
15. Deng, H., Stathopoulos, G., Suen, C.Y.: Error correcting output coding for the convolutional neural network for optical character recognition. In: Proceeding of the 10th International Conference on Document Analysis and Recognition, pp. 581–585 (2009)
16. Bluche, T.: Deep Neural Networks for Large Vocabulary Handwritten Text Recognition (2015)
17. Chollet, F. Keras: the Python deep learning API, https://keras.io/. Accessed 23 Feb 2020

Comparing of Multi-class Text Classification Methods for Automatic Ratings of Consumer Reviews

Jantima Polpinij[1(✉)] and Bancha Luaphol[2]

[1] Intellect Laboratory, Department of Computer Science, Faculty of Informatics, Mahasarakham University, Talat, Thailand
jantima.p@msu.ac.th
[2] Department of Digital Technology, Faculty of Administrative Science, Kalasin University, Kalasin, Thailand
bancha.lu@ksu.ac.th

Abstract. Consumer reviews show inconsistent ratings when compared to their contents as a result of sarcastic feedback. Consequently, they cannot provide valuable feedback to improve products and services of the firms. One possible solution is to utilize consumer review contents to identify the true ratings. In this work, different multi-class classification methods were applied to assign automatic ratings for consumer reviews based on a 5-star rating scale, where the original review ratings were inconsistent with the content. Two term weighting schemes (i.e. *tf-idf* and *tf-igm*) and five supervised machine learning algorithms (i.e. *k*-NN, MNB, RF, XGBoost and SVM) were compared. The dataset was downloaded from the Amazon website, and language experts helped to correct the real rating for each consumer review. After verifying the effectiveness of the proposed methods, the multi-class classifier model developed by SVM along with *tf-igm* returned the best results for automatic ratings of consumer reviews, with average improved scores of accuracies and F1 over the other methods at 11.7% and 10.5%, respectively.

Keywords: Consumer reviews · Inconsistent ratings · Multi-class classification · Automatic ratings

1 Introduction

The recent growth of Internet usage among consumers has generated huge content of online social media sources such as review websites, blogs and product fan pages. Online customer reviews can now be posted as text by customers to express their emotions, sentiments and expressed their experiences for purchased products and services. These emotions or sentiments can be positive, negative or neutral. Today, customer reviews are playing a major role in consumer purchase decision-making for products and services [3]. Feedback is useful for companies to recognize their strengths and weaknesses, and generate new ideas to improve products and customer service [10,14,19].

© Springer Nature Switzerland AG 2021
P. Chomphuwiset et al. (Eds.): MIWAI 2021, LNAI 12832, pp. 164–175, 2021.
https://doi.org/10.1007/978-3-030-80253-0_15

However, customer reviews are often inconsistent in their ratings. Negative and sarcastic reviews are not beneficial and do not help or assist companies to do better. Therefore, rating prediction studies are important [7,8]. Many previous studies focused on consumer feedback as ratings or reviews separately and ignored data inconsistency [21]. To rectify this problem, Shi and Liang [21] assessed inconsistent reviews based on text sentiment analysis and support vector machines, while Geetha et al.. [9] identified consistency between customer ratings and actual customer feelings. Dai et al.. [5] addressed this problem by extracting prevalent topics from online reviews and automatically rating them on a 5-star scale.

Shi and Liang [21] mentioned that customers may be inclined to write their true feelings in reviews; thus, it is possible to utilize consumer review content to identify its real rating. This idea was followed up by Dai et al.. [5]; however, they only presented their ideas as a framework. Here, multi-class classification methods of giving automatic ratings for consumer reviews relating to movies were presented where original review rating might be inconsistent with its content. Two term weighting schemes (i.e. *tf-idf* and *tf-igm*) and five supervised machine learning algorithms (i.e. *k*-NN, MNB, RF, XGBoost and SVM) were compared. Meanwhile, a dataset used for this study was downloaded from the Amazon website. All movie reviews in the dataset were verified by language experts and gave them the correct rating based on a 5-star scale.

The paper is organized as follows. In Sect. 2, it is the related work. Section 3 presents the datasets used for this study. Meanwhile, the proposed method is presented in Sect. 4 and the experimental results and discussion are presented in Sect. 5. Finally, the conclusion is in Sect. 6.

2   Related Work

Due to various reasons, some customers give inconsistent ratings and reviews on commercial websites. Existing studies focused on consumer feedback as either ratings or reviews separately and ignored the inconsistencies between them. Consumers cannot always satisfactorily express complex opinions by ratings but they tend to display their true emotions in written reviews [10]. Copious research has addressed this problem with some chosen examples below.

Xiaojing Shi and Xun Liang [21] harvested 852,071 ratings and corresponding reviews from the Taobao website. They resolved the inconsistencies based on text sentiment analysis and support vector machines. Their method improved the existing online customer feedback system by intelligently resolving conflicting ratings or reviews from customers, and also provided decision supports for both consumers and shopkeepers.

Geetha et al.. studied the relationship between customer sentiments in online reviews and customer ratings for hotels [8]. They explored customer sentiments and expressed them in terms of polarity. Their results determined consistency between customer ratings and actual customer feelings across hotels belonging to premium and budget categories. However, they mentioned that their study was not exhaustive and other factors like customer review length and review title sentiment could also be analyzed for their impacts on customer ratings.

Dai *et al..* [5] presented a framework for extracting prevalent topics from online reviews and automatically rating them on a 5-star scale. Their framework consisted of five modules including linguistic pre-processing, topic modeling, text classification, sentiment analysis and rating. Topic modeling was used to extract prevalent topics that were then used to classify individual sentences against the relevant topics. A word embedding method was used to measure the sentiment of each sentence. Two types of information associated with each sentence are its topic and its sentiment. They combined these to aggregate the sentiment associated with each topic. The overall topic sentiment was then projected onto the 5-star rating scale. They used the dataset of Airbnb online reviews to demonstrate proof of concept. The proposed framework was simple and fully unsupervised. It was also domain-independent and, therefore, applicable to all other domains of products and services.

Later, Cuizon *et al.* [4] applied text mining to analyze customer reviews and automatically assign collective restaurant star ratings based on five predetermined aspects as ambiance, cost, food, hygiene and service. Text reviews were tokenized into sentences, with noun-adjective pairs extracted from each sentence using the Stanford Core NLP Library, and associated to aspects based on the bag of associated words fed into the system. Sentiment weight of the adjectives was determined through the AFINN library. Overall restaurant star ratings were computed based on individual aspect ratings. They also generated a word cloud to provide a visual display of the most frequently occurring terms in the reviews. Increased feedback improved the reflective sentiment score for restaurant performance.

3   Dataset

10,000 movie reviews for several films based on the 5-star rating scale was gathered from the Amazon website during February 2020, formatted as XML files with different lengths. Each rating group consists of 2,000 reviews (Fig. 1).

Fig. 1. An example of movie review with inconsistent rating

Firstly, we randomly selected 1,000 movie reviews as a test set. Each rating group in the test set consists of 200 reviews. This test set is used to evaluate the obtained multi-class classifier models. The results of evaluation are considered again by the experts to verify the correctness. After obtaining the test set, the rest of movie reviews is used as a training set.

To obtain the most appropriate multi-class text classifiers for automatically rating of movie reviews, a 10-fold cross validation was also applied, where this technique is used to evaluate predictive models by partitioning the original sample into a training set to train the model, and a validation set to evaluate it. It is noted that language experts verify the movie reviews in the training set and assigned them the correct rating based on the 5-star rating scale.

4   The Method of Multi-class Classifiers Modelling

This section describes for the method of multi-class classifiers modelling. It consists of four main processing steps i.e. pre-processing of movie reviews, features selection and movie review representation, term weighting, and multi-class classifiers modelling. Each processing step can be described as follows (Fig. 2).

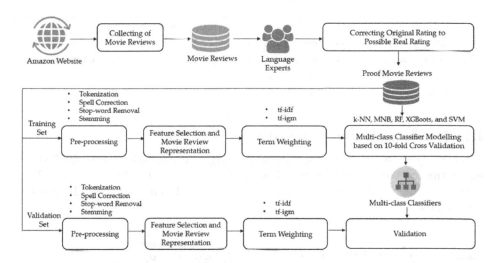

Fig. 2. The method of multi-class classifiers modelling

4.1   Pre-processing of Movie Reviews

Tokenization: The process of tokenization involves dividing the remaining text into tokens. In this study, the tokens are "words". Therefore, this process can be called word segmentation.

Spell Correction: Movie reviews are written by customers and often contain spelling mistakes or typo errors. Spelling mistakes were corrected in the pre-processing step.

Stop-Word Removal: Movie reviews usually include constructive terms (e.g. prepositions) and special symbols (e.g. punctuation). These terms and symbols are called "stop-words" that are considered meaningless and do not contribute to sentiment classification of movie review. Therefore, these terms and symbols were filtered out.

Stemming: Stemming is the process of removing a part of a word, or reducing a word to its stem or root. This might not necessarily mean reducing a word to its dictionary form. Advantages include shortening the vocabulary space, thus drastically improving the size of the index (or feature space). Stemming also helps to reduce language ambiguity during processing time. This work applied the snowball stemmer to map variant word forms to their base form or their word stem [18] (Table 1).

Table 1. An example of movie review pre-processing

Original text	"He is very good in this twist on the classsic story"
Tokenization	'He', 'is', 'very', 'good', 'in', 'this', 'twist', 'on', 'the', 'classsic', 'story'
Spell correction	'He', 'is', 'very', 'good', 'in', 'this', 'twist', 'on', 'the', 'classic', 'story'
Stop-word removal	'good', 'twist', 'classic', 'story'
Stemming	'good', 'twist', 'classic', 'stori'

4.2   Feature Selection and Text Representation

After pre-processing, the information gain (IG) [17] technique was applied to select the most relevant features of each class based on the filter method. The threshold used for filtering irrelevant features was 0.1. The formula of IG can be represented as:

$$ig(t) = -\sum_{i=1}^{m} p(c_i) \log p(c_i) + p(t) \sum_{i=1}^{m} p(c_j|t) \log(c_i|t) + p(\bar{t}) \sum_{i=1}^{m} p(c_j|\bar{t}) log(c_i|\bar{t})$$

(1)

where c_i represents the i-th class, $P(c_i)$ is the probability of the i-th class, $P(t)$ and $P(\bar{t})$ are the probabilities that term t appears or not in the documents, $P(c_i|t)$ is the conditional probability of the i-th class given that term t appears, and $P(c_i|\bar{t})$ is the conditional probability of the i-th class given that term t does not appear.

Finally, the obtained customer review features were represented as a vector space model (VSM) [1,20] describing the occurrence of words within a customer review.

4.3   Term Weighting

To obtain the most appropriate term weighting technique for sentiment classifier modeling, two different term weighting schemes were compared. The first was an unsupervised term weighting, represented as a *term frequency-inverse document frequency (tf-idf)* [6], while the second was a supervised term weighting represented as a *term frequency-inverse gravity moment (tf-igm)* [2].

Term Frequency - Inverse Document Frequency (tf-idf): This is one of the earliest and most common unsupervised term weighting schemes and is often used in text classification. In this scheme, *tf* can be presented as $tf(w_i, d_j)$, where it defines the number of times w_i occurs in d_j. Meanwhile, $idf(w_i)$ shows a frequently used keyword within a document collection. The equation of $idf(w_i)$ is:

$$idf(w_i) = \log\left(1 + \frac{N}{df(w_i)}\right) \qquad (2)$$

where N is the total number of documents in the whole collection, and $df(w_i)$ is the number of documents in the collection containing w_i. Then, $idf(w_i)$ is used to evaluate how important a word is to the collection by giving the highest score to the rarest term.

Term Frequency - Inverse Gravity Moment (tf-igm): This term weighting scheme measures the non-uniformity or concentration of the inter-class distribution of terms that reflect the distinguishing power of term classes. The standard *igm* equation assigns ranks (r) based on the inter-class distribution concentration of a term that is analogous to the concept of *"gravity moment (igm)"* in physics. The igm can be presented as:

$$igm(w_i) = \left(\frac{tf_{w_{i1}}}{\sum_{r=1}^{M} tf_{w_{ir}} \times r}\right) \qquad (3)$$

where $(r = 1, 2, ..., M)$ is the number of documents containing the term w_i in the r-th class sorted in descending order. Thus, tf_{w_i} represents the frequency of w_i in the class in which it most often appears.

In reality, λ is added into the *igm* factor as an adjustable coefficient used to maintain the relative balance between global and local factors in the weight of a term. The λ coefficient has a default value of 7.0 but can be set as a value between 5.0 and 9.0. The equation of *tf-igm* can be represented as:

$$tf\text{-}igm(w_i) = tf(w_i, d_i) \times (1 + \lambda \times igm(w_i)) \qquad (4)$$

To reduce the effect of high tf_{w_i}, the original *tf-igm* takes the square root of tf_{w_i} to obtain a more reasonable term weighting.

4.4   Multi-class Classifiers Modelling

In this section, features vectors obtained by the previous processing step were used to model the multi-class classifiers that are used to assign real rating to movie review. To obtain the best sentiment rating classifier, we compared five machine learning methods consisting of k-NN, MNB, RF, XGBoost, and SVM.

k-NN is a lazy learning, non-parametric algorithm. It is one of the most used learning algorithms due to its simplicity [22]. k-NN ranks the nearest k neighbors of the labeled examples from the training set and uses the categories of the highest-ranked neighbors to derive a class assignment. The more near neighbors with the same category, the higher the confidence in that prediction. In this study, we take the case of $k = 3$.

Multinomial Naïve Bayes (MNB) is one of the simplest probabilistic classifier models that is computationally very efficient and easy to implement [15]. The classifier estimates a class-conditional document distribution $P(d|c)$ from the training documents and applies Bayes' rule to estimate $P(c|d)$ for test documents, where the documents are modeled using their terms. To efficiently compute the conditional probabilities, MNB assumes all features to be independent. For small sample sizes, MNB can outperform the most powerful alternatives. MNB is highly scalable and can easily handle large datasets.

Random Forest (RF) is an ensemble learning method composed of different decision trees [12]. It uses bagging and feature randomness when building each individual tree to create an uncorrelated forest of trees whose prediction by committee is more accurate than that of any individual tree. One of the biggest advantages of random forest is its versatility. RF can be used for both regression and classification tasks. RF can also reduce overfitting of data to improve accuracy. In this study, we generated 100 decision trees for our forest.

EXtreme Gradient Boosting (XGBoost) is a decision tree based ensemble method, where ensemble learning offers a systematic solution to combine the predictive power of multiple learners [11]. XGBoost applies a gradient boosting framework to enhance performance. The gradient boosting framework is designed to be highly efficient, flexible and portable; it provides parallel tree boosting to solve many problems in a fast and accurate way. This algorithm can help to prevent model over-fitting. It has fast processing to handle missing values and improves tree pruning effectiveness.

Support Vector Machine (SVM) is a linear model for classification and regression problems [13]. This algorithm creates a hyperplane and decision boundary to separate data into classes. SVM finds the points closest to the hyperplane that are called support vectors, and computes the distance between a line and the support vectors, called the margin. The goal is to maximize the margin. The hyperplane for which the margin is maximum is called the optimal hyperplane. If the maximum margin is obtained, the decision boundary used to separate classes is as wide as possible. Consequently, this can more clearly separate classes. In this study, the RBF is used as kernel function for the SVM algorithm, where this kernel function have been confirmed by many studies that it can return an appropriate results [13].

5   Experimental Results

The first experiment evaluated the performance of classification methods to select the most appropriate. Well-known metrics namely accuracy, recall, precision, F1 and AUC were used. The area under the curve (AUC) was used to evaluate the performance of sentiment classification [16]. The AUC distinguishes the quality of a prediction by measuring the two-dimensional area underneath the entire receiver operating characteristic curve (ROC) [16]. We also used the 10-fold cross validation procedure to evaluate the performance of multi-class classification methods. The 10-fold cross validation procedure was applied as a possible solution to prevent overfitting. Results of the first experiment are presented in Table 2 and the overall picture of the results in Table 2 can be also shown as a graphical representation (See in Fig. 3).

Table 2. Evaluation of automatic ratings to consumer reviews based on 10-fold cross validation

Algorithms	Term weighting scheme	Accuracy	Recall	Precision	F1	AUC
k-NN	tf-idf	0.62	0.62	0.62	0.62	0.62
	tf-igm	0.64	0.64	0.64	0.64	0.64
MNB	tf-idf	0.74	0.73	0.75	0.74	0.73
	tf-igm	0.76	0.75	0.77	0.76	0.75
RF	tf-idf	0.74	0.73	0.74	0.73	0.73
	tf-igm	0.74	0.73	0.74	0.73	0.73
XGBoost	tf-idf	0.74	0.73	0.74	0.73	0.73
	tf-igm	0.74	0.73	0.74	0.73	0.73
SVM with RBF	tf-idf	0.76	0.76	0.76	0.76	0.76
	tf-igm	0.78	0.78	0.78	0.78	0.78

Table 2 presents the results of automatic ratings to consumer reviews using different text classification methods. The performances of our classifier models were not very high because our training set had some classes that contained many similar words with the same class predicting power. Thus, it was difficult for the classifier models developed by this dataset to predict the class precisely.

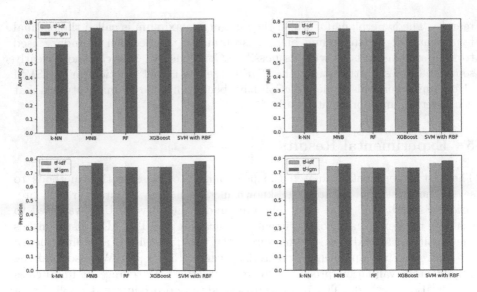

Fig. 3. The overall picture of the results in a graphical representation

The highest accuracy, recall, precision, F1 and AUC scores were achieved by the SVM with RBF kernel function, performed using the *tf-igm* term weighting scheme (Table 2), while *k*-NN gave the lowest performance.

Firstly, considering the term weighting schemes used in this study (i.e. *tf-idf* and *tf-igm*), *tf-idf* returned the lowest scores when performing with any of the algorithms. The *tf-idf* is an unsupervised term weight that cannot effectively overcome imbalanced sentiment classification because it does not take class information into account. The *tf-idf* weighting scheme is unable to entirely specify the class discriminative power of each word. By contrast, *tf-igm* can precisely calculate the distinguishing class of a term, especially for multi-class problems. Results in Table 2 show that choosing an appropriate term weighting scheme was important because the term weighting scheme plays a crucial role in extracting the most classical features as an input to the classifier. This improved the performance of automatic ratings for consumer reviews based on the multi-class classification method. However, term weighting had no effect on RF and XGBoost because they are usually robust to outliers and can handle them automatically. Therefore, they might not require scaling features with any special term weighting scheme.

Secondly, considering the classification algorithms used in this study (i.e. *k*-NN, MNB, RF, XGBoost and SVM), the highest evaluation scores were achieved by the SVM algorithm, performed using both *tf-idf* and *tf-igm* term weighting schemes. This algorithm works relatively well when there is a clear margin of separation between classes and is more effective in high dimensional spaces. MNB, RF and XGBoost gave lower performances of automatic ratings to consumer reviews. The RF and XGBoost algorithms required more time than the other

Table 3. Evaluation of automatic ratings to consumer reviews with test set

Algorithms	Term weighting scheme	Accuracy	Recall	Precision	F1
k-NN	tf-igm	0.60	0.60	0.60	0.60
MNB	tf-igm	0.72	0.71	0.73	0.72
RF	tf-igm	0.72	0.71	0.72	0.71
XGBoost	tf-igm	0.72	0.71	0.72	0.71
SVM with RBF	tf-igm	0.74	0.74	0.74	0.74

algorithms for training and validating classifier models because they are based on the bagging algorithm that uses the Ensemble Learning technique. However, if the number of trees in RF and XGBoost are inappropriate, it is possible that the classifier models might be ineffective for class prediction. Consequently, the results of RF are lower than the results of SVM and MNB. For MNB, its results are also lower than the SVM algorithm. This is because the predictors used for developing classifier models might not be independent, and this decreased its performance. Lastly, the k-NN algorithm returned the poorest for this study. This is because it does not work well with high dimensional data and has difficulty calculating the distance in each dimension. The k-NN algorithm is also quite sensitive to noise in the dataset.

We chose the best model of each algorithm by considering the AUC scores, with final experimental results of the entire test set presented in Table 3.

Results in Table 3 were consistent with results in Table 2. Highest evaluation scores were still achieved by the SVM with RBF kernel function, performed with the *tf-igm* term weighting scheme for the same reason as mentioned above.

6 Conclusion

Consumer reviews are often inconsistent in their ratings. They might contain sarcastic comments that are not beneficial and do not help or assist companies to do better. As a result, automatic rating predictions are required to utilize consumer review contents and identify their true ratings. This study presented automatic ratings for consumer reviews using the multi-class text classification method. We also compared different classification methods to obtain the most appropriate. Two term weighting schemes (i.e. *tf-idf* and *tf-igm*) and five supervised machine learning algorithms (i.e. k-NN, MNB, RF, XGBoost and SVM) were compared. A total of 10,000 movie reviews were downloaded from the Amazon website with 2,000 reviews per class. We randomly selected 200 reviews per class and used them as the test set. Meanwhile, the rest of movie reviews is used as the training set that is used for modelling multi-class classifiers based on 10-fold cross validation. Language experts corrected the movie reviews in the training set with the real ratings based on a 5-star scale. After obtaining the most appropriate model of each algorithm, it is evaluated by the test set. Then, the results are verified the correctness by the language experts.

After verifying the effectiveness of the proposed methods, the multi-class classifier model developed by SVM along with *tf-igm* returned the best results for automatic ratings of consumer reviews. After testing with test set, it can be found that the SVM classifier improved the accuracy and F1 scores of MNB classifier at 2.78%, while it improved the accuracy and F1 scores of XGBoost classifiers were 2.78% and 4.23%, respectively. Meanwhile, the multi-class classifier model developed by k-NN returned the poorest results.

References

1. Caropreso, M.F., Matwin, S.: Beyond the bag of words: a text representation for sentence selection. In: Lamontagne, L., Marchand, M. (eds.) AI 2006. LNCS (LNAI), vol. 4013, pp. 324–335. Springer, Heidelberg (2006). https://doi.org/10.1007/11766247_28
2. Chen, K., Zhang, Z., Long, J., Zhang, H.: Turning from tf-idf to tf-igm for term weighting in text classification. Expert Syst. Appl. **66**, 245–260 (2016)
3. Constantinides, E., Holleschovsky, N.I.: Impact of online product reviews on purchasing decisions. In: International Conference on Web Information Systems and Technologies, vol. 2, pp. 271–278. SCITEPRESS (2016)
4. Cuizon, J.C., Lopez, J., Jones, D.R.: Text mining customer reviews for aspect-based restaurant rating. Int. J. Comput. Sci. Inf. Technol. (IJCSIT) **10** (2018)
5. Dai, X., Spasic, I., Andrès, F.: A framework for automated rating of online reviews against the underlying topics. In: Proceedings of the SouthEast Conference, pp. 164–167 (2017)
6. Domeniconi, G., Moro, G., Pasolini, R., Sartori, C.: A comparison of term weighting schemes for text classification and sentiment analysis with a supervised variant of tf.idf. In: Helfert, M., Holzinger, A., Belo, O., Francalanci, C. (eds.) DATA 2015. CCIS, vol. 584, pp. 39–58. Springer, Cham (2016). https://doi.org/10.1007/978-3-319-30162-4_4
7. Ganu, G., Elhadad, N., Marian, A.: Beyond the stars: improving rating predictions using review text content. In: WebDB, vol. 9, pp. 1–6. Citeseer (2009)
8. Ganu, G., Kakodkar, Y., Marian, A.: Improving the quality of predictions using textual information in online user reviews. Inf. Syst. **38**(1), 1–15 (2013)
9. Geetha, M., Singha, P., Sinha, S.: Relationship between customer sentiment and online customer ratings for hotels-an empirical analysis. Tour. Manage. **61**, 43–54 (2017)
10. Ghose, A., Ipeirotis, P.G.: Estimating the helpfulness and economic impact of product reviews: mining text and reviewer characteristics. IEEE Trans. Knowl. Data Eng. **23**(10), 1498–1512 (2010)
11. Hanif, I.: Implementing extreme gradient boosting (xgboost) classifier to improve customer churn prediction. In: ICSA 2019: Proceedings of the 1st International Conference on Statistics and Analytics, ICSA 2019, 2–3 August 2019, Bogor, Indonesia, p. 434. European Alliance for Innovation (2019)
12. Islam, M.Z., Liu, J., Li, J., Liu, L., Kang, W.: A semantics aware random forest for text classification. In: Proceedings of the 28th ACM International Conference on Information and Knowledge Management, pp. 1061–1070 (2019)
13. Joachims, T.: Text categorization with support vector machines: learning with many relevant features. In: Nédellec, C., Rouveirol, C. (eds.) ECML 1998. LNCS, vol. 1398, pp. 137–142. Springer, Heidelberg (1998). https://doi.org/10.1007/BFb0026683

14. Karakaya, F., Barnes, N.G.: Impact of online reviews of customer care experience on brand or company selection. J. Consum. Mark. (2010)
15. Kibriya, A.M., Frank, E., Pfahringer, B., Holmes, G.: Multinomial Naive Bayes for text categorization revisited. In: Webb, G.I., Yu, X. (eds.) AI 2004. LNCS (LNAI), vol. 3339, pp. 488–499. Springer, Heidelberg (2004). https://doi.org/10.1007/978-3-540-30549-1_43
16. Liu, Y., Zhou, Y., Wen, S., Tang, C.: A strategy on selecting performance metrics for classifier evaluation. Int. J. Mob. Comput. Multimedia Commun. (IJMCMC) 6(4), 20–35 (2014)
17. Oreški, D., Novosel, T.: Comparison of feature selection techniques in knowledge discovery process. TEM J. 3(4), 285 (2014)
18. Porter, M.F.: Snowball: a language for stemming algorithms (2001)
19. Qiao, Z., Wang, G.A., Zhou, M., Fan, W.: The impact of customer reviews on product innovation: empirical evidence in mobile apps. In: Deokar, A.V., Gupta, A., Iyer, L.S., Jones, M.C. (eds.) Analytics and Data Science. AIS, pp. 95–110. Springer, Cham (2018). https://doi.org/10.1007/978-3-319-58097-5_8
20. Salton, G., Wong, A., Yang, C.S.: A vector space model for automatic indexing. Commun. ACM 18(11), 613–620 (1975)
21. Shi, X., Liang, X.: Resolving inconsistent ratings and reviews on commercial webs based on support vector machines. In: 2015 12th International Conference on Service Systems and Service Management (ICSSSM), pp. 1–6. IEEE (2015)
22. Trstenjak, B., Mikac, S., Donko, D.: KNN with TF-IDF based framework for text categorization. Procedia Eng. 69, 1356–1364 (2014)

Improving Safety and Efficiency
for Navigation in Multiagent Systems

Chattrakul Sombattheera[(⊠)]

Multiagent, Intelligent and Simulation Laboratory (MISL), Faculty of Informatics,
Mahasarakham University, 44150 Khamreang, Kantarawichai, Thailand
`chattrakul.s@msu.ac.th`

Abstract. Multiagent system concept can be deployed in many real
world applications. A good example is unmanned aerial vehicle (UAV).
While UAV deployment in real world has gained more popularity, many
areas of research are still needed for more efficient, more useful, safer and
more environment-friendly deployment of UAVs. The first and foremost
issue is the navigation problem. Here, we investigate how to navigate
UAVs through congested 3D sphere towards their individual destinations
efficiently and safely. Our approach is based on 3D reciprocal velocity
obstacle (3DRVO) and intelligent agent's Belief-Desire-Intention (BDI)
architecture. We represent UAVs by intelligent agents using 3DRVO at
low level navigation for safety, and BDI at high level planning for efficiency. The simulation results show that agents can travel safely to their
destinations. The results also show that the agents can travel efficiently,
i.e., while the number of agents increases, the elapsed time for simulation
and the simulation rounds increase in much lower rates.

1 Introduction

In recent years, we have witnessed that the deployment of UAV in real world has
been gaining more and more popularity. Google has been trying to use UAVs to
deliver medical supply to the patients outside hospitals. Amazon has been trying
to use UAVs in logistics system. Furthermore, UAVs are also widely deployed
in non commercial areas, including search and rescue mission, weather forecast,
surveillance, tracking systems, etc. As this trend grows steadily and rapidly, the
areas of research involving UAVs are still needed for more efficient, more useful,
safer and more environment-friendly deployment of UAVs. We are interested in
efficiency and safeness aspects of UAV navigation through congested 3D sphere
towards their individual destinations.

To serve with safety issue, we base our solution on 3DRVO, which is very
efficient approach for collision avoidance. However, 3DRVO only consider surrounding agents in close proximity. This ends up in low efficiency because it
create congested areas, which takes a lot of both time and computation power
for navigating agents through and out of the areas. To serve with efficiency issue,
we use BDI architecture to help agents plan to avoid congestion by collection

P. Chomphuwiset et al. (Eds.): MIWAI 2021, LNAI 12832, pp. 176–187, 2021.
https://doi.org/10.1007/978-3-030-80253-0_16

surrounding information and adjust their plans accordingly. In our work, we assume perfect information, i.e., each UAVs has the information about other UAVs' position, direction and speed. In reality, UAVs need sensing equipment to acquire information about the surrounding agents. Another approach could be to allow UAVs to communicate among themselves.

The remaining of the paper is structured as following. We discuss both 3DRVO and BDI. Since there are a lot of agents in our system, we need to handle the exchange of information among themselves wisely. We therefore discuss k-d tree in which we manage agents. We discuss the experiment then conclude the paper.

2   Fundamentals

This section discusses under-pinning algorithms comprising the basis of our work. At the very low level of automatic navigation of agents, we deploy 3DRVO, a collision avoidance algorithm. 3DRVO is based on the reciprocal velocity obstacle concept, which we also briefly discuss first. Then we discuss a higher level of navigation, namely, BDI architecture (Believe, Desire, Intension). This architecture allows for agents to repeatedly observe the ever changing environment and adapt plan accordingly. In the sections below, we present the aforementioned concepts.

2.1   Reciprocal Velocity Obstacles (RVO)

The reciprocal velocity obstacle [9] considers that other agents are moving obstacles. Each agent scans for other obstacles in front of it, predict their trajectories and try to avoid them. Therefore, an agent take half of the responsibility for avoiding a collision, while assuming other agents involved reciprocates by taking care of the other half. When choosing a new velocity for robot A, the average is taken of its current velocity v_A and a velocity outside the velocity obstacle $VO_{A|B}$ induced by the other robot B. The reciprocal velocity obstacle for agent A induced by B, written $RVO_{A|B}$, is defined as

$$RVO_{A|B} = \{v|2v - v \in VO_{A|B}\}.$$

As shown in Fig. 1, RVO guarantees that if both agents A and B select a velocity outside the reciprocal velocity obstacle induced by the other, and both robots choose to pass each other on the same side, then the trajectories of both robots will be free of collisions.

2.2   3D Reciprocal Velocity Obstacle (3DRVO)

RVO is then extended for 3D environment, namely 3DRVO [1]. Let A be a simple-airplane and let B be an obstacle moving in the space $\mathbb{R}^3$. Assume A and B to have collided if do not change direction. Let p_A and p_B denote the current

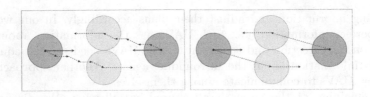

Fig. 1. Reciprocal Velocity Obstacle helps avoid collision between agents.

positions of the reference points of A and B, respectively. Let v_B be the velocity of moving obstacle B. The VO for simple airplane A induced by moving obstacle B for the window of time τ, written $VO\tau_{A|B}$, is the set of all velocities of A that will cause a collision between A and B at some moment before time τ, assuming that B maintains its velocity v_B.

2.3   Three Dimensional Collision Avoidance

To incorporate the reactive behavior of simple-airplanes with respect to each other and avoid oscillations, we use 3DRVO, introduced in [1]. It is briefly discussed below.

Let simple airplanes A and B have velocities v_A and v_B, respectively, and let the velocity obstacle of A induced by B for the window of time τ be $VO^\tau_{A|B}$. Moreover, let the relative velocity $v_A?v_B$ be in $VO^\tau_{A|B}$, from which it follows that A and B will collide at some point in time before τ if they maintain their current velocities. Let **w** be the vector from $v_A - v_B$ to the closest point of the boundary of the velocity obstacle $\partial VO^\tau_{A|B}$. Therefore, **w** is the smallest change needed to avoid collision during the window of time τ. A adjust its velocity by $\alpha\textbf{w}$ and B takes care of the remaining fraction to avoid collision. The set of permitted velocities for a simple-airplane A induced by simple-airplane B for the window of time τ, denoted $ORCA^{\tau,\alpha}_{A|B}$ is the half-space in the direction of n starting at the point $v_A + \alpha\textbf{w}$,

$$ORCA^{\tau,\alpha}_{A|B} = \{v|(v - (v_A + \alpha\textbf{w})) \cdot n\}.$$

The value of $\alpha = \frac{1}{2}$ used by [9] prescribes that A and B take equal responsibility. It is important to note that while $VO^\tau_{A|B}$ contains velocities that will cause a collision in the window of time τ, the velocities within $ORCA^{\tau,\alpha}_{A|B}$ are those which are collision-free for time τ.

3   Believe-Desire-Intention Architecture

Believe-Desire-Intention (BDI) architecture is one of, if not, the most well-known software agent development paradigm. The architecture allows for agents to gather ever changing environment status as its belief. The task given to the agent is regarded as the desire of the agent. In other words, the agent has a desire to achieve its goal, i.e., completing the given task. Intention is the deliberation of plans for achieving its goal. As shown in Fig. 2, the agent monitors changes in its environment and update its belief about it accordingly. This information is used to evaluate whether the plan needs to be revised. The agent then follows the updated plan to achieve its goal.

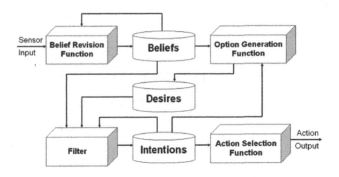

Fig. 2. BDI Architecture

Here, we bring about the BDI paradigm into our 3DRVO-based simulation to enhance the performance of executing agent simulation. Although 3DRVO constantly monitor the status of environment in front of the agent, it appears to be the low level mechanism that cannot solve the congestion efficiently. 3DRVO merely allows for agents to move towards and get out of the congestion slowly. This simply means that it will consume a lot of computation power for the agents to go through and get out of the congestion. As a consequence, it takes a lot of wasted time for agents to go through and get out of congestion. In addition, it is considered not intelligent enough that such congestion could have been avoided.

3.1   Planning Strategy with Sub-goal

In order to get a better understanding of our BDI agents, consider a simple situation shown in Fig. 3. Agent A wants to move from position a_0, to a_5. Its original plan is to go through, a_1, a_2, X, a_4 and then to a_5. Agent B wants to move from position b_0, to b_5. Its original plan is to go through, b_1, b_2, X, b_4 and then to a_5. Each of these positions is simple sub-goal for agents and is kept in each agent's plan stack.

In discrete simulation, the agent will move one step closer to the destination in each iteration. Let assume the time unit is .25 s. The atomic action of agent A is moving from a_0 to a_1, and so on. The atomic action of agent B is moving from a_0 to a_1, and so on. For each iteration, the agent is moved closer to its sub-goal, while low-level 3DRVO is used to avoid collision. Once each agent reaches its sub-goal, it will be removed and the next position in the plan stack will be placed as its new sub-goal. This process is repeated until agent A reaches a_2 and agent

B reaches b_2. If both agents maintain their movement as per plans, they will reach X at about the same time. 3DRVO can be used to navigate both agents just around position X, merely enough to avoid collision. This works alright with a small number of agents. However, a few hundreds of agents moving in this manner pass position X can be costly. BDI architecture allows for agents to look ahead and re-plan, in this case: agent A goes to a_3 then a_4, and agent B goes to b_3 then b_4.

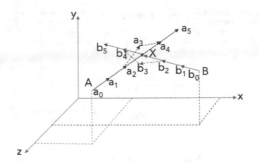

Fig. 3. Agent movement with BDI Architecture

The question here is how far away should a_3 and b_3 be from X? In this research, we minimize the distance that both agents have to deviate from their original plans. Given a simple scenario like this, the difference cannot be seen clearly. When the number of agents increases up to a few hundreds, the deviation is larger. In our experiment, we try to minimize the deviation and observe how tight is the congestion which agents can still go through and pass efficiently.

4   K-D Tree Algorithms

One of the key elements of simulating a large number agents in 3D sphere is a data structure for storing them and their information, and a set of efficient algorithms for accessing surrounding agents when simulating each agent's move. Because there are multiple repetitions for calculating the movement, the performance of 3D graph traversing algorithms is very important.

4.1   3D-Tree Algorithms

Insert Node. Inserting an element operates similar to inserting into a typical binary tree. The pseudocode is shown above. The initial call is $root = insert(x, root, 0)$. We assume that the dimensions are indexed $0, 1, \ldots, DIM - 1$. The parameter cd keeps track of the current cutting dimension. We advance the cutting dimension each time we descend to the next level of the tree, by adding one to its value modulo DIM. (For example, in the plane this value alternates

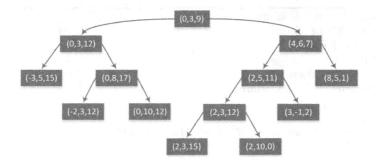

```
1:  procedure INSERT(x, t, cd)
2:      if t == null then
3:          t = newKDNode(x)
4:      else if (x == t.data) then
5:          Print"Error!"                                        ▷ error! duplicate
6:      else if (x[cd] < t.data[cd]) then
7:          t.left = insert(x, t.left, (cd + 1)%DIM)
8:      else
9:          t.right = insert(x, t.right, (cd + 1)%DIM)
10:     end if
11:     return t
12: end procedure
```

between 0 and 1 as we recurse from level to level.) We assume that the + operator
has been overloaded for the cutting dimension to operate modulo DIM. Thus,
when we say $cd + 1$ in the pseudocode, this a shorthand for $(cd + 1)\%DIM$.
Note that if a point has the same coordinate value as the cutting dimension it
is always inserted in the right subtree.

Find Minimal. Given a node t in a kd-tree, and given the index of a coordinate
axis i we wish to find the point in the subtree rooted at t whose i-th coordinate is
minimum. This is a good example of a typical type of query problem in kd-trees,
because it shows the fundamental feature of all such query algorithms, namely
to recurse only on subtrees that might lead to a possible solution.

For the sake of concreteness, assume that coordinate is $i = 0$ (meaning the x-
axis in the plane). The procedure operates recursively. When we arrive at a node
t if the cutting dimension for t's data point. On the other hand, if t's cutting
dimension is any of other axis (the y-axis, for example) then we cannot know
whether the minimum coordinate will lie in its right subtree or its left subtree, or
might be t's data point itself. So, we recurse on both the left and right subtrees,
and return the minimum of these and t's data point. We assume we have access
to a function $minimum(p1, p2, p3, i)$ which returns the point reference p_1, p_2, p_3
which is not null and minimal on coordinate i. The pseudocode is shown above.

```
procedure FINDMIN((T, dim, cd))                        ▷ empty tree
    if T == NULL then
        return NULL
    end if
    if cd == dim then
        if t.left == NULL then
            return t.data
        else
            return Findmin(T.left, dim, (cd + 1)%DIM)
        end if
    else
        return              minimum(findmin(T.left, dim, (cd        +
1)%DIM), findmin(T.right, dim, (cd + 1)%DIM), T.data)
    end if
end procedure
```

Delete. The algorithm needs to consider a number of different cases. If the node is a leaf, the algorithm deletes the node. Otherwise, its deletion would result in a "hole" in the tree. The algorithm need to find an appropriate replacement element. In both the 1-child and 2-child cases, the algorithm finds a replacement node. Assuming that the right subtree is non-empty, the replacement key was taken to be the smallest key from the right child and recursively deleted the replacement. To generalize this to the multi-dimensional case, the algorithm finds the point, whose coordinate along the current cutting dimension is minimum. If the cutting dimension is the x-axis, the replacement key is the point with the smallest x-coordinate in the right subtree. The findMin() function does this job. To prevent error when the right subtree is empty, the algorithm will select the minimum (not maximum) point from the left subtree, and move the left subtree over and becomes the new right subtree. The left child pointer is set to null.

Nearest Neighbor Search. Given a set of points S stored in a k-d tree, and a query point q, we want to return the point of S that is closest to q. The algorithm has three important elements of range and nearest neighbor processing. Partial results: Store the intermediate results of the query and update these results as the query proceeds. Traversal order: Visit the subtree first that is more likely to be relevant to the final results. Pruning: Do not visit any subtree that can be judged to be irrelevant to the final results. The algorithm maintains an object, which contains the partial results of the query. For nearest neighbor search this has two fields, *close.dist*, the distance to the closest point seen so far and *close.point*, the data point that is the closest so far. Firstly, *close.point* is set to null and *close.dist* is set to INFINITY. This structure will be passed in the recursive search procedure, and will be returned from the procedure. There are two other arguments: the cutting dimension cd, which as always, cycles among the various dimensions, and a rectangle object r that represents the current node's cell and is used to determine whether we should visit a node's descendents. This also helps

```
procedure DELETE(x, T, cd)
    if T == NULL then
        Error point not found!
    end if
    next_c d = (cd + 1)%DIM
    if x = T.data then
        if t.right! = NULL then
            t.data = findmin(T.right, cd, next_c d)
            t.right = delete(t.data, t.right, next_c d)
        else if T.left! = NULL then
            t.data = findmin(T.left, cd, next_c d)
            t.right = delete(t.data, t.left, next_c d)
        else
            t = null
        end if
    else if x[cd] < t.data[cd] then
        t.left = delete(x, t.left, next_c d)
    else
        t.right = delete(x, t.right, next_c d)
    end if
    returnt
end procedure
```

```
procedure NN(Q, T, cd, BB)
    if T == NULLordistance(Q, BB) > bestDist then
        return
    end if
    dist = distance(Q, T.data)
    if dist < best_d ist : then
        best = T.data
        best_d ist = dist
    end if
    if Q[cd] < T.data[cd] then
        NN(Q, T.left, next_c d, BB.trimLeft(cd, t.data))
        NN(Q, T.right, next_c d, BB.trimRight(cd, t.data))
    else
        NN(Q, T.right, next_c d, BB.trimRight(cd, t.data))
        NN(Q, T.left, next_c d, BB.trimLeft(cd, t.data))
    end if
end procedure
```

prune the search space. When the algorithm arrives at a node t, it determines whether the associated cell r is close enough to provide the nearest neighbor, otherwise return immediately. Then the associated data point $t.data$ is tested whether it is closer to the query q than the current closest. If so, the current closest is updated accordingly. Finally, the subtrees are searched, starting with the subtree whose cell is closer to q. The algorithm recursively searches this subtree first and then visit the farther subtree second. Each call updates the nearest neighbor result.

5   Experiment and Results

We are interested in safety of agents and efficiency of simulation. Therefore, we investigate on i) the time consumption of agents in moving through the scenes, and ii) the path of agents in moving through crowded area.

5.1   The Scenes

Here, we consider merely one extreme scene. Agents are distributedly located on the surface of a virtual sphere of radius 400 units. They are to move towards the center of the sphere to the opposite position. The agents are represented by a small sphere of radius 10 units. The distance between each pair of the agents on the surface is not exactly equal but is approximately close to each other. The ratio between the radius of agents and the radius of the sphere indicates the how quickly the agents will enter the congested zone where all the agents are about to touch each other. This affects the navigation of the agents as they try to avoid colliding other agents. The experiments were carried out on a Pentium i5-4690 CPU @ 3.50 GHz machine running 64-bit Windows 10 with 32 GB ram. We experimented 200, 400, 600 and 800 agents. The aforementioned ratios are 20, 40, 60 and 80 respectively.

5.2   Results

First, we consider the overall picture of the simulations. We are interested in elapsed time and rounds of simulation because they tell us how costly it is to navigate agents to their destination both practically (elapsed time) and theoretically (simulation round). Table 1 shows the figures collected from our experiments. As the number of agents grows from 100 up to 800 agents, the elapsed times increase. When we consider the increasing ratios from t_1 to t_2, $\frac{t_2 - t_1}{t_1}$, of elapsed time, we find that the trend also increases. Between 100 and 200 agents, the increasing ratio is 1.29, which is more than that of the number of the agents. Between 200 and 300, the increasing ratio is 0.71, which is also more than that of the number of the agents. This trend holds through 800 agents. However, the increasing number of agents trend is not consistent – they are actually decreased, from 1, .5, .33, .25, .2, .17, .13, .12. This decreasing behavior is consistent with the elapsed time increasing ratio except for the 800 agents.

Elapsed time per agents also increases when the number of agents increases. Note that the increasing rates are quite consistent except for the case of 700 agents. This could be just random. This behavior holds for the simulation rounds even in the case of 700 where the increasing ratio is minus. We can interpret the overall behavior that the algorithm perform reasonably well. The elapsed time and the simulation round do not dramatically increase (or decrease) when the number of the agents increase (or decrease). In other words, it is safe to use this algorithm to simulate agent navigation and observe their behavior as well as the efficiency of the system.

Note that in scenes where number of agents are smaller, it will take more time for agents to reach the crowded zone, where agents have to deviate from their original paths.

Table 1. Simulation results.

No. Agent	Elapsed time	Elapsed Time Inc. Ratio	Elapsed Time Per Agent	Ela. Time Per Agent Inc. Ratio	Sim. Rounds	Sim Rnd Inc. Ratio
100	41564	–	415.64	–	1782	–
200	95267	1.29	476.34	0.15	1847	0.04
300	163244	0.71	544.15	0.14	1938	0.05
400	242453	0.49	606.13	0.11	2049	0.06
500	337397	0.39	674.79	0.11	2163	0.06
600	439423	0.30	732.37	0.09	2286	0.06
700	533081	0.21	761.54	0.04	2264	−0.01
800	676845	0.27	846.06	0.11	2337	0.03

Second, we are interested in individual behavior of agents in crowded zones. Due to limited space, we choose to show results of 10 agents in 200, 400, 600 and 800 agents scenes. Note that the position of agents are distributed over the surface of the virtual space. However they may not look so due to scaling.

Figure 4 shows the track results of simulate 200 and 400 agents. For the scene of 200 agents, the crowded zone is very small, within 100 unit diameter. Agents have to diverge from their original paths. The diversion does not look too bad that they can be navigated towards their destinations without moving back. For the scene of 400 agents, the crowded zone is slightly larger than the previous scene. The diversion is also worse. Although it does not look too bad in the figure, as we track the recorded actual paths of these agent, we find that some agents have to move back to avoid collision. On the other hand, some lucky agents can almost maintain their original paths.

For the scene of 600 agents, it is obvious that the crowded area is larger – around 400 units in diameter. All agents diverge from their original paths. As the crowded area is quite large, it can be noted that the diversion of agents begin sooner rather than later. The move back behavior can be found more often. For the scene of 800 agents, the crowded zone is around 600 units in diameter. It becomes a chaos for some agents because they have to move backward and forward to get out of the crowded zone. There are still some lucky agents which manage to go through the crowded zone with minimal diversion. Most agents steer themselves around the crowded zone. This results in reasonable simulation rounds with respect to the increased number of agents.

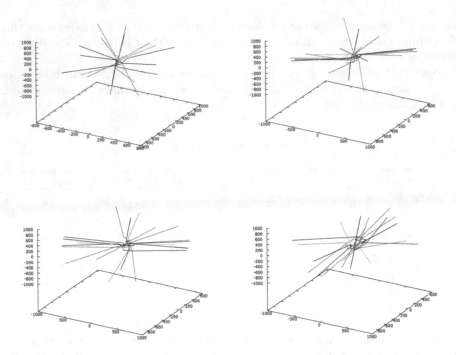

Fig. 4. Tracked path of 10 selected agents in the 200 (top left), 400 (top right), 600 (bottom left) and 800 (bottom right) agents scenes.

From computation perspective, the algorithm is cheap and efficient. While the number of agents increase, the elapsed time also increases in relative low rate. The simulation round also is also have the same behavior. It does not take dramatically more time to navigate agents to their destinations. Therefore, this algorithm is suitable for navigating agents both in research and in real world.

6   Conclusion and Future Work

The research deploys 3DRVO to help navigate agents through congested area safely and incorporate BDI architecture to help improve efficiency of simulation. In the experiments, all agents are distributed on the surface of the virtual 3D sphere and moves towards the opposite positions. The results show that agents can reach their destination safely and efficiently. With respect to safety, there was no collision between agents at all. With respect to efficiency, the results are satisfactory. Both elapsed time and simulation rounds increase when the number of agents increases. However, the increasing ratios both in elapsed time and simulation rounds seem to be consistent. The increasing number of agents does not cause any problem to the algorithm. The results also show that while the number of agents increases and the crowded zone become larger, most agents can steer themselves around the congested area. Some agents are able to maintain their planned paths but some unlucky agents are trapped in the chaotic crowded zone. From computation perspective, the algorithm is cheap and efficient. While the number of agents increase, the elapsed time also increases in relative low rate. The simulation round also have the same behavior. It does not take dramatically more time to navigate agents to their destinations. Therefore, this algorithm is suitable for navigating agents both in research and in real world.

Acknowledgement. We thank the Faculty of Informatics, Mahasarakham University, Thailand for their financial support in fiscal year 2559.

References

1. Snape, J., Manocha, D.: Navigating multiple simple-airplanes in 3D workspace. In: IEEE International Conference on Robotics and Automation, Anchorage, Alaska (2010)
2. van den Berg, J., Lin, M.C., Manocha, D.: Reciprocal velocity obstacles for real-time multi-agent navigation. In: Proceedings of the IEEE International Conference on Robotics and Automation, Pasadena, California, 19–23 May 2008, pp. 1928–1935 (208)
3. Bentley, J.L.: Multidimensional binary search trees used for associative searching. Commun. ACM **18**(9), 509 (1975)
4. Kareem, A.: Numerical simulation of wind effects: a probabilistic perspective. J. Wind Eng. Ind. Aerodyn. **96**, 1472–1497 (2008)
5. Torreño, A., Onaindia, E., Sapena,Ó.: A flexible coupling approach to multi-agent planning under incomplete information. Knowl. Inf. Syst. **38**(1), 141–178 (2014)
6. Berman, P., DasGupta, B., Muthukrishnan, S., Ramaswami, S.: Improved approximation algorithms for rectangle tiling and packing. In: Proceeding SODA 2001 Proceedings of the Twelfth Annual ACM-SIAM Symposium on Discrete Algorithms, pp. 427–436 (2001)
7. Dimopoulos, Y., Moraitis, P.: Multi-agent coordination and cooperation through classical planning. In: IEEE/WIC/ACM International Conference on Intelligent Agent Technology, IAT 2006 (2006)
8. Boutilier, C.: Planning, learning and coordination in multiagent decision processes. In: TARK 1996 Proceedings of the 6th Conference on Theoretical Aspects of Rationality and Knowledge, pp. 195–210 (1996)
9. van den Berg, J., Lin, M.C., Manocha, D.: Reciprocal velocity obstacles for real-time multi-agent navigation. In: Proceedings of the IEEE International Conference on Robotics and Automation (ICRA) (2008)
10. van den Berg, J., Guy, S.J., Lin, M., Manocha, D.: Reciprocal n-body collision avoidance. In: Pradalier, C., Siegwart, R., Hirzinger, G. (eds.) Robotics Research. Springer Tracts in Advanced Robotics, vol. 70, pp. 3–19. Springer, Heidelberg (2011). https://doi.org/10.1007/978-3-642-19457-3_1

Correction to: Thai Handwritten Recognition on BEST2019 Datasets Using Deep Learning

Rapeeporn Chamchong⬤, Umaporn Saisangchan,
and Pornntiwa Pawara⬤

Correction to:
Chapter "Thai Handwritten Recognition on BEST2019
Datasets Using Deep Learning" in: P. Chomphuwiset
et al. (Eds.): *Multi-disciplinary Trends in Artificial Intelligence*,
LNAI 12832, https://doi.org/10.1007/978-3-030-80253-0_14

The word 'encoded' has been updated to 'decoded' in section 4.3 of the chapter. The ground truth of image 6 in Table 3 has been updated from สุบภาพแข็งแรงนะคร้าบ to ทุกสิ่งทีเกิดปืนมักมีเหตุผลเสมอ.

The updated version of this chapter can be found at
https://doi.org/10.1007/978-3-030-80253-0_14

Author Index

Printed in the United States
by Baker & Taylor Publisher Services